ATLANTIC STUDIES ON SOCIETY IN CHANGE

NO. 89

Editor in Chief, Béla K. Király
Associate Editor in Chief, Peter Pastor

János Mazsu

The Social History of the Hungarian Intelligentsia, 1825–1914

Translated from the Hungarian by
Mario D. Fenyo

Social Science Monographs, Boulder, Colorado
Atlantic Research and Publications, Inc.
Highland Lakes, New Jersey

Distributed by Columbia University Press, New York
1997

EAST EUROPEAN MONOGRAPHS, NO. CDLXV

The publication of this volume was made possible by grants from
Postabank és Takarékpénztár [Postal and Savings Bank], Budapest
and *Nemzeti Kulturális Alap* [National Cultural Foundation].

Library of Congress Catalog Card Number 96-61477
ISBN 0-88033-362-6

Printed in the United States of America

Contents

Contents

Contents

Contents

Tables

Tables

Tables

Tables

Tables

Tables

Tables

Tables

Preface to the Series

The present volume is a component of a series which, when completed, will constitute a comprehensive survey of the many aspects of East Central European society.

The books in the series deal with the peoples whose homelands lie between the Germans to the west, the Russians to the east and the Mediterranean and Adriatic seas to the south. They constitute a particular civilization, one that is at once an integral part of Europe, yet substantially different from the West. The area is characterized by a rich variety in language, religion, and government. The study of this complex area demands a multidisciplinary approach and, accordingly, our contributors to the series represent several academic disciplines. They have been drawn from the universities and other scholarly institutions in the United States and Western Europe, as well as East Central Europe. The author of this monograph is professor of history at Kossuth Lajos University in Debrecen.

The Editor in Chief, of course, takes full responsibility for ensuring the comprehensiveness, cohesion, internal balance, and scholarly quality of the series. He cheerfully accepts this responsibility and intends this work to be neither a justification nor condemnation of the policies, attitudes, and activities of any persons involved. At the same time, because the contributors to the series represent so many different disciplines, interpretations, and schools of thought, his policy in this, as in the past and future volumes, is to present their contributions without major modifications.

Béla K. Király

Preface

Several factors motivated me in the early 1980s to undertake the study of the social structure of the Hungarian intelligentsia. One of these factors may be traced to certain traditions in Hungarian historiography: as an outcome of research on the institutions of political administration in the period of the Dual Monarchy, historians have been able to adequately reveal the structure, character, operation and functions of these institutions in their political and constitutional aspects. Furthermore, the economic historiography which evolved after World War II focused on analyzing the organizations in charge of the objective management of the economy, which was heading toward a capitalist mode of production. There remained many questions, however, the answers to which could not be anchored on similarly extensive and high quality research. For instance, how could the occupation groups of the intelligentsia numbering mere tens of thousands in mid-nineteenth century grow, in little over half a century, into a body of over three hundred thousand, and evolve into a social stratum distinct from all other social groups? Nor could we answer questions about the evolution of the occupation structure of this stratum, or about which segments of Hungarian society would serve as reserves for this intelligentsia, and to what extent? In other words, how was this dynamically growing stratum recruited? How was it structured, what were the material conditions, the ideological and ethical values, the traditions that shaped its formation? What were the psychological profiles of these groups? And finally, how was this intelligentsia integrated into the bourgeoisie and what role did it play in the processes of industrial modernization and in the shaping of modern Hungarian society in general?

These questions are not original, and attempts have been made to answer them: suffice it to think of the radical social scientists at the beginning of the century whose investigations did not lack historical perspective, or of the relevant works of Gyula Szekfű, Ferenc Erdei, István Bibó and, in the following generation, Péter Hanák and Tibor Huszár. Nevertheless, it was precisely the variety of answers that intimated how little we know about the basic structural processes in the evolution of the intelligentsia in Hungary. And without a more accurate knowledge of these processes it is hardly possible to critically assess the conclusions regarding its historically changing social role, or even to provide a more authentic and nuanced picture of these processes. On the other hand, it is true that revealing the basic processes in the social structure of the intelligentsia can only be the beginning of the analysis of more complex, comprehensive issues.

The other factor which prompted me to undertake this investigation was a practical consideration pertaining to the structural analysis of the Hungarian intelligentsia: the nature and composition of the sources available to us.

The basic sources for a study of the changes in the social makeup of the intelligentsia in the period of the Dual Monarchy, are the censi, and reports and statistics from institutions, ministries, including the office of the prime minister, regarding officials and other white-collar employees. These statistical sources enable us to analyze the effectives, the transformation of the structure of trade or occupation groups, the changes in its religious and ethnic composition and, in certain cases, even their income, housing, landowning, etc., relations. These compact and comprehensive series of data, however, seldom enable us to undertake a detailed, fine, or reciprocally relevant analysis; hence, in practice, we can only undertake the analysis of the processes of change of the social stratum as a whole from particular aspects, which can then be used to shed light on other aspects.

Where the censi and similar statistical sources proved insufficient to answer questions—for instance, about the recruitment of the intelligentsia, or about several aspects of social mobility and living conditions—I attempted to bridge the gaps by including analyses of other sources. I discuss these sources and the pertinent methodological issues in the introduction and in the course of the relevant analyses within the main text.

My research and analyses being primarily macrostructural, the case study regarding the construction and apartments of a building in Debrecen may seem out of place. Nevertheless, it is an organic part of this work, due to the fact that there are no sources at all appropriate for a more comprehensive analysis of the housing relations of the contemporary intelligentsia; moreover, this case study, truly prompted by this research project, enabled me, given my familiarity with the location, to carry out not only some sort of in-depth analysis, but also to include nuances deriving from personal experiences which cannot be achieved at the macro level.

Within the framework of this investigation I did not consider it my task to include the history of the concept of intelligentsia, or a comprehensive social history of the stratum to which this concept is applied. I could not, however, bypass at least a schematic overview of the relevant international literature. This line of thought, dealing with the specialized literature in the field and conducive to reformulating certain basic issues, had to be placed at the beginning of the investigation, along with certain discussions on methodology, as a matter of logic.

In my analyses of the sources I have relied to a large extent on the research in sociology and social history undertaken since the 1970s—primarily the work of Domokos Kosáry, Károly Vörös, László Katus, Tibor Hajdu, Tibor Huszár and Péter Hanák. Moreover, it is inspired by the discussions and conferences sponsored by the István Hajnal Circle (later Association), which tackled the scientific endeavors of my own generation.

Furthermore, I have received invaluable assistance from the critique provided by university colleagues and friends, for which I am grateful.

I am especially thankful for the personal and professional help provided by János Veliky in the choice of the topic and its initial analysis, and to Péter Hanák who provided the most valuable leads for the research embodied in this book. I am also grateful to Professor Mario D. Fenyo of Bowie State University, for his untiring effort in translating this work faithfully and idi-

Preface

omatically, and to Professor Peter Pastor of Montclair State University in New Jersey, for recognizing the value of my contribution and for making the publication of this book possible.

I also wish to thank László Gönye for his assistance with the English translation of architectural terms and Edit Völgyesi for editorial help and typesetting.

Debrecen, April 1997

INTRODUCTION

The Historical Debate Regarding the Concept Intelligentsia

The term intelligentsia is one of the most widely used and abused terms in historical and sociological literature. Although extensively investigated by social scientists, it has given occasion to countless misunderstandings. The reason for these misunderstandings, of course, is that it has been used vaguely, without a consensus regarding its definition, or has been defined incorrectly. Other historical and sociological works have used the concept in only one or a few of its many significant aspects.[1]

The sociology of knowledge, and scholars focussing on cultural history, have used the concept intelligentsia from the perspective of accumulation of knowledge, placing the producers and communicators (perhaps even the consumers) of principles, values, cultural goods at the core of their research. The protagonists of this perspective are the creative intellectuals, more or less removed from the socio-historical context determining them, disembodied from their relation to social hierarchy, to

---

[1] Alexander Gella, ed., *The Intelligentsia and the Intellectuals* (Thousand Oaks, Ca, 1976); Ron Eyerman, Lennart G. Svensson, and Thomas Soderqvist, eds., *Intellectuals, Universities, and the State in Modern Western Societies* (Los Angeles, 1987); George B. Huszár, *The Intellectuals—A Controversial Portrait* (Glencoe, 1960); Tibor Huszár, ed., *Korunk értelmisége* [The intelligentsia in our age] (Budapest, 1975); Tibor Huszár, ed., *Fejezetek az értelmiség történetéből* [Chapters from the history of the intelligentsia] (Budapest, 1977); Tibor Huszár, ed., *Értelmiségiek, diplomások, szellemi munkások* [Intelligentsia, members of professions, intellectual workers] (Budapest, 1978); and Tibor Huszár, ed., *Értelmiségszociológiai írások Magyarországon 1900–1945* [Writings on the sociology of the intelligentsia in Hungary] (Budapest, 1981); György Konrád and Iván Szelényi, *The Intellectuals on the Road to Class Power* (New York, 1979); Iván Szelényi, *Új osztály, állam, politika* [New class, state and politics] (Budapest, 1990); Mária M. Kovács, *Liberal Professions and Illiteral Politics: Hungary from the Habsburgs to the Holocaust* (New York, 1994); Milenko Karanovich, *The Development of Education in Serbia and Emergence of Its Intelligentsia, 1838–1858* (Boulder, 1995).

political power.[2]

The concept of "intellectual" is also a manifestation of the self-perception of the social scientist: "...in all ages (the intellectual leads in) the passionate yearning for knowledge, the expression of truths, the readiness for perpetual renewal, the urge to create, serving idealistic values bereft of all vested interest, with moral purity, with indifference toward what in the intellectual's eyes appears as nothing but base political considerations."[3]

The approach of the social historian generally sets out from the premise that the intelligentsia is a distinct social group or stratum, which came about during the process or in the age of industrial modernization. Beyond this premise, however, even social historians diverge widely in their definition of the concept.[4]

It might help us find our way amidst this diversity if we took a philological approach which, on the surface of it, may appear astonishing: when and where did the concept intelligentsia first appear as a designation for a discrete social category? Even though a good many sociologists and historians show a predilection for using the term "professional" or "intelligentsia" in referring to Egyptian and Sumerian clerics, when it comes to works about the mandarins of China, or about the civil servants of the period of enlightened absolutism[5] the application of the concept is of relatively recent date. Following the dispersion of the Romance languages the term "intelligence" became a commonly used psychological or philosophical category to designate degree of understanding, level of knowledge, or capacity to learn.[6] Of course, in everyday language as well as in scientific literature, literate people have always played a role as learned persons, or as highly educated members of professional groups. They were designated, however, not as intellectuals or

[2] Gella, "An Introduction to the Sociology of the Intelligentsia," in Gella, op. cit., pp. 9–34.

[3] Huszár, ed., *Korunk értelmisége,* p. 8.

[4] Gella, op. cit.

[5] Huszár, ed., *Korunk értelmisége*; Jürgen Habermas, *The Structural Transformation of the Public Sphere: An Inquiry into a Caterory of Bourgeois Society* (Cambridge, Mass., 1989).

[6] Huszár, ed., *Korunk értelmisége,* p. 7.

intelligentsia, but rather as literati, clerks, sages, or even as doctors, judges, poets, or philosophers.

The designation intelligentsia, as applied to a social group, was unknown before the nineteenth century.[7]

Some of the confusion in the historical appearance of the concept intelligence and intelligentsia derives from the fact that in West European and Anglo-American social thought the expression intellectual extensively overlaps with the categories and meaning of "professional" in English, or "intellectuel" in French.

The expression "intellectuel" entered into European consciousness in connection with the Dreyfus affair, then the term was popularized by Julien Benda.[8]

This category "intellectual," however, does not correspond to the one we are seeking to examine. According to the definition given by Hugh Seton-Watson, Western societies have used, and continue to use, this concept to refer to "a small inner elite society made up of writers and representatives of culture who live according to their style."[9]

Where "intelligentsia" is not confused with the terms professional or intellectuel, its meaning is very different from the one in Hungary. A good example of this is encountered in the research of Lewis Feuer, according to which the meaning of "intellectual" in the 1920s acquired a demonstrably pejorative content: Americans used the term to denote leaders of groups within the workers movement, usually members of the urban petty bourgeoisie, brought up on the Lower East Side of Manhattan, political wind-mill fighters, who had nothing to do with "professionals" engaged in respectable bourgeois occupations.[10]

In Anglo-American literature the term "intelligentsia," to this day, is colored by the assumption that the term and its meaning made its appearance in the Western world, along with the Russian exiles belonging to the professions, in the aftermath

---

[7] Gella, op. cit., p. 14.

[8] Huszár, ed., *Korunk értelmisége*, p. 11.

[9] Peter Allen, "The Meanings of 'An Intellectual': Nineteenth- and Twentieth-Century English Usage," *University of Toronto Quarterly* 55, no. 4 (Summer 1986), pp. 343–358.

[10] Lewis S. Feuer, "What is an Intellectual?" in Gella, op. cit., pp. 48–50.

of the Bolshevik Revolution.

We cannot find the answer to "when and where" on the basis of research carried out in Western societies; rather, there has been a regular contest among successive waves of Polish, Russian and German historians to determine how this term first appeared as a designation for a social grouping—whether in the Russian empire, on Polish territory, or somewhere in Germany. A string of Russian historians have reiterated that the term was coined by the Russian writer Peter Boborykin in 1860, at least until the Polish historian Vaclav Lednicki demonstrated that that the term had been used by V. G. Belinskii already in 1846.[11] Richard Pipes represents the views of those focussing on the term in its German form (Intelligenz), used as early as 1849, "as a social group distinguished from the mass of population by its education, its way of life, and a general sense of affinity with the Western cultural community."[12] According to Alexander Gella, a sociologist of Polish extraction, it was Karol Liel who first used the term in Polish literature in 1844.[13]

Our only contribution to this debate, which took place in the decades of the 1960s and 1970s, is that Lajos Kossuth used the term "értelmiség," referring to the "intelligentsia" or "honoratior" stratum, as early as 1843, in the daily Pesti Hírlap, in an article on suffrage in the municipalities.[14]

A detailed etymological analysis would unquestionably reveal interesting ramifications regarding when and where the concept was first used. The social historian, however, is more concerned with examining why the social group, which came into existence about simultaneously with the designation "intelligentsia," appears precisely in areas that were backward or peripheral to industrially modernizing Europe, around the mid-nineteenth century. What are the specific characteristics of social

---

[11] Gella, op. cit., p. 12.

[12] Richard Pipes, "The Historical Evolution of the Russian Intelligentsia," in The Russian Intelligentsia, ed. Richard Pipes (New York, 1961), p. 48.

[13] Alexander Gella, "The Life and Death of the Polish Intelligentsia," Slavic Review 30, no. 1, p. 4.

[14] Pesti Hírlap, March 26, 1843.

development in Central and Eastern Europe that explain the formation of a social group whose function, system of values, and mentality were distinct from those of other strata, and which had a consciousness of its own?[15]

On the basis of research in various countries,[16] and with divergent approaches, we have come up with the following schematic answers applicable to the region as a whole:

a) Although the levels of development in the region may have varied, it was nevertheless the basically feudalistic, backward, barely urbanized agrarian societies that were swept into the increasingly powerful stream of industrial modernization.

b) The structure of the feudal society, divided into estates, could not undergo a gradual process of dissolution, as it had in the West. Thus the various estates, the inter and intra-group relations, the ingrained systems of values and of mental and cultural attitudes, the institutions of rule and social hegemonic relations underlying the surface of constitutional arrangements were integrated into the rapidly evolving new societies, called "bourgeois national," with minimal modifications. After the dissolution of the network of feudal institutions, the social structures and groups, instead of creating advanced market relations, were integrated primarily through the bureaucratic superstructure of the state, deeply imbedded into the economic and social processes.

c) Beyond the reorganization and legitimation of the socio-political rule and administration, and beyond the development of a professional ruling class, the development of an administration capable of serving the needs of economic modernization became part and parcel of the in many ways successful economic

---

[15] According to Gella, the so-called classic nineteenth century intelligentsia is a sui generis phenomenon in Eastern and Central Europe. See, *The intelligentsia*, p. 23.

[16] In addition to the works already cited, see Andrej Borucki, "Sudy of the Socio-Occupational Position of the Pre-War Intelligentsia in People's Poland," *Polish Sociological Bulletin*, nos. 1–2 (1962), pp. 131–140; Jozef Chalasinski, "A lengyel értelmiség társadalmi eredete [The social origins of the Polish intelligentsia], in Huszár, ed., *Korunk értelmisége*, pp. 173–223; Alexander Hertz, "The Case of an Eastern European Intelligentsia," *Journal of Central European Affairs*, (1951), p. 11; Allan Pollard, "The Russian Intelligentsia: the Mind of Russia," *California Slavic Sudies*, no. 3 (1964); Marc Raeff, *Origins of the Russian Intelligentsia: the Nineteenth-Century Nobility* (New York, 1966); Klaus Vondung, *Das Wilhelminische Bildungsbürgertum*, (Göttingen, 1976).

emulation in the area.

The etatist habits of enlightened absolutism were revived during this process, the state assuming significant functions not only in modernization, but also in the formation of a fledgling bourgeois society where vested interests were undeveloped, where autonomies remained at a low level. The well-developed bureaucracy of this "new bourgeois state" not only performed the function of governing, not only organized and managed some of the tasks of the underdeveloped market, but required and formed a hitherto unheard-of mass of trained people, who would then promote within its institutions and offices a particular esprit de corps—the birth of a corporate social (group) ethos.

d) In Central and Eastern Europe economic modernization took place in the half a century preceding World War I, to a large extent within illiterate societies, at a low level of mass culture. From Russia to the German-speaking lands, between ninety to thirty percent of the population could neither read nor write in the middle of the nineteenth century.

Thus, before World War I, the acquisition of basic culture, or lack thereof, could create strata and as a result, even under capitalist conditions, the general culture acquired at the secondary school level could become an active factor in restructuring society and in its ethical makeup.

Regarding the latter, Alexander Hertz wrote: "Neither in the United States nor in England does it [education] provide social distinction in the same degree as do personal success, fortune, or even birth. In neither country are there sharp differences between the educational levels of the upper and lower income groups. In both countries access to school training is a relatively easy matter. And, finally, in both countries a college graduate may be a member of an 'intellectuel' group—a faculty, a learned society, a professional association, the bar, etc.—but by no means does his education make him regard himself as a member of a separate social class or caste bound to lead the nation on the road to its destiny. In most cases he defines his social status as that of the middle classes."[17]

Once the old order in Central and Eastern Europe disintegrat-

---

[17] Hertz, op.cit., p. 13.

ed, a diploma or completion of high school assumed the function of the patent of nobility of yore in the process of social organization.

e) Moreover, it is important from the point of view of our topic, that the half a century of industrialization was also the period of formation of national communities. The relatively extensive intelligentsia became called upon, in these backward, partly illiterate societies, to create the political ideologies and national cultures of the new nation-states. In almost every society this formed the intelligentsia's sense of mission, which was only enhanced by the fact that the system of political institutions replaced, with the public role of the intelligentsia the autonomies of the undeveloped and undifferentiated national-bourgeois societies.

The consciousness of a national mission and the task of substituting for "immature" social autonomy, also became a basic factor in the development of an independent social traits mentality and consciousness of this class.

Of course the German *Bildungsbürgertum* of the nineteenth century or the *Beamtenintelligenz* at the beginning of the next century, extensively analyzed by Max Weber, bear only a distant resemblance to the Russian service nobility or the revolutionary intelligentsia. Precisely for this reason it may be important to examine the peculiarities of the German variant, from several aspects.

The Stratifying Function of the School System and Literacy in the Industrial Age

By industrial age we are referring to a particular era, namely the period from the 1780s to World War I, when the first great wave of the industrial revolution swept across the economies of Europe and which has been referred to, in the works of György Ránki, as the "long nineteenth century."[18] We are interested in studying the process of literacy primarily as it relates to economic

---

[18] Iván T. Berend and György Ránki, *Gazdasági elmaradottság, kiutak és kudarcok a XIX. századi Európában* [Economic backwardness, solutions and failures in nineteenth-century Europe] (Budapest, 1979).

development deriving from industrialization, reappraising or modifying that optimistic perception which permeate works in economic history, usually without any attempt at empirical verification: namely, that the precondition for economic achievement in this period was the high educational level of the labor force and, moreover, that there is a direct correlation between the process of industrialization and the rise in working class culture.[19]

Furthermore, we need to decide what is meant by literacy, and how could it prove useful if it is nothing more than the dissemination of a knowledge of reading and writing. Indeed, the above is a close enough definition of literacy, but this approximation requires a word of explanation. To define more precisely: literacy is the development of a mass culture that is no longer or not exclusively based on the forms and means of oral transmission of information. Thus the essence of this mass culture is the elimination of illiteracy, the spread of the aptitudes for and means of using written information systematized through formal schooling.

And although, logically speaking, the opposite of illiterate is "one who knows how to read and write," this very expression is the product of a particular view, the result of a centralized and planned educational system as promoted in the period of enlightened absolutism.[20] This expression, even in the Hungarian language, camouflages the fact that, until the beginning of the nineteenth century, in England even until mid-nineteenth century, universal schooling at the primary level focussed on merely teaching how to read, eventually complemented by numeracy, while the teaching of writing was limited mainly to handwriting skills. Thus the English expression "literacy" means both a certain basic culture and a knowledge of reading

---

[19] E. G. West, *Education and the Industrial Revolution* (London, 1975); Carlo M. Cipolla, *Literacy and Development in the West* (Baltimore, 1969); R. Aldrich, *An Introduction to the History of Education* (London, 1982).

[20] Ernő Fináczy, *A magyarországi közoktatás története Mária Terézia korában* [The history of public education in Hungary in the age of Maria Theresa], vol. 1 (Budapest, 1899); Áron Kiss, *A magyar népiskolai tanítás története* [The history of public school education in Hungary] (Budapest, 1881–1883), vols. 1 and 2.

and writing.[21] From our point of view, the category literacy is precise enough, however, since it indicates a historical process which includes, at its more advanced stage, the knowledge of reading and writing. This more advanced stage was reached, at the primary school level, in the second half of the nineteenth century in Europe.

Along with clarifying the concept, certain observations regarding research methods are warranted: the literature in the field excludes from the rank of illiterates all those who for physical or mental reasons are incapable of interpreting or understanding written symbols. These include two important categories: infants, that is children usually under the age of six, and those who are physically or mentally challenged.[22]

The investigation of the issue of cultural illiteracy, that is, the challenges faced in reading and writing the dominant language by those who are literate only in the language of a minority group would constitute a separate task.

In the period preceding modern census-taking statistics devised in the last third of the nineteenth century, most societies produced three types of records for determining the pro-portion of the literate among the general population: registers of marriage, military enlistment records, and judicial proceedings.[23] The latter category applies only to a particular segment of the population, but the former two may prove helpful, if appropriate correctives are applied, in determining the rate and progress of literacy among the population at large.

Because of the divergent sources and varying analyses, the research results bearing on the first half of the nineteenth century and earlier are appropriate only for determining general and lasting tendencies and for comparative studies.

Modern census records from before World War I do not allow us to make comparisons with regard to illiteracy among adults; hence the literature in the field does not insist on one hundred percent as absolute literacy, but rather considers that this has been

---

[21] Richard Aldrich, op. cit.; Richard Hoggart, *The Uses of Literacy* (Baltimore, 1958).

[22] János Afra Nagy, "Az írástudatlanok Budapesten" [Illiteracy in Budapest], *Statisztikai Közlemények* [Statistical Publications] 63, no. 1, pp. 5–29.

[23] Ibid., pp. 10–15.

achieved when the rate of illiteracy among adults drops to below
ten percent.

The Hungarian census of 1869, directed by Károly Keleti, was
a pioneer venture in modern census-taking, for it was the first one
to examine cultural conditions—albeit it is true that he included,
among the literates, those who were able to write "somewhat."[24]

From the point of view of literacy, the long nineteenth century
may be divided into two clearly separate stages on the basis of the
research results available to us. We have consistent data available for analysis for the period 1780 to 1840 for England, Scotland
and France.[25] At the time of the industrial revolution in England
about two-thirds of the adult male population, and somewhat over
one third of adult women, that is approximately one half of the
entire adult population was able to read, count and, to some
extent, write. In the two centuries following the spread of the
printing press, the rise of the rate of literacy in England was relatively rapid; according to the estimates, by 1675 the rate of literacy among men had risen to forty percent: it was about two-thirds
among the urban population and, even in the most backward
rural areas, one tenth of the population was literate. Beginning
with the last third of the seventeenth century the increase in the
rate of literacy slowed down, but surged again in the two or three
decades preceding the industrial revolution.

In the same period the literacy rate among adult males in
Scotland rose from eighty to about ninety percent and, in
France, from forty-five percent to about fifty-five percent. The
difference between the rates in England and France corresponds
more or less to the difference in economic development between
the two countries, but this does not apply to Scotland at all.

In spite of the differences at the start, the process of literacy
shows uniformity in all three countries at the time of the industrial revolution. A slowing down, almost a stagnation, may be
observed in France for a relatively short period, between 1800

---

24 Károly Keleti, *Hazánk és népe* [Our country and its people] (Pest, 1871).

25 Lawrence Stone, "Literacy and Education in England, 1640–1900," *Past
and Present* 42, pp. 69–139; François Furet and Jacques Ozouf, "Literacy and
Industrialization: the Case of the Département du Nord in France," *Journal of
European Economic History* 5 (1976), pp. 5–44.

TABLE 1

**Literacy among the Adult Male Population in France,
Scotland, and England (1600–1900)[27]**

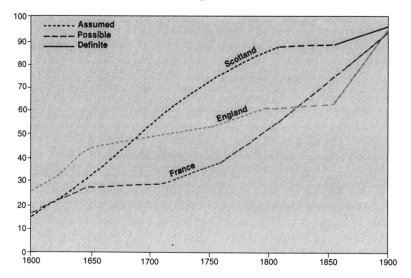

and 1820, in England from 1790 to 1840, in Scotland to the middle of the nineteenth century.[26]

The historical evolution of obvious differences in cultural levels between the northern and the southern regions of England was modified in these decades by a decline in the industrial regions, a dramatic decline according to many researchers.[28] Although, except for some locations, such as Halifax, we do not have exact data tracing the drop in the ratio of the literate in certain industrial centers, the absolute numbers of illiterates definitely increased, and rapidly at that. On the other hand, in the industrially developing areas, albeit at a slow rate, the gap between literacy among males and females was increasing, which indicates that, in the first phase of industrialization, literacy fo-

---

[26] Furet and Ozouf, op. cit., p. 15.

[27] Stone, op. cit., p. 121.

[28] Michael Sanderson, "Literacy and Social Mobility in the Industrial Revolution in England," *Past and Present* 56, pp. 75–104.

cused primarily on men, aggravating the economic inequities between the genders. In connection with the basic traits of the spreading of literacy in England, we must also mention that in the early stage of the industrial revolution, the division of labor in the large industrial plants and the introduction of the assembly line did not require a literate work force at first. In addition to the illiterate mass of hired hands, however, there was a significant rise in the number and education of foremen, technicians, engineers who belonged to the lower middle class; hence we may assume that practical training and technological culture beyond the elementary level played an important role in English economic achievement. In other words, the protagonist of the industrial revolution in England was the technician, whereas the illiterate manual laborers played the role of the "extras."[29]

Around 1840 English economic development was unquestionably the most advanced in Europe, yet the rate of literacy among the adult population barely exceeded fifty percent. If we compare this figure to data from other regions of Europe it turns out that it was not only in Scotland that literacy surpassed the British but in all of Western Europe, including Prussia and the western parts of the Habsburg empire.[30] This warrants at least mentioning other factors that, while not strictly economic, may have influenced the evolution of literacy in Europe.[31]

Factors deriving directly from the relations between the educational system and social structure:

For many centuries during the Middle Ages literacy did not entail social status, for most lords, oftentimes the very ruler could not read. On the contrary, it was "knowledge of writing" that created a separate social condition for the clergy and the small number of secular writers.

From the seventeenth century on we may observe how the dif-

---

[29] Charles Arnold Anderson and Mary Jean Bowman, "Education and Economic Modernization in Historical Perspective," in *Schooling and Society: Studies in the History of Education,* ed., Lawrence Stone (Baltimore, 1976), pp. 3–19; Sanderson, op. cit.

[30] Afra Nagy, op. cit., pp. 16–17; Peter Lundgreen, "Educational Expansion and Economic Growth in Nineteenth-Century Germany," in Stone, op. cit., pp. 20–68.

[31] Stone, op. cit., pp. 83–92.

ferentiated educational system catered to various levels of society, as a result of which lack of an education or illiteracy becomes a significant dividing line between the lower and upper classes.

With the elimination of illiteracy in the developed countries by the beginning of the early twentieth century the lines of social division have been displaced beyond or above the primary school level.[32]

The impact of work opportunities, or the labor market were:

The character of the labor market in the societies of classical industrialization was quite different from its character in the societies of bureaucratic or centralized industrialization. In the the former (e.g., in England) schooling was a rational investment, whereas in the latter (e.g., in Prussia) formal learning, the acquisition of a diploma became far more valuable in the eighteenth and nineteenth centuries, precisely because market conditions were not operative.[33]

Clearly, the spread of child labor had an impact on primary schooling; the stagnation in the elimination of illiteracy in England in the first decades of the industrial revolution was due to some extent to the increase in child labor. The ratio of schooling dropped as a result of all-day factory work, while, because of the dramatic spread of Sunday schools, the knowledge of mere reading was again on the rise. The negative effect of child labor in agricultural work in the less developed regions must also be taken into account.[34]

Perhaps religion was the most important factor in the spread of education in the period preceding the nineteenth century. The dissemination of the Bible and of religious literature in general was also the main impetus for the evolution of the printing press and literacy. The Reformation and the Protestant churches centered on the vernacular, and on the Bible-reading, virtuous, God-

---

[32] Ibid.

[33] See Konrad H. Jarausch, ed., *Transformation of Higher Learning, 1860 –1930* (Chicago, 1983); also, K. Detlef Muller, Fritz Ringer, and Brian Simon, eds., *The Rise of the Modern Educational System* (Cambridge, 1987).

[34] *Magyar Statisztikai Közlemények* [Hungarian Statistical Publications], new series, vol. 64, 86–92; Afra Nagy, op. cit., p. 46.

fearing person, accounting for the spread of literacy.

The Protestant churches and Protestant countries were the first to introduce mandatory universal schooling: mandatory schooling for children was introduced in Saxony in 1642, in 1649 in Württemberg. Edicts issued in Prussia in 1717 and 1736 required attendance at schools. No illiterates remained in the Protestant cantons of Switzerland, judging from the registers of marriage, by the middle of the eighteenth century.[35]

In Hungary, too, it was the spread of Reformation that elicited the development of primary schooling; as early as 1548 the law promulgated by Ferdinand I required the church hierarchy to establish schools according to their competence.

A series of laws adopted by the beginning of the eighteenth century indicate the recognition of the significance of education in the competition for the allegiance of the believers. In the same century, the cities with Protestant residents began to regulate some issues of mass education by means of statutes.[36]

The Presbyterian Church of Scotland is a special case, for already in 1560 it developed a specific plan for establishing a nationwide schooling system. In 1646 a law was adopted mandating schooling in Scotland, fully implemented by the beginning of the next century; the taxes paid by landowners and renters of land financed the widespread education of the less fortunate. It was mainly owing to the Presbyterian church that over four-fifth of Scottish society could read and write by the beginning of the English industrial revolution.[37]

In general it can be asserted that the rivalry between the churches for the souls of the faithful promoted the spread of literacy. In other words, the evolution of religious pluralism was a decisive factor in the spread of education and basic culture throughout Europe up to the middle of the nineteenth century. Vice-versa, where religious pluralism did not evolve (for instance, in the areas of Orthodox Christianity) literacy remained at a low level.

The positive and negative impacts of social control and of

---

[35] Afra Nagy, op. cit., pp. 8, 18–20, and 34; Stone, op. cit., p. 80.

[36] J. Scotland, *The History of Scottish Education*, (London, 1969).

[37] Ibid.

power are:

In the Middle Ages, the fear of literacy was widespread; among the establishment the notion prevailed that schooling would put an end to the convenient moral and cultural dependence of the lower classes. Suffice to mention an extreme modern example: until the Civil War in the United States, in most slave-owning states the teaching of the alphabet to the slaves was forbidden by law and a punishable offense. Both the English and the French Revolutions elicited waves of a similar conservative perspective on popular education. In the period of the spread of factory work these views were reinforced, because it was believed that workers who benefit from primary schooling would no longer be willing to perform boring tasks or heavy physical labor.

At the same time, the absolutist regimes who found their military position shaken (Prussia, the Habsburg empire and, much later, Russia after the Crimean War), emphasized the development of primary schooling as part of economic modernization, with varying results. The goal of the absolutist state was to remove primary schooling from the control of the churches and to deal with it as a political issue. The Prussian education system, designed to be universal, was rather effective: according to the data from marriage registers only 16.2 percent of the men and 39.5 percent of the women who were marrying in the 1840s remained illiterate. In the 1860s data about literacy were no longer even reported on the rosters of military enlistment, the assumption being that everyone was literate.[38]

As we know, absolutism in Russia was far less efficient even in this respect. Military and power considerations also played a role in the rather belated British law of 1870 regarding universal education. The victory of the North over the South in the United States, or the victory of Prussia over Austria merely confirmed the notion that a better system of universal education improves chances for military victory. Memories of Sedan and the desire for revenge played a role in the evolution of French laws on public education. In the process of formation of modern bourgeois

---

[38] Afra Nagy, op. cit., pp. 18–20.

nations, the national movements regarded public education as an important tool for creating national unity, placing state education above state religion.[39]

Social control and power considerations also played important roles, albeit lesser ones, in promoting literacy. In the aftermath of the Enlightenment it was commonly believed that universal primary schooling is capable of halting the spread of crime, a positive approach to the dilemma whether to build more schools or more jails?[40] Adam Smith also held the notion that a general education would preserve nations from superstition and from the influence of utopian radicals, from social anarchy. The persistence of this notion is illustrated by the general opinion entertained by the British political elite after the Russian Revolution, that it was its good schools and general culture that saved England from Bolshevism.

Demographic processes, strategies and customs also had an impact on primary education. Suffice to mention but two: under traditional demographic conditions it was too risky to invest in the schooling of children because of the high death rate. The drop in the death rate in Western Europe at the end of the eighteenth century had a demonstrable effect on the rise of literacy. The first phase of industrialization was accompanied by a kind of demographic revolution. The sudden increase in population created tensions which could not be relieved in the short run by the educational system. (In addition to immigration, the rise in the birthrate was the main cause of the rise of illiteracy in the industrial centers in England.)

The above factors explain why the industrial revolution did not come about in the countries with the most advanced system of general education; in other words, in the first phase of industrialization there is no clear-cut evidence of a positive correlation between industrial revolution and literacy. On the other hand, it can be asserted on the basis of factual data that there is a positive correlation between industrialization and literacy in that, until the middle of the nineteenth century, the ratio of literates

---

[39] Emil Niederhauser, *A nemzeti megújulási mozgalmak Kelet-Európában* [The movements of national renewal in Eastern Europe] (Budapest, 1977).

[40] Stone, op. cit., p. 90.

among adults exceeded forty percent in those societies where there was an industrial takeoff. (The significance of this ratio is confirmed by data from the developing countries in the 1950s.)[41]

From the middle of the nineteenth century rate of literacy in Europe reached a new stage: rise is evident in every country, as a result of which illiteracy is eliminated in the developed countries of Europe by the beginning of World War I.[42]

By the turn of the century the process was complete in Switzerland and Germany, followed, at the beginning of the twentieth century, by Great Britain and even Ireland. Complete literacy was achieved somewhat later, but still before World War I, in the Austrian and Czech lands of the Austro-Hungarian Monarchy, and in Northern Italy—although illiteracy remained around sixty percent in the Mezzogiorno. The process was particularly rapid and perhaps most complete in Scandinavia, reaching practically one hundred percent. Regarding the nature and rate of literacy, Estonia can be classified with Scandinavia.

The Hungarian realm, Spain, the areas inhabited by Poles and Lithuanians and, on the average, Italy may constitute a grey area. It was immediately before the turn of the century that these areas transcended the threshold of forty percent, but the rate of evolution was too slow to result in the complete elimination of illiteracy before World War I. The rate of illiteracy was still about one third of the adult population in Hungary, about forty percent in Poland, and 45.6 percent in Spain, which was at the bottom of the list.[26] Merely for the sake of comparison, barely thirty percent of the African American population remained illiterate in this same period, while literacy had become general in 1860s among white Americans. (It is true that widespread "functional" illiteracy is bemoaned in the United States, and not just among minorities.)

Finally, among the most backward areas, even up to World War I we find Portugal, Serbia, Greece, Romania, European Russia, and southern Italy. These areas rarely achieved a forty

[41] Anderson and Bowman, op. cit., p. 5.

[42] Afra Nagy, op. cit., pp. 16–19; Hartmut Kaelble, *Industrialization and Social Inequality in Nineteenth Century Europe* (New York, 1986), pp. 86–104.

percent literacy rate, if that much. The most developed countries of Central and South America—especially Argentina, Uruguay, Chile—had reached or exceeded that level.[44]

While we cannot ascertain a clear correlation between universal primary education and the first phase of European industrialization until 1840, in the second phase industrial competition becomes the most powerful factor in promoting the educational system. General education—along with a more developed university system—becomes the handmaid of economic progress in the developed countries, rendering the relationship between mass culture and development unequivocal.[45]

Data from the areas that caught up in this period indicate that while their school system may have evolved historically for different reasons in the earlier period, it nevertheless became a catalyst or an organic component of economic achievement.

From the middle of the previous century to World War I, Hungary achieved spectacular progress in the elimination of illiteracy, especially after the 1868 Act on Public Education. The characteristics of this process include a pronounced variation in the rate of growth from decade to decade, including a definite rise in the rate of illiteracy in most cities (in most industrial centers as well between 1880–1890), and a temporary increase in the gap between genders, religions, and ethnic groups, which make Hungary resemble England during the industrial revolution rather than other countries that were catching up.[46] Thus, if there is such a thing as a model of literacy, the Hungarian process in the fifty years preceding World War I is closer to the British model of an earlier period than to the Scandinavian or German in the same period.

---

[44] Ibid.

[45] Miller, Ringer, and Simon, eds., op. cit.

[46] Afra Nagy, op. cit., pp. 169–187.

CHAPTER I

Social Mobility among Professionals: Literature and Sources

Several factors played a part in shaping the issues to be examined. For one thing, numerous assertions and stereotyped statements have currency in historical literature regarding the social background of professionals or certain groups of professionals, mainly because of an uncritical adoption of types frequently mentioned in the literary works and journalism of the period.[1] The lack of a quantitative study on the social background of professionals in the period of the Dual Monarchy is probably owing to the fact that no data containing the basic information for such an investigation, towit the occupation of the father, had been collected before 1930.[2]

On the other hand, in the 1970s, in Hungary as elsewhere, research undertaken on social mobility discovered the type of source—statistics on education—which could compensate for the above-mentioned lack of information, and could, if not systematically shed light on social mobility, at least shed some light on and even facilitate a quantitative analysis of intergenerational mobility affecting the professional stratum for the pre-1930 period. This research, however, again on grounds of lack

---

[1] János Mazsu, "A dualizmus kori értelmiség társadalmi forrásainak főbb változási tendenciái" [Main tendencies in the change of the origins of the intelligentsia in the period of the Dual Monarchy], *Történelmi Szemle,* no. 2 (1980), pp. 289–308.

[2] After the partial censi of social strata in Budapest in the late twenties, the first nationwide collection of data which covered these factors was the census of 1930. See the *Magyar Statisztikai Közlemények*, new series, vol. 114.

of sources, stretched back only as far as 1899 and restricted itself, for no particular reason, to higher education, thus equating intelligentsia with the person who has earned a degree.[3]

The professional class evolved as a result of structural changes incurred in mid-nineteenth century,[4] as a stratum with a specific lifestyle, as a numerically determined integral part of the gentry and educated middle class. Therefore, if we disregard the processes of mobility prior to this period, our perception of the historical formation or evolution of the professional stratum remains hopelessly limited.

Another problem involved in this research is whether completion of higher education did, indeed, signify formal preparation for categories belonging to the professional class. An examination of this issue led to the conclusion that in the period of the Dual Monarchy the completion of four years of the eight-year gymnasium or secondary school was sufficient to qualify one as a member of the intelligentsia, whereas the upper stratum of the professionals was composed of the thin but influential layer of those who had completed higher education, two categories usually difficult to differentiate in the sources.[5]

This recognition, moreover the fact that the professionals who obtained degrees also had to go through the channels of secondary education, led to the conclusion that a comprehensive examination of the intelligentsia in the Dual Monarchy must be based primarily on the study of the social background of those who had attended secondary school, to be complemented by a study of those who attended university. We could not avoid the issue: what proportion of high school graduates actually ended up in some intellectual occupation? On the basis of the career choices of high school graduates it could be ascertained that eighty-five to ninety percent of those with a high school diploma,

---

[3] Rudolf Andorka, "Az értelmiség mobilitásának történeti alakulása" [The historical evolution of the mobility of the intelligentsia], in Huszár, op. cit, pp. 71–96; also, his "Az egyetemi és főiskolai hallgatók társadalmi összetétele, 1898–1942" [The social background of students at institutions of higher learning], *Statisztikai Szemle* [Statistical Review], no. 2 (1979), pp. 176–98.

[4] Mazsu, op. cit., pp. 289–301.

[5] Ibid.

and about three-quarters of those who attended high school but did not graduate, entered directly or eventually on intellectual careers.[6]

As regards the social background of students in secondary and tertiary education, the central concern of socio-historical research in Western Europe, with traditions longer than in Hungary, provides a new approach to formulating the basic issues. This central concern of social and cultural history was revived as a consequence of the student rebellion and the ensuing political debates in the late 1960s: namely, how did access to secondary and higher education on the part of the various strata and classes of society change between the pre-industrial and the industrial periods, as a consequence of the dynamic vertical restructuring of society? Although the results of such research regarding the inequality of access to instruction or training and the causes and extent of changes in accessibility diverged significantly, even when applied to the selfsame society, there was nevertheless a common trait in all this body of research: it did not specifically deal with the issue of how access to education or training affected social mobility.[7]

The reason for this oversight is not to be sought primarily in the political motivation for this body of research, but rather in the fact that, in the nineteenth century, the educational system in Western countries played a function different from the one it played in Hungary; school was not designed to become a "reproducer" or a new social combination, there was no considerable overlap between the replacement function of those completing secondary education as compared to those studying in institutions of higher learning.

On the basis of these schematic considerations the issues of our research can be rephrased as follows:

What sources may be used, and with what degree of validity, regarding the social background of the intelligentsia in the period of the

---

[6] *Magyar Statisztikai Évkönyv*, new series, no. 9, p. 331; ibid., 17, p. 363; 23, p. 258; Vallás és Közoktatási Minisztérium, *Report 11*, p. 243; ibid., *Report 17*, vol. 2, p. 38; ibid., *Report 20*, vol. 2, pp. 52–53; and ibid., *Report 25*, pp. 349–51.

[7] For a summary of the topic see H. Kaelble, *Historische Militatforschung* (Darmstadt, 1978), pp. 73–93.

Dual Monarchy—in other words, what sources can be used to examine the process of intergenerational mobility heading towards the professional class?

What opportunities were historically available to given social groups, and how did these opportunities change.

Sources of Research

In the second half of the nineteenth century, secondary education was made up of two principal functional units. One was the "gimnázium" (middle school and high school) of eight grades leading to an examination qualifying for a diploma. The other, from 1878 on, was the "reáliskola" (middle school and high school) without a classical curriculum. The latter was created by the so-called Thun reform of education. Almost half of the secondary schools in the period of the Compromise were partial institutions (with four or, in some cases, six forms), more or less the equivalent of American middle schools or junior high schools, and only gradually did most of these schools evolve into complete high schools, to satisfy the requirements of the law of 1883, which required a secondary education for many civil service jobs. The so-called public schools [polgári iskola], stressing commercial subjects, were created by the 1868 Act on Public Education. These entered a stage of dynamic development only in the 1890s, and took the place of these "middle schools."[8]

The periodical reports published by the schools, first under the name *Tudósítvány* (later as *Értesítő*), which reported on the operation of the secondary schools and on the activities of the teachers, were prompted by the empire's organization plan promulgated in Hungary in 1850. Because of paragraph 116 of this *Organisations-Entwurf*, in addition to the more or less systematic roster of students, their religious affiliation and the marks obtained were included in the reports which were becoming more and more topically inclusive as time went on.[9] From the

---

8 Mazsu, op. cit.

9 Regarding the topics covered by school reports, see István Medreczky, "Az iskolai értesítők szerkezete" [The components of school transcripts], *Magyar Középiskola* [Hungarian secondary schools] (1909), p. 115.

late 1860s, in addition to data regarding students' perfor-
mance in the schools, these reports included a so-called statistical section which, while omitting names, published data on
the students' religion, their mother tongue and place of residence.

The categories used for determining the students' religion
were identical with those used in the censi of the period; in
accordance with the liberal spirit of the age, but at variance
with the system used in the census of 1869, the data included a
statement regarding the student's mother tongue along with the
language actually spoken, until the introduction of the 1883 Act
on Secondary Schools. From then on the category of language
spoken was reduced to two: namely, "speaks Hungarian" or
"speaks only Hungarian." Unfortunately, the data regarding
place of residence—consisting of the categories, local, from the
county, from a different county, from Croatia and Slavonia, from
another country—do not contain information useful for analysis
today. Beginning with the academic year 1878–1879, the secondary schools under the supervision of the Ministry of
Education, that is public and Roman Catholic institutions, in
compliance with instructions spelled out by the Ministry,
included the "civilian occupation" of the parents of the student.
Secondary schools under denominational supervision introduced this practice from the academic year 1881–1882.[10]

Before returning to the methodological problems occasioned
by the category of civilian occupation, later merely occupation of
the parents or guardians, we must mention another level of statistics in education. According to paragraph 148 of Act XXXVIII
of 1868, the minister of religion and education was to report to
Parliament annually on the state of public education in
Hungary. The periodical publication, printed from 1870 on,
included nationwide summaries of the statistics submitted by
individual secondary schools, along with the statistics, compiled
under different categories, submitted by primary and tertiary

---

[10] See the catalog of school reports of the Széchenyi Library, the catalog of
the National Educational Library and Museum, as well as collection of school
reports held by the Central Library of Kossuth Lajos University, Debrecen.

institutions.[11] The annual reports of the Ministry constitute a source that can be used in conjunction with the school bulletins, since they were based on the data provided by the individual schools. The significance of this source is affected by the fact that it soon swelled to unmanageable proportions, even though the reports remained incomplete.

The annual reports of the Ministry after 1899 were merged with the government reports mandated by paragraph 5 of Act XXXV of 1897; statistics regarding education were published as appendices to the government reports in the annuals on statistics, and they were also printed, in the same format, in the volumes of the *Magyar Statisztikai Évkönyv* [Hungarian statistical yearbook].[12]

From 1878, the statistics on national education, much as the bulletins, included data on the social background of the students in schools under government control and, from 1881, the data were extended to cover all secondary schools. The data regarding the position or occupation of the parents followed the categories used in the contemporary censi, with a time lag and minor differences.[13]

Sets of Categories Used to Indicate Job or Occupation in Educational Statistics

1878
professional
independent farmer
self-employed tradesman and merchant

---

[11] *Reports from the Hungarian Royal Minister of Religion and Education Regarding the State of Public Education, Presented to Parliament* [in Hungarian], nos. 1–27, (Pest, 1871–1873; Budapest, 1874–1898).

[12] A magyar *királyi kormány 1900. évi működéséről és az ország állapotáról szóló jelentés és statisztikai évkönyv* [Statistical yearbook regarding the operations of the Hungarian royal government in 1900. See also yearbooks for 1908–1918, and a report regarding conditions in the country] (Budapest, 1901).

[13] Regarding the statistics on occupations in the population censi see Zoltán Tóth, "Az egyén társadalmi státusza és foglalkozása az osztrák és a magyar társadalomstatisztikákban" [The individuals' social status and occupation in Austrian and Hungarian social statistics], manuscript, 1986.

clerical employee
workers and household employee

1881

self-employed professional
independent farmer
tradesman and industrialist, merchant, entrepreneur, etc.
civil servant
clerical employee
household help, worker

1890

farmer
independent
large landowners and lessees
smallholder and lessees
employee
tradesman
independent
large landowner
small tradesman
employee
merchant, entrepreneur
self-employed
wholesaler
retailer
employee
clerical employee
civil servant
clerk and white collar
military
other professional (doctor, lawyer, clergyman, etc.)

1908

farming
large, mid-size, and smallholder or lessee
smallholder (small lessee), day laborer
other agricultural worker (sharecropper, caretaker, gardener, fisherman)
farm manager

other farming personnel, servant
mining and industry
miner or industrialist
white collar
other (foreman, apprentice, worker)
commerce and transportation
merchant or entrepreneur
white collar
other personnel (noncommissioned officer, apprentice, servant)
civil service and the professions
civil servant or clerk hired by the day
priest, professor or teacher
other professional and his employee
civil servant or other white-collar, servant
officer in the military (honvéd, gendarmes)
noncommissioned officer (honvéd, gendarmes)
day laborer in various branches
pensioner, private individual living on revenues, recipient of alimony
other or of unknown occupation
children from orphanages

1915–1918

---

farming
independent farmer
employee
worker and servant
mining, industry, commerce, banking and transportation
self-employed
white collar
other employee
professional
civilian and military clerk
priest, professor, teacher
other self-employed
civilian and military noncommissioned officer and servant
day laborer in various branches
pensioner, capitalist, alimony receiver, privately employed
other and unknown
children from orphanages

The first methodological problem associated with this two-tiered categorization derives from its statistics: the data regarding occupation, dissociated from other factors determining the social status of the individual (e.g., religion, ethnic background), and dissociated from the individual (i.e., the roster of names), refer to the student population of the whole secondary school, thus making it impossible to relate the various elements to the individual, to reconstruct the real historical and social stratification of the student body, or rather of their parents.

The other important methodological problem is that the abstract statistical categories lump together various groups and occupations belonging to different social classes:

Until 1890, under self-employed, we find large and mid-size landowners lumped together, the peasant population who own farms of various sizes, the big and small entrepreneurs in industry and transport; the workers in agriculture, industry, and communications (commerce, transport, banks) are lumped together as providing personal services; the intelligentsia (including professionals, civil servants, priests, teachers, etc.) with the business administrators. All these categories belonging to different social strata are lumped together even in subsequent periods.

After 1890 the branches of occupation listed approximate social stratification more accurately—separating large from smallholders, big from small entrepreneurs, the employees of various branches and day laborers from servants, moreover by further subdividing the groups belonging to the intelligentsia—but even at this level the various categories cover rather divergent social groups. (The division between great and small entrepreneurs causes further problems, since the censi did not make such a distinction.)

From 1908 the breakdown of categories took a significant step forward—further refinement of the category of smallholders, the differentiation of business administrators by branch, the separation of noncommissioned officers in the military and in the civil service from the officer class—but at the same time there was a big step backward, for landowning and entrepreneurial categories are once again under the same heading.

Finally, the third methodological problem is caused by the frequent shifts in categories, making it difficult to study the various periods comparatively.

If follows from the above, that the analysis of students in secondary schools as the reserve for replacement of the intelligentsia is bound to remain at the macrostructural level; instead of significant groups of social strata all we have at our disposal, are rough and indirect data for statistical analysis.

The reorganization of the categories was done by the combined application of two approaches:

Creating categories to make it possible to compare different periods in such a way that the finer distinctions would still allow us to reconstruct the rougher categories.

Creating a universally understandable set of statistical categories which, hopefully, correspond better to the actual social stratification.[14]

In consideration of the aforementioned limitations, the research issues are modified as follows:

What was the ratio of the various social groups, from 1878 to the World War I, in providing a base for the intelligentsia, and what changes did this base undergo?

In seeking a clearer picture of the process of social mobility, the examination of the makeup of the student body in public secondary schools as compared to universities comes in handy at this point, enabling us to draw conclusions regarding the peculiarities of mobility into the lower ranks of the civil service versus mobility directed at professional careers. At this stage of analysis data regarding religion and ethnic background would have come in handy, to elucidate the relationship between occupation categories and social groups.[15]

What was the secondary schooling of various social groups, and their mobility, in the period under examination, what social

---

[14] For the rearrangement of the categories, see Mazsu, op. cit. On similar methodological problems and their solutions, see Ferenc Földes, "Munkásság és parasztság kulturális helyzete Magyarországon" [The educational status of workers and peasants in Hungary], in Ferenc Földes, *Válogatott írások* [Selected writings] (Budapest, 1967), pp. 13–95; also, Andorka, op. cit.

[15] Mazsu, op. cit.

distances between intelligentsia and other categories are signalled by their varying access to opportunities?[16]

It is not possible, on the basis of these sources, to combine various elements determining status and, moreover, the approximation of the occupation categories listed in the statistics to the historical and social stratification in society—thereby putting an end to the abstract nature of the investigation or to expanding the validity of our conclusions.

It is not further rearranging of statistical categories, or possibly bringing in related data that enhance the validity of the examination on a large scale, but rather the inclusion of sources which are organically related to our two-tiered educational statistics, and which can shed light on the results of the analysis at the macro level by samples from the micro level. This type of source is represented by the "registers" of secondary schools, seldom used for research in social history.

These secondary school registers include sections on the general social status of the individual (occupation of parents, religious affiliation, mother tongue, home address), and data for identification (i.e., the surname), making it possible to include other sources (registries, titles to land, inheritance papers, surviving census reports, tax returns, leases etc.) in identifying the social status of the student and parents. Moreover the empirical job terminology in these registers also gives us access—through an interpretation of the occupational categories in the school reports—to information regarding the historical evolution of the abstract categories.[17]

---

[16] Accepting Parkin's thesis, that the inequalities in social mobility are directly proportionate to the length of the course of mobility, this is how distances and dividing lines between social groups are indicated. Frank Parkin, *Class Inequality and Political Order* (London, 1971). To examine the opportunities for training I used the index of secondary school students per 1,000 wage-earners, relying on data in the censi from 1890, 1900, and 1910. For the mobility of ethnic and religious groups, I used an index based on numbers of secondary school students and proportions within the overall population.

[17] An examination secondary schools registers for Debrecen and the Hajdúság may entail a double distortion. In the value system of the locals the abstract categories had been reinterpreted, thereby significantly diverging from the practice of classification according to the codes in the censi, but beyond the parents' occupation, the classification took into consideration factors that were commonly known in the locality, such as wealth, prestige, noble background, etc.

Since we are limited in the extent to which we can build upon research based on an analysis of the school registers for several reasons (the unwieldy mass of registers, lack of access to such registers in neighboring countries), it is the internal relationship between statistical sources on education and the registers (indices to the reports, similarities in student population) that provide opportunities for choosing our samples, and shed light on the relationship between macro and micro research, regarding the social background of secondary school students in the period of the Dual Monarchy and, through it, on the upward social mobility into the intelligentsia.

Social Background of Secondary School Students during the Age of Dualism

Methodological Schema

Levels of sources	I.	II.	III.
Sources	Reports of the Ministry of Religion and Education, 1878–1898. Reports of thegovernment in the statistical yearbooks, 1899–1900.	Report cards from secondary schools, 1878–.	Registers from secondary schools.
Research data	Nationwide statistical summaries. Discrete data regarding segments of the social background of students in general.	Statistical summaries from the schools regarding segments of the social background of the student body in general.	Rosters pertaining to individual students indicating status (occupation of parents, ethnic background, religion, place of residence, etc).
Elements connecting levels of sources	Identical categories of statistics.	Identical statistical categories. Student rosters.	Student rosters.

Levels of sources	I.	II.	III.
Research possibilities deriving from connecting levels of sources	Position in macro level processes.	Distribution by school, type of school, by providers (parents), by place of residence, by type of settlement, by region. Revealing the classification of students by statistical categories (The peculiarities of these categories).	Revealing the contents of statistical categories (empirical classification of occupation groups). Identification of microgroups by historical, ethnic and religious affiliation, the identification of types. Extending the period of research to before 1878.
Connections to other sources and research procedures	Research on careers (memoirs, diaries, belletristic sources, the press).	Non-statistical data from school report cards (history of institution, schedule of courses, grades, etc.,).	Registers of schools, land registries, wills, summaries of censi, tax returns, apartment leases, etc.

CHAPTER II

The Character and Growth of the Intelligentsia

In Hungarian society, as in others, professional careers and the larger groups that assumed intellectual functions within the social division of labor accompanied industrialization and the evolution of bourgeois society, although the beginnings of the process reach back to the eighteenth and the first half of the nineteenth centuries.[1]

Thus research bearing on groups that perform intellectual functions or tasks in society must begin by taking this into consideration, i.e., the historical roots of this social group and concept. Consequently, it must also consider that "the social role and function of the intelligentsia can only be grasped and analyzed in depth, realistically at the general level."[2]

In our approach historicity does not mean merely that the intelligentsia makes its appearance as a social stratum at a given degree of social development, at the time of the evolution of bourgeois society—even though the distinctive character of groups performing intellectual functions does have precedents

---

[1] Tibor Huszár, "Értelmiségtörténet—értelmiségszociológia" [History and sociology of the intelligentsia], in Huszár, op. cit. p. 5; Károly Vörös, "A modern értelmiség kezdetei Magyarországon" [The beginnings of a modern intelligentsia in Hungary], *Valóság*, no. 10 (1975); Károly Vörös, "A társadalom és iskolaügy a pannon térségben" [Society and the issue of education in Western Hungary], in *Nemzetközi kultúrtörténeti szimpózion, Mogersdorf, 1976* [International symposium on cultural history] (Szombathely, 1978), pp. 14–42; Domokos Kosáry, "Értelmiség és kulturális elit a XVIII. századi Magyarországon" [Intelligentsia and cultural elite in eighteenth-century Hungary], *Valóság*, no. 2 (1981) pp. 11–20.

[2] Tibor Huszár, "Gondolatok az értelmiség szociológiai jellemzőiről és fogalmáról" [Notions regarding the concept of intelligentsia and its sociological traits], *Valóság*, no. 2 (1972); Tibor Huszár, *Fejezetek az értelmiség történetéből* [Chapters from the history of the intelligentsia] (Budapest, 1977), pp. 9–21.

reaching further back—but it also signifies the duality: that though the continuity of the production process makes it possible, nay presupposes the continuous in motion of accumulated experience, hence the continuity of intellectual functions, roles and of the groups performing these, yet the intelligentsia in its quality and character changes together with the structural modification of social division of labor, power relations and culture.

Our first task, mandated by our approach—before a more specific analysis or as a prerequisite for these—is the development of a concept of intelligentsia which, on the one hand, corresponds to the differentiation in the social organization of labor of a given period and to the formation of groups deriving from it, on the other hand, reflects the contemporary social recognition, both materially and prestige-wise; after all the presence or absence of this may have helped or hindered the realization of groups performing intellectual functions as an intelligentsia.

During the eighteenth century secular culture gained momentum in Hungary, and one of its essential elements was that the intellectuals within the churches performed increasingly multiple and differentiated functions (teaching, healing, book publishing, scientific research, etc); moreover, this inner secularization tied in with the gradual broadening of intellectual functions outside the churches, its differentiation, and the intellectualization of a series of tasks that earlier had been tackled empirically.[3]

Among the causes of this process, slow at first, but gaining momentum in the second half of the century, the most important were the attempts at modernization on the part of the enlightened absolutist state, the growth in the production of cash crops by the nobility, the expertization of the administration of the estates regime at the county level, and an end to the stagnation of towns.[4] All these causes account for the fact that by the beginning of the nineteenth century, in addition to the intellectual functions that had been taken care of by the churches

3 Kosáry, op. cit., p. 13.
4 Ibid., pp. 12–13.

and the priesthood, there developed a body of officials employed by the specialized bureaucratic institutions of the centralized administration, a corps of officials in the counties and the larger cities—mainly free towns chartered by the king—dealing with financial or economic matters, a body of managers employed in the complex administration of the large estates, and a cultural elite, which remained mainly within the framework of public education or which was tied by its umbilical cord and dependent on the activities of the magnates as patrons. It can already be noted how little room and demand there was for the practitioners of the so-called free professions, who are the most numerous in industrialized societies. The role of the physician in Hungary was performed, in a manner accessible to the masses, by barbers, medics, or midwives in public employ; any proliferation of lawyers, beyond the limited financial opportunities, was hampered by the restricted rights of the overwhelming majority of the population; even the satisfaction of literary and artistic yearnings deriving from a bourgeois lifestyle did not require a large number of writers or artists.[5]

Yet it is difficult to determine what was the proportion of those practicing the professions for a living, or the ratio of intellectuals among the nobility, just like it is not possible to draw a clear line of division between the two social groups. The essence of the difference between them, however, was obvious in feudal society: "on one side you have social rank, wealth and political role and a certain right to decide—on the other side intellectual work performed as a trade, the main source of income."[6]

It is even more difficult to determine from what strata of society came the groups who were to perform the tasks belonging to the intelligentsia. Considering the family background of the students in secondary institutions in Hungary in the eighteenth century,[7] as well as the impact of the patents issued by Joseph II

---

[5] Vörös, op. cit., pp. 22–23.

[6] Kosáry, op. cit., p. 16.

[7] Zoltán Ambrus-Fallenbüchl, "Magyarország középfokú oktatási viszonyai a XVIII. században" [Secondary schools in Hungary in the eighteenth century], in *Történeti statisztikai évkönyv 1965–1966* [Yearbook of historical statistics 1965–1966] (Budapest, 1966), pp. 174–240.

in 1785, we cannot be far off the mark if we estimate that approximately forty percent of the estimated twenty thousand earning[8] their living as intelligentsia around eighteen hundred did not come from the ranks of the nobility. This estimate is reinforced by the transformation of the meaning of the term "honoratior" in the first decades of the nineteenth century: until the 1820s this term applied to professionals who, although the majority of them came from noble background, were living from the salaries; but the increase in the numbers of honoratior who did not come from the ranks of the nobility had the impact that in the 1830s this designation began to be applied to intellectuals of non-noble background while, because of their actual activities and the similarity in lifestyle, the intellectuals of non-noble background (now called honoratior), their legal status, the jurisdiction of the court, their exemption from taxes, now approximated those of noble[9] background.

In the 1840s some elements of the bourgeoisie also had an impact on the proliferation of those performing intellectual tasks, in the differentiation of those tasks, and in the increase in the rate of growth of their absolute numbers. Yet the majority of those earning salaries as intellectuals were still tied to production under feudal conditions and the feudal social structure: among the sixty to sixty-six thousand persons earning their living as intelligentsia, the largest group were the intelligentsia members of churches (ca. twenty thousand), and in second place we find the civil servants (ca. sixteen thousand). About half as many (ca. ten thousand each) were the camps of the intendants and teachers, mostly in the public schools, while the lawyers numbered about five thousand—even though only a fraction of them actually functioned as lawyers. All those involved in the modern professions (physicians, pharmacists, journalists, writers, artists, engineers) numbered no more than the lawyers.[10]

The particularities of the organization of professions do not

---

[8] Kosáry, op. cit., p. 18.

[9] János Varga, "Megye és haladás a reformkor derekán (1840–1843)" [County and progress at the height of the Age of Reform], *Somogy megye múltjából* [From the past of Somogy County] 11, (1980), pp. 234–236.

[10] Vörös, *A modern értelmiség.*

reflect, in and of themselves, the three basic traits of the development of Hungarian intelligentsia:

a) The intellectual tasks of its rule were performed in large part by the nobility, as was the establishment and administration of its cultural institutions; a group of magnates and lesser nobility with European culture also assumed a significant role in other areas of public life, although their social position, the formation of their groups, their network was still determined by their origins, their place in the system of feudal estates, rather than by the position they occupied within the social organization of work.[11]

We refer to this phenomenon and social group as the non-professional intellectuals even though they did not form an actual group within the aristocracy or the nobility.[12]

b) The intellectual functions of knowledge in the field were performed mainly by non-nobles who were not part of the group above; within the framework of the feudal estates, they were listed as having the status of "honoratior" (neither commoners, nor nobility).[13]

c) In accordance with the above, in the first half of the nineteenth century—given the level of the social division of labor and in harmony with the particularities of social organization in the period—the concept of grouping those fulfilling intellectual functions into a single social group never even occurred to anyone. It is typical, from this point of view, that the concept which eventually was adopted to designate such a group, the

---

[11] Ferenc Erdei, "A magyar társadalom a két világháború között" [Hungarian society between the two wars], *Valóság* 1, no. 4 (1976), p. 47; Huszár, "Értelmiségtörténet," pp. 7–8.

[12] Huszár, op. cit., p. 7.

[13] István Hajnal, "Az osztálytársadalom" [Class society], in *Magyar művelődéstörténet* [The history of education in Hungary] (Budapest, 1941), vol. 5, pp. 165–172.

term "intelligence" first occurred in Hungarian literary usage in 1831, and still with the meaning of "understanding, the ability to understand."[14] It is typical that in 1843 Kossuth still referred to the intellectual "as an abstract concept."[15]

In the second half of the 1840s the growing manifestations of change become significant, not because they dominate, but because of the prospects for the development of a Hungarian intelligentsia. We must stress again that these changes may be explained in part by some elements of a rising bourgeois society, most important among which were: the development of the cultivation of cash crops, the direction and operation of a fledgling industry, a modernizing system of transport and commerce, the transformation in the structure of culture and public access to it, the beginnings of expertise in administration, as well as the development of education and health service serving these ends.[16]

The hitherto weak process of professionalization became stronger as a result of the modification and innovation of intelligentsia functions engendered by embourgeoisement. In addition to the body of elected county officials made up of the landowning nobility, the category of civil servants who lived off their salaries now became numerically significant. This was the period when the right of the ""honoratior" class to hold office was beginning to have an impact.[17]

Rapidly growing institutions of cultural life, moving from the courts of the nobility into towns and cities—the press, book publishing—finally made it possible for those who owned no significant amounts of land or other source of wealth to make a living from their creativity. This was also the time in the evolution of the intelligentsia when the privately employed white-collar worker made its appearance in industry and especially in banking.

---

14 Huszár, "Értelmiségtörténet," p. 7.

15 *Pesti Hírlap*, 26 March 1843.

16 Vörös, *A modern értelmiség*, p. 3.

17 Péter Hanák, "Magyarország társadalma a századforduló idején" [Hungarian society at the turn of the century], in *Magyarország története 1890–1918* [History of Hungary 1890–1918], ed. Péter Hanák (Budapest, 1978), p. 453.

Section 2/d. of Act V of the 1848 March Laws, which laid the constitutional groundwork for the bourgeois transformation of society, did not undertake to define the intelligentsia, merely enumerating all those intellectual occupations that were to provide for their practitioners greater public influence in the future. These were "scientists, surgeons, lawyers, engineers, academic artists, professors, members of learned societies, pharmacists, clergymen, assistant clergymen, notary publics and teachers." It is typical that those who drafted this modern law, which took as its basis the activity performed in the social organization of labor, also felt that economic and legal independence were a condition *sine qua non* of this evolution, and it was on these grounds that they excluded the managers of estates, even though they were to change their mind shortly.[18]

In his study of the beginnings of the intelligentsia in Hungary, Károly Vörös felt the following concept of the intelligentsia would be applicable for empirical research pertaining to the first half of the nineteenth century: the modern intelligentsia "refers to the stratum that performs intellectual, or at least non-manual work evolving as a result of economic development, and in harmony with the nature of this evolution, and finds positions increasingly in new job areas within the framework of the middle-class, or as a result of the expansion of middle-class jobs."[19] Hence the range of jobs fills intellectual functions, that is, one of the main characteristics of the modern intelligentsia, according to Vörös, would be filling intellectual tasks as a matter of occupation. If we give the broadest possible definition to the intellectual functions of social tasks, the historical characteristic of the evolution of the intelligentsia in this early period would be that the intellectual functions are as yet undeveloped and undifferentiated; any narrowing of the definition would limit the examination of the process and the possibility of arriving at meaningful generalizations. His concept of the intelligentsia—considering the contemporary system of education and the amount of training required to fill certain intellectual occupations—is not limited by years of schooling either.

---

18 Vörös, op. cit., p. 10.
19 Ibid., p. 2.

The qualification "modern" implies, even if not explicitly, a traditional intelligentsia which still played a significant role at that time, the majority of whom did not have specialized training and were not tied to an intellectual role as regards their social position or livelihood.

The conclusions of the study of Vörös confirm that his definition is appropriate for empirical research; we feel, however, that it would premature, in the first half of the nineteenth century and even in the 1840s, to consider the groups filling intellectual functions—whether traditional or modern—as a distinct social stratum within the framework of the feudal order of social organization.

The process which began within this feudal order determined the evolution of the Hungarian intelligentsia in subsequent periods in two ways. On the one hand, the intellectual occupations or activities that developed by the first half of the nineteenth century carried with them organically and retained the traits of the feudal order and the prestige of those individuals who filled most of these functions.[20] On the other hand, the training of members of the intelligentsia who filled traditional occupations (government officials, clergymen, managers, lawyers, etc.) had already developed, or had reach high levels in certain cases, while the occupations necessitated by the launching of capitalist development started at a lower point or at a level without any tradition, and reached a higher level only as a result of the gradual transformation of the system of education—a level high enough to earn them the status of intelligentsia according to the social criteria of the time.

Mid-century was a turning point for the whole of Hungarian society, including the evolution of the intelligentsia: the feudal and administrative obstacles to the process of embourgeoisement so relevant to the evolution of the intelligentsia, and more directly to the process of joining the intelligentsia, were practically liquidated.

The following traits of the period from mid-century to the year of the Compromise (1867) are relevant as regards the development of our concept of intelligentsia:

---

[20] Hajnal, op. cit., p. 165–172.

a) As a result of the losses suffered in the war and through emigration, the traditional aristocratic and noble intellectuals who still played a decisive role in the first half of the century were relegated into the background, as regards their significance and their numbers, in comparison with the rapidly growing professional intelligentsia groups.

b) The relative acceleration of capitalist development, as well as the modernization of the state (although the latter was designed to serve the interests of the empire), gave rise to a systematic development of specialized institutions, which organized and subordinated the intelligentsia groups.

c) Parallel to these processes, groups of the intelligentsia began to organize along occupation lines or common interests, basically according to the function they occupied in the division of labor.[21]

It may be pointed out, however, that the first sign of organization of this social stratum was the formation of the National Association of Hungarian Officials [Magyar Tisztviselők Országos Egyesülete], as late as 1874, for this was the first social organization which assumed as its objective the collaboration and representation of every occupation group involved in intellectual work. Regardless of the results achieved by the Association the initial appeal clearly reflects the intelligentsia's consciousness as a stratum: "The Association seeks to promote the interests, resolve the social problems, and improve the oppressing economic situation of all civil servants, at the federal, local or community levels, and of white collar employees in institutions, corporations or private service, and of all those associ-

---

[21] Sándor Peres, *A magyarországi tanítóegyesületek története* [The history of teacher's associations in Hungary] (Budapest, 1896); *Pesti Napló*, 4 March 1866, p. 6; Antal Szaladi, *A magyar hírlapirodalom statisztikája 1780–1880-ig* [Statistics on the Hungarian press from 1780 to 1880] (Budapest, 1896).

ated with them" [meaning those in the liberal professions—J. M.];
not for a moment has the Association lost sight of those obstacles it has to overcome in order to achieve these objectives."[22]

It would be one-sided, however, if in our depiction of two
decades of the transformation of the intelligentsia we were to
note only the tendencies of development, and neglected the factors of continuity, or the fresh contradictions that surfaced at
this time—contradictions referred to succinctly, in the above
appeal, as obstacles to social organization. The most basic difficulty was that society as a whole did not transform itself into a
bourgeois-national society. What more, even the social estates
from before 1848 merely fell apart and, while some of its segments were able to join the process of capitalist development,
others were not: in the case of peasantry and of the gentry, the
overwhelming majority did not. In the case of ethnic groups, the
imperial tendencies merely enhanced the processes of dissolution and divergence.[23] The extent to which the techniques of
bourgeois social organization were unable to reconstitute the
disintegrating social elements into a new estate, is revealed in
the analyses of contemporaries, based on direct experience.
Among these the analysis and conclusion of Gyula Schwarcz at
the end of the period is the most fitting: "Hungarian society, as
we have seen, does not yet exist in an organic sense: the individual strata of the Hungarian nation are nothing more, to this
day, than more or less isolated remnants of those estates that
were already in existence before forty-eight...."[24]

Intellectual occupation groups presented a picture no more
harmonious. In addition to their porous, fragmented origins, their

---

[22] *Magyar Tisztviselő* [Hungarian official], 18 October 1874, p. 2.

[23] György Szabad, "Az önkényuralom kora (1849–1867)" [The age of arbitrary
rule], in *Magyarország története 1848–1890* (Budapest, 1979), pp. 525–608;
Huszár, "Értelmiségtörténet," p. 8.

[24] *A közoktatásügyi reform mint politikai szükséglet Magyarországon* [Educa-
tional reform as political necessity in Hungary] (Pest, 1869), p. 181. As for
Károly Keleti, he refers to the process of social disintegration as nothing less
than the formation of a caste system. *Hazánk és népe a közgazdaság és a társadalmi statisztika szempontjából* [Our country and its people from the point of
view of economics and social statistics] (Pest, 1871), p. 152.

segmentation according to ethnic group and denomination, according to whether they belonged to hierarchical institutions or to institutions of objective function, or whether they owed their allegiance to the empire as a whole or to some division of it, they were also divided by levels of education, levels of income or wealth, and by level of social prestige.[26]

Strong fragmentation and heterogeneity on the one hand, homogeneous professionalization of social existence on the other —this explains why the occupation groups filling the functions of the intelligentsia were seen by the public, and even in the specialized literature, in a contradictory manner or as containing partial truths as a social group and as a concept.

The concepts developed by the public may be traced through contemporary dictionaries and encyclopedias. The *Little Italian Interpreter* of Antal Ágoston, published in 1864, did not include any collective noun to identify the intelligentsia as a whole, it merely included terms for particular occupations such as judge, lawyer, doctor, surgeon, etc.[27]

The dictionary published by Czuczor and Fogarasi in the same period is more thorough, for it includes the term "értelmiség" (intelligentsia) and its meanings: "General meaning: power of intellect, the sum of intelligent men"—in other words, it is no more than a synonym for the earlier term "intelligence."[28]

As an indication of the confusion of values deriving from traditions of Hungarian social history rather than of the peculiarities of the evolution of the intelligentsia and its stratification, three decades later the *Great Encyclopedia of Pallas*, and even the *Great Révai Encyclopedia* published the year World War I broke out could not come up with anything better as regards the meaning of the term "értelmiség."[29]

---

[26] Schwarcz, op. cit., p. 181.

[27] *Kis olasz tolmács* [Little Italian interpreter] (Pest, 1864).

[28] Gergely Czuczor and János Fogarasi, *A magyar nyelv szótára* [Dictionary of the Hungarian language] (Pest, 1864) vol. 2, p. 539.

[29] *A Pallas nagy lexikona* (Budapest, 1895), vol. 9; *Révai nagy lexikona* (Budapest, 1908), vol. 10.

In Schwarcz's *Educational Reform* the meaning of the term "közértelmiség" (general intelligentsia) barely differs from the second definition contained in the Czuczor and Fogarasi dictionary; yet we know that he was aware of the main tendencies of transformation of the intelligentsia as we had sketched them above, not only because of the nuances in his analysis, but as indicated in explicit language: "They play a nasty game in our country with the term 'értelmiség.' Quite often they refer to the ownership of a few hundred acres of land as 'értelmiség,' as if these two things were necessarily identical."[30] The occupation categories listed in the census of 1869 reflect one of the basic traits of the transformation that had taken place, namely the diversification of careers in the intelligentsia by the addition of private white-collar employees in the modern sector of the economy, although they were not yet listed among those with "intelligentsia income."[31]

The preface to the census also reflects the confusion in evaluations, even in scientific circles, caused by the dimensions and quality of the change:

> Perhaps it is the heading "earnings of the intelligentsia" that requires most explanation, and here too it may be mostly the heading that could be criticized. It is natural that, in public life, the farmer, the craftsman or industrialist, the merchant also be ranked among the so-called intelligentsia.
>
> We do not mean to begrudge them this title, but the difference between them and those counted under this column is that their occupation is attached to objects: the land, the industrial plant, a trade, the store, etc., while under intelligentsia we have classified mostly members of the so-called free professions or those related to them.[32]

---

[30] Schwarcz, op. cit., p. 45.

[31] *A magyar korona országaiban 1870 elején végrehajtott népszámlálás eredménye* [The results of the census conducted in the countries of the Hungarian crown at the beginning of 1870] (Pest, 1871).

[32] Ibid., p. 254

Thus the census, conducted at a more advanced stage of the process, provides us with a working point of reference. The starting point of the authors of the volume compiling the results of the first really modern Hungarian census, that of 1890, was an analysis of the structure of Hungarian society, defining the category intelligentsia in the following terms: "all those segments of the population whose earnings [i.e., their specialized training and knowledge—J. M.]...form the basis of their livelihood, whether in the service of the state and society, or as practitioners of the so-called free professions, or employed in the economic sector—that is, in agriculture, mining, industry, transportation and communication, carrying on the pertinent intellectual labor."[33] Under "intelligentsia" the instructions attached to the census sheets gave a list of specific occupations, on the basis of the principle enunciated:

> *actual intelligentsia:* all civil servants (even clerks), teachers and professors, clergymen, monks, nuns, doctors, midwives, staff of hospitals, pharmacists, lawyers, private and other engineers, artists;

> *intelligentsia in the economic sector:* agricultural engineers, forestry rangers, estate managers, railroad engineers and other railroad white-collar employee, public engineers, mining engineers, white-collar employee in industry, chemists, draughtsmen, bank clerks.[34]

Near the end of the century, and at the beginning of the twentieth century, we encounter increasing signs that the rapidly growing intelligentsia may rightly be considered a separate stratum within the framework of the "gentry and educated middle-class"—separate from other classes and strata of society, because of their social organization, the formation of a particular intellectual profile[35]—rather

---

[33] *Magyar Statisztikai Közlemények,* new series, vol. 2, p. 83.

[34] Ibid.

[35] Tibor Huszár, "Az értelmiségszociológia és szociográfia hazai történetéhez" [Contribution to the history of Hungarian sociology of the intelligentsia], in *Értelmiségszociológiai írások Magyarországon 1900–1945* [Writings on the sociology of the intelligentsia in Hungary] (Budapest, 1981), pp. 8–32.

than merely a collective statistical category or a description of kind of work.[36]

We deem the following to be the most important among the processes of social stratification:

a) the process of how the intellectual function became a bourgeois occupation, or became professionalized, took on a very specific form in Hungary in the nineteenth century (probably true about most "third world" countries in the twentieth century). Since the state assumed a significant role in creating conditions favorable to capitalist development, and especially since large foreign concerns appeared on the Hungarian economic scene rather early,[37] the most typical member of the intelligentsia was the government employee living off his salary.

In spite of the rapid growth, during the four decades following mid-century, of the ratio of so-called free professionals who depended on market relations, they never exceeded ten percent of all members of the intelligentsia. After the industrial takeoff, the intelligentsia became even more pronouncedly a class of employees: in 1910 less than eight percent of them were independent as regards their earnings. See table 2.

---

[36] Zsuzsa Ferge, *Társadalmunk átrétegződése* [The transformation of the stratification of our society] (Budapest, 1969), pp. 81–2.

[37] Szabad, op. cit., pp. 542–548, 566–570, 572–580; Iván T. Berend and György Ránki, "A modern tőkés gazdaság kialakulása—az ipari forradalom kora (1848–1914)" [The formation of modern capitalist economy—the age of the industrial revolution], in *A magyar gazdaság száz éve* [A hundred years of Hungarian economy] (Budapest, 1972), pp. 17–105.

TABLE 2

White-Collar and Intelligentsia Occupations in Hungary in 1900–1910[38] (Excluding Croatia-Slavonia)

Occupation Group	1900	1910
Government employees	76,930	95,767
In church service	48,948	54,107
Employees of private companies and institutions	75,324	122,325
In the professions	17,227	23,620
Government Employees		
Legislation	278	202
Administration	34,135	41,442
Justice	11,184	11,209
Education	8,418	13,814
Public health	3,110	4,879
Armed forces	7,888	9,684
State owned enterprise	11,917	14,537
In Church Service		
Priests, monks, nuns	18,003	18,637
Laymen employed by churches	2,896	2,388
Teachers, professors including community level	28,049	33,082
Employees of Private Companies, Institutions		
Agriculture (plus forestry)	11,350	10,604
Industry (plus mining)	17,328	32,167
Commerce	25,839	44,881
Transportations, postal services	10,706	17,194
Private schools	1,220	1,682
Health maintenance doctors	272	370
Scientific and public societies	1,220	3,550
Paralegals and clerks	4,201	7,905
Assistant pharmacists	1,274	2,283
Other white-collar and clerical	1,863	1,684
In the Professions		
Lawyers	4,190	6,443
Physicians (including Veterinarians)	2,696	2,580
Literature and the arts	3,870	5,304
Self-employed tutors, professors	5,565	7,821
Engineers	858	1,409
Self-employed secretaries, counselors	48	63

38 *Magyar Statisztikai Közlemények,* new series, vol. 27, pp. 240–247, vol. 62, p. 211, and vol. 64, pp. 205–211; *A m. kir. kormány 1900. évi működéséről és az ország közállapotairól szóló jelentés és statisztikai évkönyv* [Report and statistical yearbook on the activities of the Hungarian royal government in 1900 and the state of the country] (Budapest, 1901), pp. 449, 569–603, 660–710; and *A m. kir. kormány 1910. évi működéséről és az ország közállapotairól szóló jelentés és statisztikai évkönyv* [Report and statistical yearbook on the activities of the royal Hungarian government in 1910 and the state of the country] (Budapest, 1911), pp. 67, 119, 225–261, 322–385.

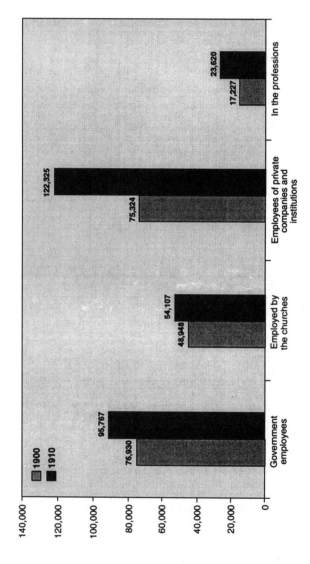

Gainfully Employed Intelligentsia by Occupation

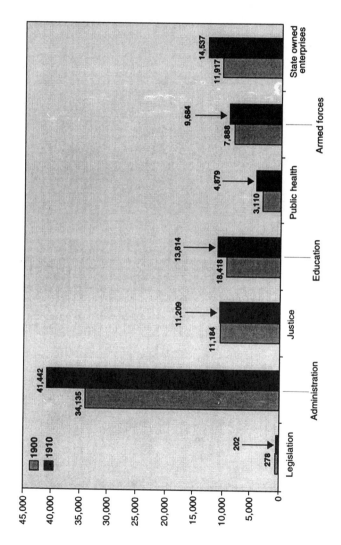

1. Government Employees

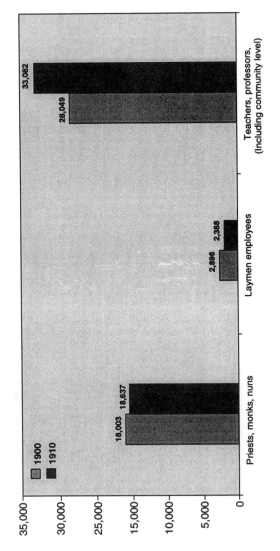

2. In Church Service

1900
1910

Priests, monks, nuns
18,003   18,637

Laymen employees
2,896   2,388

Teachers, professors,
(Including community level)
28,049   33,082

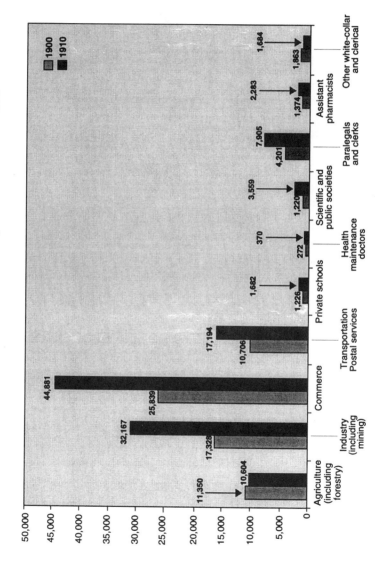

3. Employees of Private Companies and Institutions

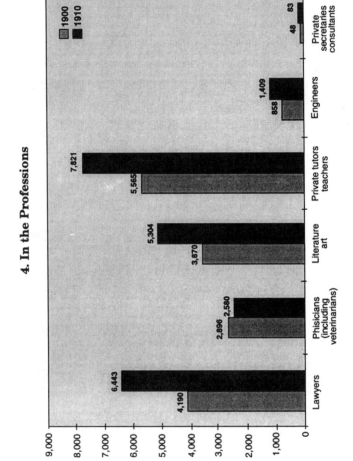

4. In the Professions

b) In the second half of the nineteenth century the evolution
of the intelligentsia occurred well above the rather low
level of mass culture: while there were differences in levels of education between urban and rural populations, as
well as between regions and genders, over one half of the
population of Hungary above six years of age could neither read nor write at the time of the census of 1869,[39]
whereas those able to enjoy serious literature and the
products of the press numbered barely 100,000, less than
one percent of the total population.[40] The cultural gap
between the intelligentsia and other social groups must
have reinforced the intelligentsia's sense of belonging, as
a negative factor of stratification.

c) The fragmentation of society in Hungary and the lack of
a national bourgeoisie embodying in its system of values bourgeois transformation as a matter of self-inter-
est compelled the theoreticians of a national-liberal ide-
ology to draft a program to overcome this lack. The
requirement that there be an "educated middle-class," a
"public intelligentsia" with the mission of promoting
embourgeoisement, the organization of a national society, and the preservation of the hegemony of Hungarian
culture became a cornerstone of the models of liberal
embourgeoisement from mid-century on and penetrated
into the consciousness of the intelligentsia itself.[41] This
sense of mission seems to have been considerably
enhanced by the restoration of the nation-state at the
time of the Compromise, for in the consciousness of the
intelligentsia with a Western culture the state "filled a
rather important role....They conceived of the state as
above narrow party struggles and above the broader
class struggle, in fact, they saw the state in the hands of
the intelligentsia, especially in the hands of the experts."[42]

---

[39] Keleti, op. cit., pp. 356–371.

[40] Ibid., pp. 386–371.

[41] Béla G. Németh, *Létharc és nemzetiség* [Struggle for survival and nation-
ality] (Budapest, 1976), pp. 280–281; Schwarcz, op. cit., pp. 181–182.

[42] Németh, op. cit., pp. 21, 27.

We must attribute a role in this relatively early stratum-
consciousness of the intelligentsia to the political and
ideological tenets it held and to its illusions regarding
the nation-state.

In order to form our concept of the intelligentsia in Hungary
based on the evolution of its historical traits we must assess two
interpretations often discussed in specialized literature, namely: excluding those white-collar who had not earned an official
high school diploma, and limiting the intelligentsia to scientists
and artists.[43] The latter interpretation may be traced to peculiar
historical reminiscences: in the second half of the nineteenth
century the term intelligentsia had often been monopolized by
groups of intelligentsia with a Western perspective, with
humanistic culture,[44] who refused to recognize the technicians,
the economists, not to mention the "apprentices" belonging to
the intelligentsia, the white-collar in the economic sector, who
remained in limbo on account of their low level of preparation.
  Those who used the term intelligentsia in this narrow sense
kept referring to two aspects of the issue: one, their awareness
of the fact that, in the second half of the nineteenth century,
with modernization and the gradual elaboration of the educational system, the school had become the only channel leading
into the intelligentsia; the other, drawing a clear-cut line at the
level of training that goes with the diploma, and cited by way of
proof, in addition to the arguments above, Act I of 1883, the law
regarding qualifications for the civil service.
  The starting premise of the former interpretation is justified,
even though it often served merely to identify the intelligentsia
with those groups of the intelligentsia who had earned degrees,
without delving into the issue; but it overlooked the fact that,
until the 1880s, the employment of officials who were literate
and no more was a common practice at mid- and lower levels of
administration, provided their background and political views
conformed with whatever served the purposes of the regime. A

---

[43] Huszár, "Értelmiségtörténet," pp. 13–15.
[44] Németh, op. cit., pp. 7–42.

clear example of this is one of the memoranda pertaining to the replacement of county officials in 1867, from the county of Esztergom: twenty-three of the fifty-eight officials selected had not attended school beyond the primary; in the column provided for justifying the selection we often find observations to the effect "experienced because of length of service," or "obtained his familiarity with legal science in his capacity of deputy sheriff," in spite of the fact that over one third of them were assigned to positions above that of clerk.[45] The bill regarding qualifications, adopted in around 1875, applied only to those who were appointed after the law went into effect; section 34 specified that it was not retroactive, that those lacking the necessary training would not be affected by it. The regulations regarding the qualifications of newly hired employees likewise did not require education beyond the high school diploma and, according to the division of labor in a given agency, required even less when it came to clerical personnel, or personnel paid by the day. According to the distinctions in the law, even at the beginning of the twentieth century only two-thirds of county officials had completed secondary school; about one third of all county employees had less education, usually four years of middle school.[46]

Only from the last decade of the Dual Monarchy do we have comprehensive sources regarding the educational background of the entire intelligentsia, and even here the categories only reveal the degree of secondary schooling and provide no information regarding those with advanced training or regarding the type of school attended. Nevertheless, we have enough information to draw the lower line regarding the historically valid limit to joining the ranks of the intelligentsia in the second half of the nineteenth century (see table 3).

---

[45] Records of the Ministry of the Interior, State Archives, vol. 148, 1867, part 3, pp. 516–1269.

[46] *Magyar Statisztikai Közlemények*, new series, vol. 40, p. 10.

TABLE 3

Distribution of the Employed Intelligentsia According to Years of Secondary Schooling in 1910[47]

Occupational group / Years of schooling	% of Salary-earning Females			% of Salary-earning Males			% of Total		
	8	6	4	8	6	4	8	6	4
White collar in agriculture and horticulture	8.70	15.22	82.61	42.89	54.77	76.08	42.73	54.58	76.11
Forestry officials			100.00	59.54	70.55	92.80	59.47	70.47	92.80
White collar in mining and smelting	8.89	20.00	91.11	61.51	70.16	87.58	60.00	68.73	87.68
White collar in industry	6.91	16.17	69.00	45.71	56.60	82.25	38.36	48.95	79.74
Banking and commerce	8.24	19.86	82.86	46.95	55.49	76.84	40.42	49.48	77.85
White collar in transportation	5.29	13.55	84.14	66.35	75.50	93.72	49.68	58.58	91.10
Public service and the professions	38.42	48.39	64.94	75.83	83.41	93.76	66.84	74.99	86.79

47 *Magyar Statisztikai Közlemények*, new series, vol. 64, p. 270. For description of the secondary school system, see pp. 91–92 and appendix 14.

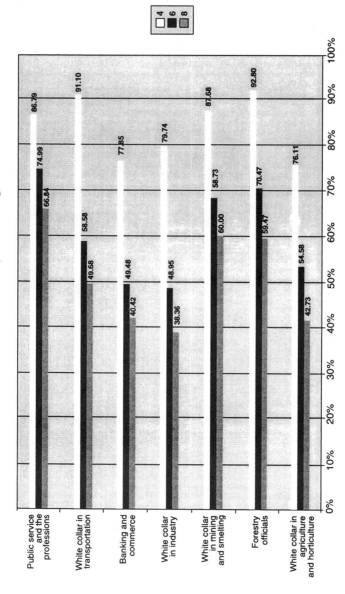

Distribution of the Employed Intelligentsia According to
Years of Secondary Schooling

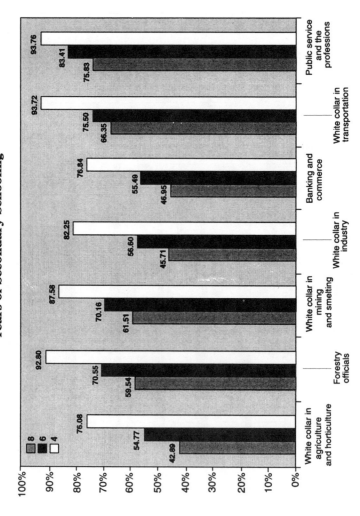

Distribution of the Employed Male Intelligentsia According to Years of Secondary Schooling

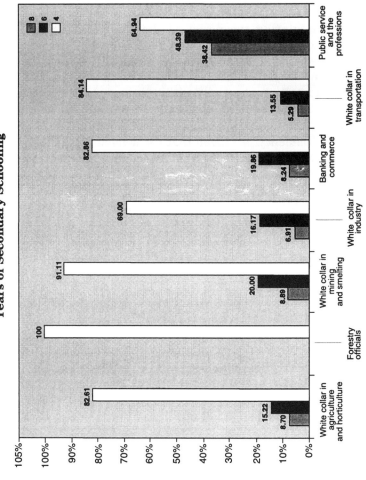

Distribution of Employed Female Intelligentsia According to Years of Secondary Schooling

The data above clearly reveal that the minimum training of the intelligentsia was four years of middle school: the overwhelming majority of the intelligentsia had at least this much schooling in the last decade of the Dual Monarchy. This was also the dividing line between the intelligentsia and other social groups.[48]

Thus, during the period of the Dual Monachy, when the bourgeois technique of social organization was becoming dominant, we feel that the hallmark of membership in the intelligentsia—in process of formation—was, in addition to performing an intellectual activity within the social division of labor as a matter of profession, the tendency to complete four years of formal training (or schooling) at the secondary school level.[49]

By "tendency" we mean that the level of expertise in certain white collar occupations (primarily white collar in the economic sector), the social organization of labor, the evolution of organizations at the plant level, and the differentiation of intellectual activities, were already in process and on the verge of becoming permanent features during this period.

Our concept of the intelligentsia requires that the censi of this period be rectified in two respects: we must include the white collar in the economic sector under the category of intelligentsia, even though they were not considered as such in the census of 1869; while the rather extensive and homogenous group of midwives, who were classified as intelligentsia in the censi, do not belong there, for only a small fraction of them achieved the level of training indicated above, even during the last decade of the period.

Dividing the intelligentsia by level of education also constitutes one of the determining factors and signifiers within the category itself—some of the occupation groups classified as "public service and professionals" (i.e. physicians, engineers, judges, attorneys, teachers, professors, clergymen) received pre-

---

[48] Ibid., the entire chart.

[49] In the census of white-collar workers conducted about thirty years later, in 1928, completion of four years of secondary school was considered the minimum qualification for belonging to the intelligentsia. *Magyar Statisztikai Közlemé-nyek*, new series, vol. 79, p. 6.

scribed higher level or specialized training. Yet this is only one of the determinants, because the associations or institutions to which the individual belonged, wealth, social background, as well as the position she or he occupied in the hierarchy of power (i.e. political life) also played determining roles in the formation of the social status of the intelligentsia and of its components.

CHAPTER III

Growth Trends of the Intelligentsia and Changes in Its Occupational Structure

The lack of contemporary sources make it extremely difficult to provide statistics on the evolution of the intelligentsia in the period between the 1840s and the Compromise of 1867.[1] The method by which the census of 1857 had been conducted renders it inappropriate not only for an examination of the shifts in the occupation of the intelligentsia, but even for registering its numbers. Thus the trends in that period can be determined only on the basis of a comparison of the data from the censi of the 1840s and of 1869, as corrected by our interpretation, using the data merely as signposts.

The data on the next page from the beginning with those from the end of this twenty year period—in spite of the divergence of the data—indicates with a satisfactory degree of probability the main proportions and characteristics of the process once the restrictions in force in the 1840s had been lifted; parallel with the modification of the functional and occupational structure of the intelligentsia there is an almost explosive growth in numbers, which did not abate until the sixties. The causes of this growth may be identified as the increasingly elaborate bureaucracy (the number of civil servants increased by 122 percent), the takeoff of a capitalist economy (a twenty percent increase in the number of white collar workers in private business), and the growing demand for skilled workers, including the intelligentsia (e.g., an increase of 172 percent in the number of teachers). How dynamic was the growth of the intelligentsia during this period is indicated not only by the fact that their numbers

---

[1] Szabad, op. cit., pp. 594–597.

just about doubled overall, but their proportions within the general population also almost doubled: while in the 1840s they represented at best 0.5 percent of the total population, by 1869 they constituted 0.91 percent and, if family members are included, over 2.5 percent of the total population!

The national averages, however, conceal significant regional differences both from the point of view of occupational structure of the intelligentsia and from the point of view of its proportion to the population.

The evolution of the counties on the left bank of the Danube were the closest to the national average, while, from the point of view of population, the southern regions were the furthest away and, from the point of view of occupational structure, Transylvania was the least dynamic. The indicators of evolution in the region between the Danube and the Tisza and, within that region, of the county of Pest-Buda make it evident that the real differences lie not so much between regions, as between urban and rural areas: while the proportion of the intelligentsia among the urban population hovered between three and five percent at the time of the Compromise, the ratio of intelligentsia to the population in lesser settlements barely exceeded 0.5 percent. As regards the occupational structure, the difference between the intelligentsia of the cities and of the country is most evident in the case of clergymen and those in commercial occupations: the ratio of the former in urban areas was between two and eight percent as opposed to fourteen to twenty percent in small settlements, whereas the ratio of the latter was thirty to forty-five percent in the cities, and only an average of six percent in small settlements. Even so, the extremely divergent proportions of intelligentsia in the professions—those which indicate the connection between urban centers and the overwhelming majority of intellectual occupations—do not fully reveal the ever-growing gap between the evolution of the intelligentsia in the cities and in the country, for the quick expansion of the demand for professionals in the capital and other urban centers did not suffice to guarantee full employment to the educated youth, thus leading to intellectual unemployment; on the other hand, "many counties are barely able to muster three or four individuals with an up-to-date preparation in the field" into the most important

TABLE 4

Growth of Intelligentsia Occupations in Hungary between the 1840s and 1869[2]

Occupational group	the 1840s (estimated)	1857	1869	Effectives in as percentages of 1840s
Clergyman	20,686	19,606	19,858	96.00
Civil servant	16,000	52,789	35,540	222.13
Teacher	10,000		27,221	272.21
Estate manager	10,000	4,958	16,063	160.63
Lawyer	4,800	3,345	4,884	101.75
Physician, pharmacist	3,000	7,267	5,295	167.05
Art, music, and literature	1,000	12,571	2,000	200.00
Technocrats	1,000			
White collar in industry			12,608	
White collar in commerce			6,566	
White collar in transportation			5,517	
Bank clerks			2,413	
Total:	66,486		137,965	207.50

[2] Vörös, *A modern értelmiség*; Szabad, op. cit., pp. 594–597; *A magyar korona országaiban 1870 elején végrehajtott népszámlálás*, pp. 257, 260–331. We have modified the data from the census of 1869: at this point white-collar personnel employed in the economic sector were not regarded as members of the intelligentsia; we regard them as such. We have not included, however, midwives among the intelligentsia, for most of them had not attained the minimum of four years of secondary schooling; we have also excluded military officers.

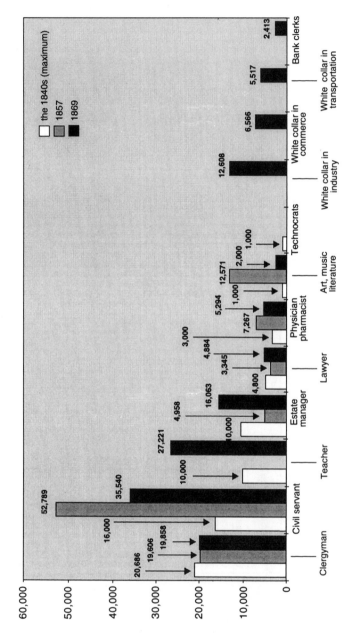

Growth of the Intelligentsia Occupations in Hungary between the 1840s and 1869

TABLE 5

Distribution of Occupation among the Intelligentsia and Its Proportion within the Population by Region[3] (without Fiume and Croatia-Slavonia)

Occupational group (%)	Left bank of Danube	Right bank of Danube	Between Danube and Tisza	Pest and Buda	Right bank of Tisza	Left bank of Tisza	Southern Regions	Transylvania	National average
Clergyman	15.62	14.97	6.82	2.04	13.93	15.07	14.56	21.94	14.60
Civil servant	22.91	19.09	30.90	33.12	24.33	25.18	25.78	30.31	26.13
Teacher	20.85	23.12	12.52	9.49	24.34	24.45	18.96	23.40	20.02
Estate manager	16.83	15.18	6.55	0.78	14.06	13.53	13.30	6.32	11.81
Lawyer	3.57	3.57	5.00	5.04	3.45	4.01	3.85	2.48	3.59
Physician, pharmacist	2.38	3.48	4.01	4.07	1.82	2.41	3.04	2.10	2.83
Art, music, literature	0.91	1.00	1.32	1.21	1.04	1.21	1.04	0.96	1.06
Technocrats	7.85	10.38	4.89	2.38	8.82	7.34	7.73	5.51	7.82
White collar in industry	2.67	0.27	0.10	0.06	3.39	1.16	1.89	2.01	1.45
White collar in commerce	2.13	3.66	15.90	26.08	1.62	1.72	4.01	1.33	4.83
White collar in transportation	2.60	3.44	8.95	12.21	1.68	2.40	4.29	2.33	4.05
Bank clerks	1.65	1.82	3.02	3.17	1.51	1.61	1.53	1.30	1.77
	Left bank of Danube	Right bank of Danube	Between Danube and Tisza	Pest and Buda	Right bank of Tisza	Left bank of Tisza	Southern Regions	Transylvania	National average
Total number of intelligentsia:	16,677	18,224	22,148	12,510	15,812	14,961	18,337	17,296	135,965*
Percentage of total population:	0.96	0.86	1.45	4.92	1.06	0.83	0.71	0.82	0.99

* Excludes the two thousand intellectuals in art, music, and literature.

[3] A *magyar korona országaiban 1870 elején végrehajtott népszámlálás*, pp. 260–331. This census included the foreign residents in Hungary, but excluded Hungarians in military service. The accepted figure for the total Hungarian population is 13.6 million.

Distribution of the Intelligentsia by Region

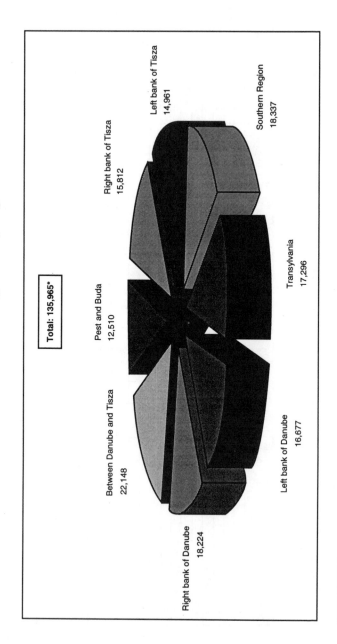

Total: 135,965*

Left bank of Tisza
14,961

Southern Region
18,337

Right bank of Tisza
15,812

Transylvania
17,296

Pest and Buda
12,510

Between Danube and Tisza
22,148

Left bank of Danube
16,677

Right bank of Danube
18,224

* Excludes the two thousand intellectuals in art, music, and literature.

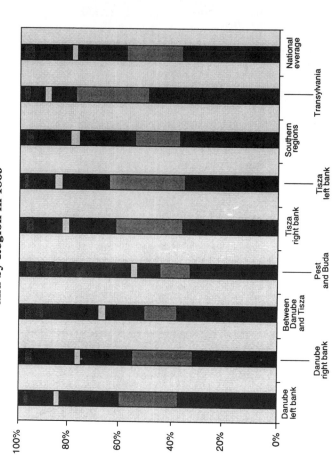

Distribution of the Intelligentsia by Occupation and by Region in 1869

Bank clerk
White collar in transportation
White collar in commerce
White collar in mining
White collar in industry
Pharmacist
Physician
Lawyer
Estate manager
Teacher
Civil servant
Clergyman

National average
Transylvania
Southern regions
Tisza left bank
Tisza right bank
Pest and Buda
Between Danube and Tisza
Danube right bank
Danube left bank

100%
80%
60%
40%
20%
0%

See appendix 16 for color version.

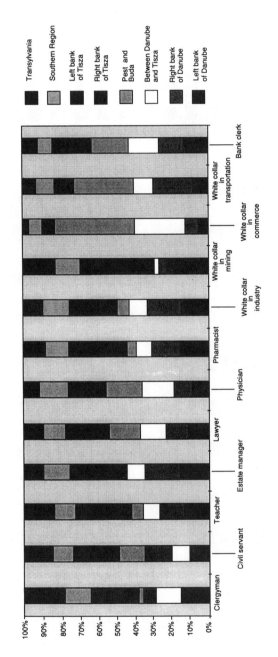

Distribution of the Intelligentsia by Occupation and by Region in 1869

positions of municipal government,[4] and it was not unusual to find in the village schools a schoolmaster who was a retired enlisted man or a fired apprentice.[5]

By restoring the nation-state and the political hegemony of the Hungarian ruling classes the Compromise modified the conditions for the evolution of the intelligentsia. The most important among these conditions was: the promotion of capitalist development and the evolution of bourgeois society. For the intelligentsia it was the ideological value system of the Hungarian political and administrative elite and its socio-political practice which served as a magnet.

Because of the shortcomings of the census of 1880—for this was the time the system of self-counting was implemented[6]—it is inadequate for measuring changes in the occupational makeup of the intelligentsia; hence once again we receive a reliable picture of these changes only over a twenty year period, on the basis of the occupational statistics provided by the 1890 census. By 1890, however, there evolved a system of gathering statistics that was to remain in place for the later period of the Dual Monarchy. In other words, the homogenous nature of the sources renders their interpretation more reliable.

---

[4] Schwarz, op. cit., p. 45.

[5] Ibid., p. 96.

[6] The reason for this was the spread of the method of self-counting: because of the inaccurate communication of data they were unable to classify 23,000 members of the intelligentsia into specific occupation groups. *A magyar korona országaiban 1880 elején tartott népszámlálás* [Census of the lands of the Hungarian crown held at the beginning of 1880] (Budapest, 1882), vol. 1.

TABLE 6

Occupational Distribution of the Intelligentsia in 1890[7]

Administration	28,874
Law enforcement	16,962
Ecclesiastic service	21,473
Education	37,139
Public health (except midwives)	7,813
Scientific societies and associations	466
Literature and art	2,483
Other professions	3,447
Agriculture	12,745
Mining and smelting	1,334
Industry	10,948
Commerce and banking	13,298
Transportation	15,654
Total:	172,636

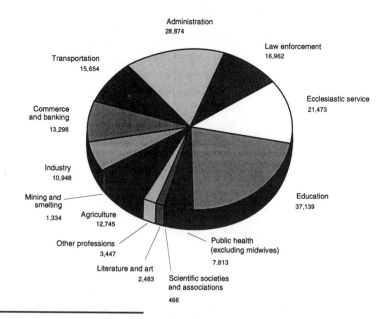

---

[7] *Magyar Statisztikai Közlemények,* new series, vol. 2, 83–110.

The comparison of the occupational makeup of the Hungarian intelligentsia on the basis of the censi of 1869 and 1890 indicates deceleration of the rate of change.[8] Not only did the rate of increase of the intelligentsia in proportion to the total population slow down—for it increased from 0.91 to merely 0.99 percent—while the population growth as a whole stagnated as well, but there was no major shift in the occupational structure either. The causes for this are to be sought in the economic crisis of 1873 and, after the recovery, in the slow "preparation"[9] for the Hungarian industrial revolution. The evolution of the intelligentsia in this period corresponds to the likewise slow but extensive transformation of the structure of Hungarian society in general.[10]

It was not in this area that the changes were truly significant; rather, the characteristics of the evolution in the earlier period gained full momentum in the twenty years following the Compromise:

Those in the professions became generally organized, and there were even attempts to organize across the professions.[11]

The typical accompaniment of capitalist development, the "free professions" akin to free enterprise, became the norm. This main trait[12] of the development of the intelligentsia in Western Europe in the period of classical capitalism became a more significant factor in Hungary at this time.[13]

---

[8] Ottó Szabolcs came to the same conclusion in "A modern értelmiség kialakulásának történetéhez Magyarországon" [Contribution to the history of the formation of a modern intelligentsia in Hungary], *Századok,* nos. 3–4 (1968), p. 593.

[9] Iván T. Berend and György Ránki, "A modern tőkés gazdaság kialakulása—az ipari forradalom kora (1848–1914)" [The formation of a modern capitalist economy—the age of the industrial revolution], in *A magyar gazdaság száz éve* [Hundred years of Hungarian economy] (Budapest, 1972), pp. 17–105.

[10] Hanák, op. cit.

[11] János Pruzsinszky, *Ötven esztendő a Magyar Köztisztviselők Országos Egyesületének életéből* [Fifty years of the existence of the National Association of Hungarian Government Employees] (Budapest, 1924).

[12] Huszár, "Értelmiségtörténet," p. 6.

[13] Part of the body of lawyers is still performing traditional activities, but the observation of Lajos Kralik applies to the majority of them: "Ninety percent of the range of activities carried out by lawyers may be described as acting as agents..." *A magyar ügyvédség múltjából* [From the past of the law profession in Hungary] (Budapest, 1904), vol. 2, p. 30.

Finally, the plant measure resulting from the concentration of capital in the modern economic sector—the group of white-collar employees in this sector and differentiated in accordance with the changes in the plant structure—went parallel with the expansion of economically oriented instruction at the secondary and tertiary levels.

From the last decade of the nineteenth century, the growth and structural change of the intelligentsia once again became dynamic as a result of a full-fledged industrial revolution.

TABLE 7

Distribution of the Intelligentsia According to Main Occupational Categories in 1900–1910[14]

	1900	1910
Administration	38,588	46,799
Law enforcement	21,512	28,097
Ecclesiastic service	23,346	23,406
Education	46,866	60,816
Public health (excl. midwives)	9,635	12,232
Scientific societies	1,290	3,793
Literature and art	4,154	5,614
Other professions	3,146	3,698
Agriculture	12,558	12,367
Mining and smelting	1,212	1,664
White collar in industry	18,011	34,086
White collar in commerce	27,174	47,892
White collar in transportation	21,670	30,796

---

14   *Magyar Statisztikai Közlemények*, new series, vol. 64, pp. 166–167. The table includes Croatia-Slavonia.

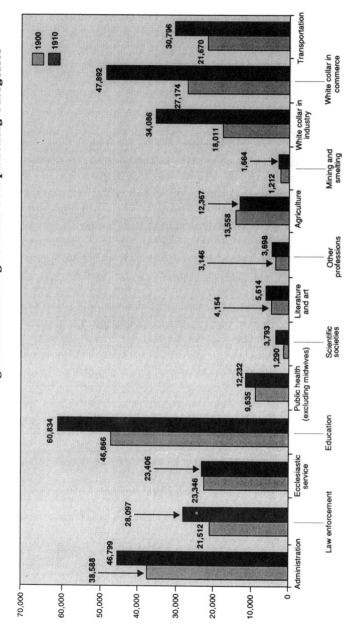

Distribution of the Intelligentsia According to Main Occupationalg Categories

The determining factor in the period 1890 to 1910, within the eighty percent growth of the intelligentsia, was the dynamic growth of white collar employees in the economic sectors: by 1910 their proportion had risen above forty percent.[15]

Although it was the numbers of white-collar workers in commerce and banking as well as in industry which grew more significantly among the intelligentsia, the eightfold growth of the intelligentsia employed by "scientific and public societies" indicates that scientific institutions were being established and became effective in this period. The increase in the number of civil servants and teachers was close to average, yet these remained the largest contingents of the intelligentsia at the turn of the century.

The capitalist transformation of the Hungarian economy and the bourgeois development of Hungarian society were largely limited to the urban centers and urban societies; the cap on and stagnation of the upward mobility of the peasantry into the middle class[16] entailed the consequence that the development of the intelligentsia promoted by capitalist development was a disproportionately urban phenomenon. Although our sources do not allow us to examine the residential preference of every group of the intelligentsia at the turn of the century, by comparing two partial approaches we gain an adequate picture of the outlines and proportions of residence and regional distribution. The first set of data covers every occupation group within the intelligentsia, but does not enable us to differentiate between municipalities and communities.

---

[15] Including estate managers, surveyors, and private engineers. Thus the intelligentsia constituted 1.7 percent of the total population in 1910 and, if we include family members and retired persons, 4.2 percent. The latter figure is based on Hanák's computations: op. cit., p. 453.

[16] Hanák, op. cit., pp. 480–501.

TABLE 8

Distribution of the Intelligentsia by Type of Settlement in Hungary in 1910[17]

Occupational group	Budapest and chartered towns	Other settlements (including towns)
Administration	16,246	30,553
Law enforcement	11,339	16,758
Ecclesiastic service	4,089	19,317
Education	17,100	43,716
Health (excluding midwives)	6,486	5,746
Scientific societies and associations	2,432	1,361
Art and literature	4,254	1,360
Other professions	2,117	1,581
Agriculture	793	11,574
Mining, industry, commerce and transport	67,546	46,892
Total:	132,402	178,858

[17] *Magyar Statisztikai Közlemények*, new series, vol. 64, p. 163 and pp. 308–313 (Croatia-Slavonia included).

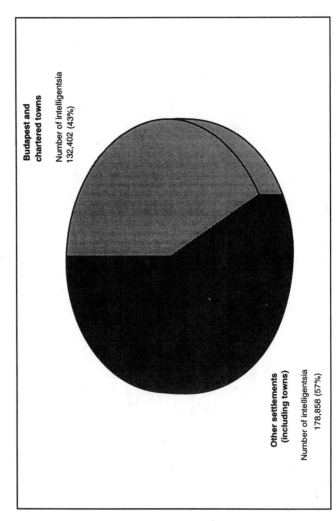

Distribution of the Intelligentsia by Type of Settlement
in Hungary in 1910

Budapest and
chartered towns

Number of intelligentsia
132,402 (43%)

Other settlements
(including towns)

Number of intelligentsia
178,858 (57%)

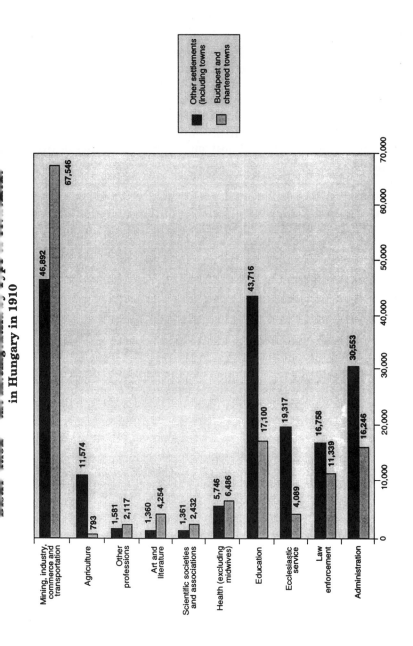

in Hungary in 1910

Other settlements (including towns)

Budapest and chartered towns

Mining, industry, commerce and transportation — 46,892 / 67,546

Agriculture — 11,574 / 793

Other professions — 1,581 / 2,117

Art and literature — 1,360 / 4,254

Scientific societies and associations — 1,361 / 2,432

Health (excluding midwives) — 5,746 / 6,486

Education — 43,716 / 17,100

Ecclesiastic service — 19,317 / 4,089

Law enforcement — 16,758 / 11,339

Administration — 30,553 / 16,246

From the data in table 7 it appears that more than two-fifths of the intelligentsia lived in the capital or in the municipalities. This concentration included physicians, pharmacists and veterinarians, scientists employed by scientific and public societies, civil servants, writers and artists, private engineers and chemists classified in the "free professions," as well as the absolute majority of white-collar workers in mining, commerce, industry and transportation. Budapest played a particularly prominent role: by 1910 almost one fourth of all intellectuals congregated there; moreover, Budapest was residence for over forty percent of all white-collar workers in industry, and for over one third of white-collar employees in commerce, banking, and transportation. The relative majority of those in scientific and artistic activities also lived and created in this environment, as did the majority of self-employed engineers.

Another set of data from the census of 1910 makes it possible for us to distinguish municipalities and settlements with over 10,000 inhabitants; on the other hand, these data did not cover white-collar employees in commerce and transportation, nor did they contain data pertaining to intellectuals belonging to the category "other" and made no distinction between the effectives of the public servants and those in the free professions.

If we collate the data from our own perspective—taking into consideration that the missing categories of intelligentsia had a higher than average concentration in the capital city and the municipalities—light is shed on the fact that, at the turn of the century, about two thirds of the intelligentsia lived in urban centers that catered to about one fourth of the total population of the country; along with its suburbs, greater Budapest was a place of concentration for about one-fourth of all intelligentsia in country.

Among the number of intelligentsia per 1,000 inhabitants in settlements with fewer than 10,000 inhabitants, there was a difference of several orders of magnitude between industrializing townships developing dynamically and close to reaching the 10,000 mark (such as Tata or Tatabánya), as opposed to traditional cultural or national centers (such as Sárospatak, Túrócszentmárton, Liptószentmiklós), seats of districts or the multitude of villages of varying sizes. According to those in charge

TABLE 9

Number and Ratio of Those in the Professions in Budapest in 1910[18]

Occupational group	National percentage	Number of the intelligentsia
Administration	15.10	7,068
Law enforcement	17.09	4,801
Ecclesiastic service	3.78	886
Education	13.94	8,483
Health (excluding midwives)	20.93	2,560
Scientific societies and associations	35.20	1,335
Art and literature	44.78	2,514
Other professions	39.43	1,458
Agriculture	2.33	288
Mining, industry	41.87	14,968
Commerce, banking	35.13	27,641
Total:	24.05	72,002

18 Gusztáv Thirring, "Budapest félszázados fejlődése 1873–1923" [Half a century of growth in Budapest], *Budapest Statisztikai Közleményei* 53, pp. 94, 127, 162–165.

**Number and Ratio of Those in the Professions
in Budapest in 1910**

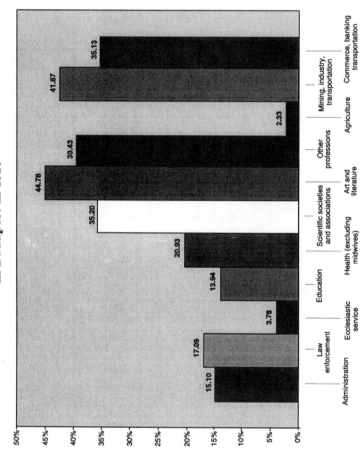

TABLE 10

Distribution of the Intelligentsia by Type of Settlement without Those Employed in Commerce, Banking, Transportation and the Category "Other Professions"[19]

Type of settlement	Total population	Public service and profess.	White collar in agriculture	White collar in industry	Total intelligentsia	Intellig. per 1,000 inhab.	Percentage of population
Budapest	880,371	492,975	270	14,968	58,991	67.01	20.12
Chartered towns (including Fiume)	1,293,009	609,550	388	5,943	47,369	36.63	16.16
Other towns and settlements over 10,000 inhabitants	2,408,932	1,029,978	942	5,774	65,237	27.08	22.26
Settlements with less than 10,000 inhabitants	13,659,844	5,616,540	8,061	5,794	121,531	8.90	41.46
Budapest with its suburbs	1,069,040	571,763	290	16,416	64,651	60.47	22.05

19 *Magyar Statisztikai Közlemények*, new ser., vol. 48. Without Croatia and Slavonia in this case. Regarding the suburbs of Budapest, see Károly Vörös, ed., *Budapest története* [The History of Budapest] (Budapest, 1978), vol. 4., pp. 529–575.

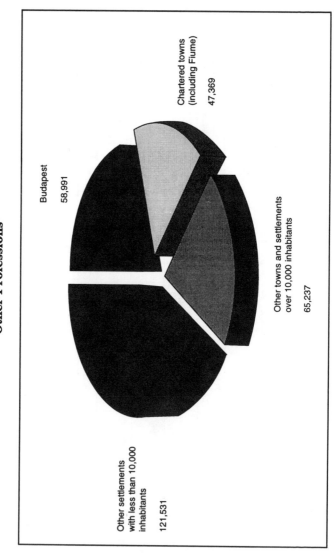

Distribution of the Intelligentsia by Type of Settlement without Those Employed in Commerce, Banking, Transportation and the Category "Other Professions"

Budapest

58,991

Chartered towns (including Fiume)

47,369

Other towns and settlements over 10,000 inhabitants

65,237

Other settlements with less than 10,000 inhabitants

121,531

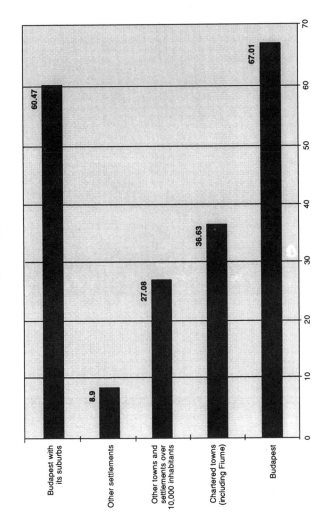

Number of Intelligentsia per 1,0000 Inhabitants
According to Type of Settlement

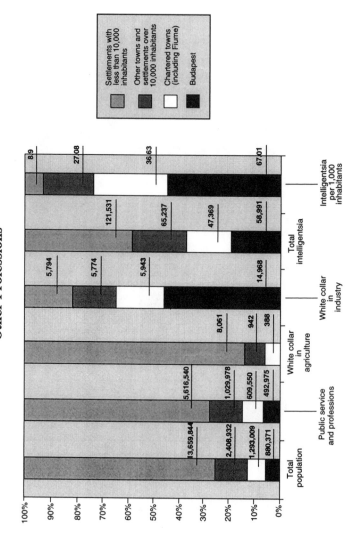

Distribution of the Intelligentsia by Type of Settlement without Those Employed in Commerce, Banking, Transportation and the Category "Other Professions"

of the census, the "series of those in professional occupations is considerably reduced" in the latter, and "made up mainly of the notary public, clergyman, teacher; occasionally the doctor or estate manager might belong to this category."[20]

The distribution by region (see appendix 1) reinforces the relationship between urbanization and the development of the intelligentsia, adding another factor, namely that the concentration of the intelligentsia in the urban centers was more pronounced in the more backward regions.

All in all, the growth of the Hungarian intelligentsia from mid-nineteenth century was very dynamic: from mid-century to 1910 the effectives of the intelligentsia increased five-fold, between the Compromise and 1910 they increased threefold, in the period of the Dual Monarchy—especially after the industrial takeoff—there was a significant shift in occupations in favor of those in the commercial sectors. The process of growth and the change in the structure of the occupations were accompanied by migration to the cities, whereas the intelligentsia of the villages remained limited to a few individuals and occupations. We must stress again that, in contrast to Western Europe, a peculiarity of the formation of the Hungarian intelligentsia and its evolution during the Dual Monarchy was that its main type and numerical majority was not the "free professions who depended from the market relations and were self-employed,"[21] but rather the civil servant living on a salary.

---

[20] *Magyar Statisztikai Közlemények*, new ser., vol. 39, p. 31.
[21] Huszár, "Értelmiségtörténet," p. 6.

TABLE 11

Growth of the Hungarian Intelligentsia
before World War I

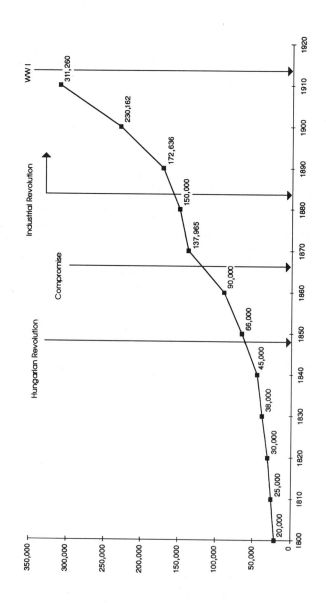

CHAPTER IV

The Social Origins of the Intelligentsia in the Age of Dualism

The social background of the evolving Hungarian intelligentsia had been pinpointed by research even before the end of World War II in 1945. In his great monograph of 1943–1944, Ferenc Erdei[1] argued that the main source of contemporary Hungarian intelligentsia was the traditional intelligentsia that had developed by the first half of the nineteenth century, when an overwhelming part was played by the nobility, which thus became the "intelligentsia of its own rule." In addition, however, although still playing a subordinate role, there was the "stratum of honoratior that had no claim to nobiliary title" and the largely plebeian body of clergyman and clergymen teachers, as well as the managerial class on the estates.[2] Moreover, they were joined in the period of absolutism by the body of officials of the Austrian Empire who were of many nationalities and without a nationality at the same time and who, after the Compromise of 1867, provided not only the overwhelming majority of the personnel of the intelligentsia in the period of the Dual Monarchy, but also its historical roots, its system of social values. According to Erdei, this inheritance was significantly modified by the fact that bourgeois, mainly assimilated, elements came to

---

[1] Ferenc Erdei, "A magyar társadalom a két világháború között" [Hungarian society between the two world wars], *Valóság*, nos. 1–2 (1976), pp. 4–5.

[2] According to László Ungár, in the 1830s two-thirds of the students in secondary schools and higher education were already of middle-class or peasant background. For lack of a precise reference we were unable to verify this assertion but, on the basis of the research carried out by Zoltán Fallenbüchl, as well as judging from sources pertaining to later periods, we feel it is exaggerated: "Szempontok a magyar polgári osztály kialakulásának vizsgálatához" [Points of view regarding research on the formation of the Hungarian middle class], *Századok* 76, (1942), p. 327.

complete the ranks of the intelligentsia in the same period.[3]

It becomes all the more important to reveal the proportions and true significance of each of these categories, as otherwise one may jump to conflicting conclusions in assessing the character and social functions of the intelligentsia.[4]

In the middle of the nineteenth century, as already mentioned, the intelligentsia numbered sixty to sixty-six thousands at most. We must agree with Károly Vörös[5] that it is not possible to determine the social background of this intelligentsia exactly, but certain indirect phenomena—such as the tradition of filling the teaching and clergy positions from plebeian strata, the Act V of 1844 which made it possible for non-nobles to hold office, as well as the issue of the social position of the honoratior—indicate that the intelligentsia was not the monopoly of the nobility even before the revolution of 1848.[6] We may note another phenomenon of the 1840s: there evolved a sizable group of people with an education unable to secure positions[7] who, in order to secure a livelihood, could not reject the opportunities offered by the absolutist regime after 1849 as their landowning compatriots had done.[8] This almost disproves the argument that the growth of the Hungarian intelligentsia in the period of absolutism was decisively or exclusively fed by a body of civil servants originating from Austria, the Czech and Moravian provinces, and of bourgeois background. This assertion

---

[3] Erdei, op. cit., part 1, pp. 47–48.

[4] Ibid.; Gyula Szekfű, *Három nemzedék* [Three generations] (Budapest, 1920).

[5] Vörös, *A modern értelmiség*, p. 19.

[6] Ibid., pp. 19–20.

[7] János Varga, "A bihari nemesség hitelviszonyai a forradalom előtt" [Credit relations of the nobility from the county of Bihar before the revolution], *Történelmi Szemle*, nos. 1–2 (1958), pp. 44–45, 51.

[8] This claim is confirmed by the roster of officials accepted as transfers at the time of the appointment of new officials in the counties in the year of the Compromise, 1867. Records of the Ministry of Interior in the State Archives, K 148, 1867, bundle 4. György Szabad arrived at the same conclusion: the leaders of the Habsburg empire "recruited large numbers of officials among the noble and middle-class intelligentsia in Hungary," but many members of the Hungarian intelligentsia forced to seek gainful employment also served in the lower and middle ranks of the police. Szabad, op. cit., pp. 460, 489.

appears all the less acceptable since, as the census data from 1869 demonstrates, the growth of the intelligentsia in the period was due to the growth in the number of teachers and estate managers. The logical conclusion of this line of thought—although the issue requires more detailed research—is that at the threshold of the Compromise the intelligentsia cannot be classified into one or two categories from the point of view of background or "main development": its reserves came, in proportions at least equal to the nobility, from the non-noble bourgeois elements of Hungarian society.[9] The feeding line in the period of the Dual Monarchy, which tripled the size of the intelligentsia, was mainly structural mobility through the educational system.[10] An analysis of this mobility sheds light on the social background of the about three quarters of the intelligentsia at the beginning of the twentieth century, whereas the remaining quarter accedes to professional careers either before the Compromise or from other sources.

The Evolution of Mobility Feeding into the Intelligentsia

The secondary school system in the period after the Compromise was divided into two major functional units. Education was provided in part by the system of secondary schools (gimnázium and reáliskola) already in existence, and in part by the middle school (polgári iskola) created in consequence of the elementary school law of 1868 which, however, did not develop until

---

[9] This process became evident even among the body of government employees at the county level, where the nobility traditionally prevailed: in 1867, after the appointment of new officials, the county of Liptó indicated their social origins: among them we find 34 of noble background, and 27 who were not. Records of the Ministry of Interior, State Archives, K 148, 1867. III–516–1785.

[10] In only two instances have we noted mass expulsion from the ranks of the intelligentsia. One of these affected a segment of the officials who held office during the autocratic rule preceding the Compromise of 1867, when a new set of officials was appointed. The other occurred on the basis of Act XVIII of 1879; by the end of the century some 2,000 public school teachers were removed for not speaking Hungarian. Ministry of Religion and Education, report 25, pp. 774–777.

the 1890s.[11] Although, according to the Act of 1883 on secondary schools, "the task of the gimnázium and reáliskola is to provide a higher general education for youth and prepare them for higher studies,"[12] in reality the lower grades of the gimnázium and reáliskola provided a middle school level education in consonance with real social needs. Evidence of this is that only one fifth of the students entering gimnázium or reáliskola received a diploma.[13] As to the proportion in which the lower grades of secondary school prepared for various professional careers we cannot determine, for lack of data. Indirectly, however, since the lower four grades of the secondary schools and the four grades of the middle schools fulfilled similar functions, albeit in different proportions, we do receive some indication regarding the distribution of choice of careers among middle school (polgári iskola) graduates.

---

[11] The acceleration in the rate of growth of public schools was largely owing to the fact that a network of specialized schools and courses had developed to meet the requirements of the social division of labor, and the four years of public school provided preparation for these. The most important among the specialized schools were the so-called higher commercial schools, authorized to award high school diplomas since 1895.

[12] Quoted in *A közoktatásügy Magyarországon* [Public education in Hungary] (Budapest, 1908), p. 113.

[13] Of the 7,338 students registered in the first year of secondary school in 1884 only 2,198 were attending the eighth grade in 1891. After the initial attrition, most of the dropping out occurred between years four and five, indicating the difference in function between the lower and upper forms. A significant fraction of the secondary schools did not even offer eight forms. Although the number of institutions that remained incomplete was diminishing gradually, 45 of the 202 high schools remained incomplete even in the academic year 1905–1906. Vallás és Közoktatási Minisztérium, *Report 20*, p. 36.

TABLE 12

Careers Chosen by Middle School (Polgári Iskola) Graduates in Hungary (Excluding Croatia-Slavonia)[14] in Percentages

1. Continued education in	1900–1901	1908–1909	1914–1915
Polgári iskola*	6.66	4.00	2.40
Gimnázium**		1.40	3.10
Reáliskola***	3.13	0.20	0.60
Girls' middle school		2.80	1.00
Middle school for commerce	12.37	23.50	29.70
Teacher's training school	16.93	11.60	11.90
Military school	1.66	0.80	1.00
Trade school	3.96	8.80	4.80
2. Occupational careers	**1900–1901**	**1908–1909**	**1914–1915**
Agricultural		1.40	1.70
Industrial	2.49	9.20	8.90
Commercial	1.70	4.30	4.20
Clerical	5.00	4.20	7.10
3. Others	**1900–1901**	**1908–1909**	**1914–1915**
Employed at home	26.80	26.60	22.30
Unknown	15.29	1.10	0.90

*   American equivalent of middle school.
**   American equivalent of middle and high school with an academic curriculum.
*** American equivalent of middle and high school with a general education curriculum.

---

[14] *Magyar Statisztikai Értesítő*, new ser. 9, p. 331; new ser. 17, p. 363; new ser. 23, p. 258.

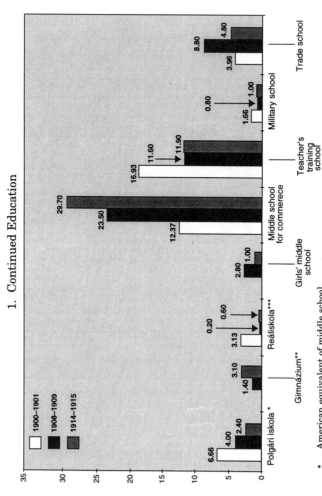

Careers Chosen by Middle School (Polgári Iskola) Graduates in Hungary (Excluding Croatia-Slavonia) in Percentages

1. Continued Education

Legend:
- 1900–1901
- 1908–1909
- 1914–1915

Categories: Polgári iskola *, Gimnázium**, Reáliskola***, Girls' middle school, Middle school for commerece, Teacher's training school, Military school, Trade school

Values:
- Polgári iskola *: 6.66, 2.40, 4.00
- Gimnázium**: 1.40, 3.10
- Reáliskola***: 3.13, 0.20, 0.60
- Girls' middle school: 1.00, 2.80
- Middle school for commerece: 12.37, 23.50, 29.70
- Teacher's training school: 16.93, 11.90, 11.60
- Military school: 1.66, 1.00, 0.80
- Trade school: 3.96, 8.80, 4.80

*   American equivalent of middle school.
**   American equivalent of middle and high school with an academic curriculum.
*** American equivalent of middle and high school with a general education curriculum.

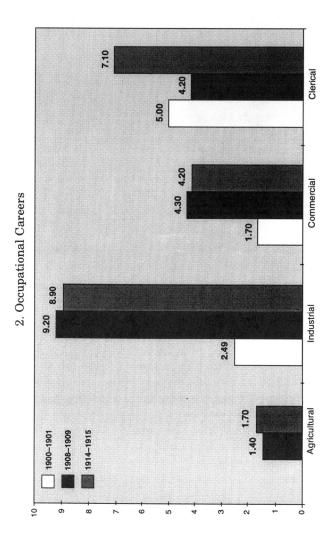

Careers Chosen by Middle School (Polgári Iskola) Graduates
in Hungary (Excluding Croatia-Slavonia) in Percentages

2. Occupational Careers

**Careers Chosen by Middle School (Polgári Iskola) Graduates
in Hungary (Excluding Croatia-Slavonia)
in Percentages**

3. Others

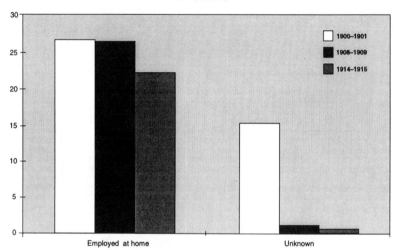

Since in the first two decades of the Dual Monarchy the ratio
of female students among those who completed four years of secondary school was negligible, those who prepared for careers in
the intelligentsia must have represented about three quarters of
those who completed secondary school without taking the gradu-
ation examination. With the increase in the number of female
students at the turn of the century, this ratio dropped to two-
thirds, while in the years immediately preceding the war, when
women were gaining access to careers in the intelligentsia, it
once again rose to three quarters. Among the careers in the intelligentsia the students who completed four to six years of secondary school gained access mainly to mid- and lower-level clerical positions in the commercial sector as well as to careers in
teaching.[15]

---

[15] We must emphasize again that from the 1890s the meaning of "completed
four years of secondary school" changed in comparison to the earlier decades,
because it included, even if not so stated, the completion of specialized schools
and courses.

The other functional unit of the system of secondary schools was the channel of educational institutions (gimnázium and reáliskola) providing eight years of schooling with comprehensive examinations at the end. We have far more reliable sources regarding their choice of career.

TABLE 13

Careers Chosen by High School* Graduates in Hungary[16] in Percentages

Career choice	1880–1881	1887–1888	1890–1891	1894–1895	1900–1901	1908–1909
Theology	22.59	21.16	18.59	14.10	12.56	11.91
Humanities	6.54	4.44	5.05	6.54	10.37	7.77
Law	25.40	21.93	26.06	28.39	26.72	21.91
Medical	16.50	11.97	10.25	7.67	6.51	12.08
Engineering	5.98	7.59	7.93	10.58	8.85	5.44
Architect	2.86	1.50	0.96	1.49	0.93	1.16
Mechanical engineer	2.76	0.95	1.57	1.49	2.43	3.05
Chemical engineer	1.12	0.72	0.61	0.69	0.91	1.83
Farming	1.17	9.49	6.36	5.61	4.85	3.72
Forestry		3.35	2.63	2.18	1.97	2.52
Mining	4.70	0.31	0.45	0.39	0.85	0.86
Industry	1.38	0.72	0.45	0.36	0.43	1.01
Commerce		2.32	2.63	2.06	1.55	6.43
Clerical		9.18	7.63	9.05	10.43	12.69
Military		4.33	7.63	5.94	5.60	3.61
Art			1.21	0.93	1.33	1.37
Other					3.71	2.67

* Gimnázium or reáliskola.

---

16 Vallás és Közoktatási Minisztérium, *Report 11*, pp. 248–249; *Report 17*, vol. 2, pp. 59–60; *Report 20*, vol. 2, pp. 67–68; *Report 25*, pp. 477–481. *Magyar Statisztikai Értesítő*, new ser. 9, p. 345; new ser. 17, p. 386.

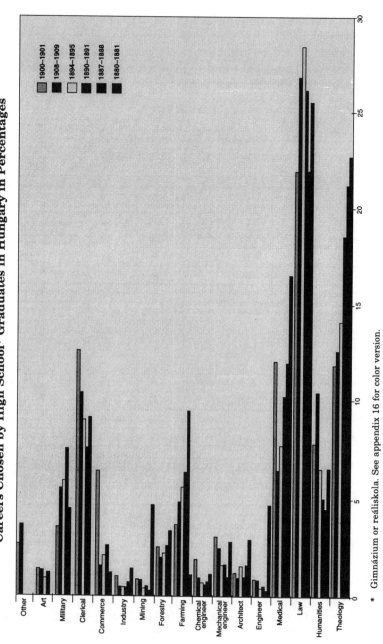

* Gimnázium or reáliskola. See appendix 16 for color version.

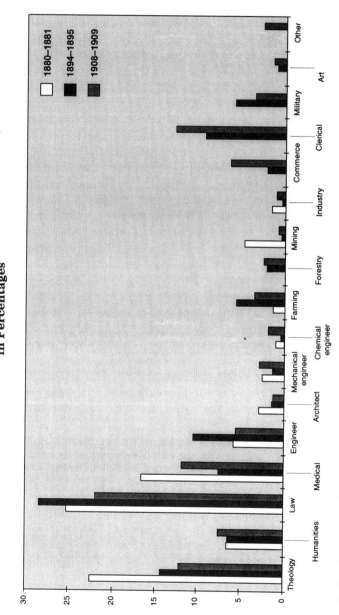

Careers Chosen by High School* Graduates in Hungary in Percentages

* Gimnázium or reáliskola.

During the whole of the period under consideration, barely 5% of all secondary school students obtained a diploma. In 1880, 16.25% among them did not opt for a career in the intelligentsia, and by the turn of the century their ratio dropped to 10% only to rise again somewhat. In 1880 two-thirds of those who did not opt for a career in the intelligentsia continued to be active in agriculture, probably as self-employed farmers, whereas in 1908 it was those who opted for a career in commerce who provided almost half of these dropouts. In 1880, 83.73% of those with diplomas, 90.35% in 1900, and 85.46% in 1908 entered careers in the intelligentsia, either directly or after attending institutions of higher learning.[17]

From an analysis of the career choices of students of secondary and public schools it becomes obvious that, in the period of the Dual Monarchy, about three quarters became members of the intelligentsia upon completion of their studies; in other words, their social relations may be understood as the social relations of the reserves of the intelligentsia. Although information regarding the social relations of students in secondary and public schools is available to us from different starting points, depending upon the type of school, and the methods of collecting information or the categories are not always conducive to identifying actual social derivation—especially as regards the students' "social status"—we can nevertheless identify the main trends of the process, its proportions and characteristics. We obtain the following general picture of the transformation of sec-

---

[17] Further breakdown of those embarking on a career as lower-ranking bureaucrats sheds light on the opportunities open to those with high school diplomas: in 1908 they numbered only 604, of whom 354 (58.61%) entered office directly, while 250 (41.39%) entered office upon completion of specialized courses.

In the railroads		23.16%
Post office and telegraph		7.91%
Other transportation		0.57%
	Total:	**31.64%**
Government office		28.82%
Local government		10,45%
Community office		25.43%
Other public office		3.67%
	Total:	**68.37%**

ondary school students according to the social status of their parents, from 1880 until the turn of the century:

TABLE 14

Socioeconomic Status of Parents of Secondary School Students [18]

Number of students	1880–1881 100%: 38,567	1887–1888 100%: 39,333	1890–1891 100%: 42,115	1894–1895 100%: 49,382
1. Landowner or renter	19.90	17.79	3.02	3.05
2. Smallholder or renter			14.34	14.48
3. Industrialist			1.09	1.36
4. Tradesman	33.99	33.48	13.30	14.84
5. Entrepreneur, wholesaler			4.93	2.04
6. Merchant			10.25	11.58
7. Public administrator	12.49	19.60	14.96	14.19
8. Private administrator	4.91	7.50	5.72	5.64
9. Military			1.06	0.98
10. Professional with higher education diploma	22.81	16.55	18.26	17.51
11. Self-employed			4.81	5.59
12. Employed in agriculture			1.59	1.77
13. Employed in industry			1.10	1.29
14. Employed in commerce			0.92	1.07
15. In private and other serv.	5.90	5.08	4.65	4.61
Total with parents from the intelligentsia	40.21	43.65	44.81	43.91

[18] Vallás és Közoktatási Minisztérium, *Report 11*, p. 243; *Report 17*, vol. 2, p. 38; *Report 20*, vol. 2, pp. 52–53; *Report 25*, pp. 349–351.

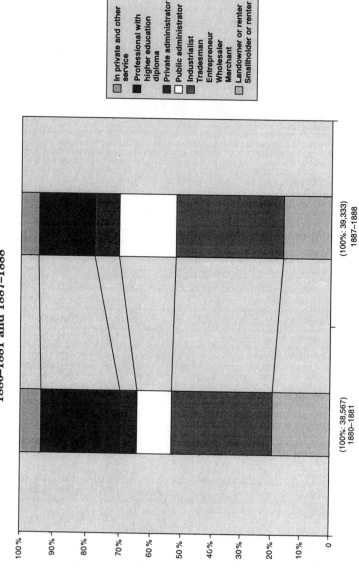

Socioeconomic Status of Parents of Secondary School Students,
1880–1881 and 1887–1888

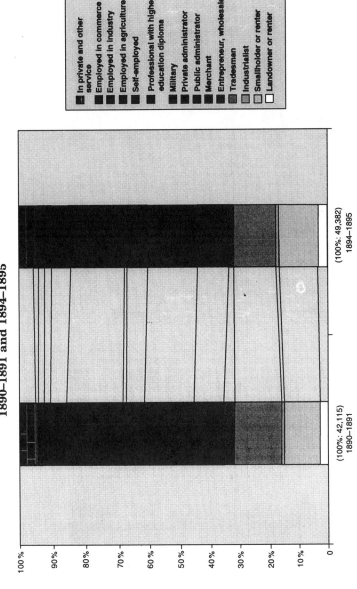

Socioeconomic Status of Parents of Secondary School Students,
1890–1891 and 1894–1895

Legend:
- In private and other service
- Employed in commerce
- Employed in industry
- Employed in agriculture
- Self-employed
- Professional with higher education diploma
- Military
- Private administrator
- Public administrator
- Merchant
- Entrepreneur, wholesaler
- Tradesman
- Industrialist
- Smallholder or renter
- Landowner or renter

(100%: 42,115) 1890–1891

(100%: 49,382) 1894–1895

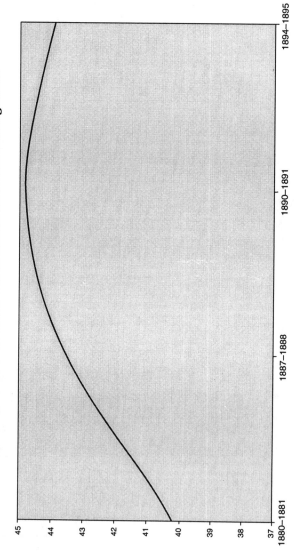

Secondary School Students with Parents from the Intelligentsia

The data enable us to identify three main trends:

1) The number of students whose family background was the intelligentsia grew along with the dynamic growth in the effectives of the intelligentsia; yet this growth was limited to a few percentage points,[19] indicating limits to the self-reproduction of the intelligentsia. The very fact that, during the first three decades of the Dual Monarchy, the intelligentsia was only able to reproduce itself below the 50% mark, is an indication of the large degree of openness of the intelligentsia to society at large.

2) It was the urban bourgeoisie which took advantage of the opportunities presented by the quick expansion in the professions: among those children whose background was not the intelligentsia, those whose background was the urban bourgeoisie had one and half majority by 1880. The data from 1890 and 1894 also indicate that over 90% of the students of bourgeois background were raised in middle-class or petty bourgeois families.

3) The third group is perhaps the most difficult to analyze from the point of view of social history. What the statistics reveal is that the proportion of students whose family were landowners or peasants who owned some land, or at least rented some, dropped evenly between 1880 and 1894 from 19.90% to 15.53%. The agricultural proletariat, whose numbers, along with family members, amounted to 4.5 million,[20] contributed only 2% of the intelligentsia.

Although, in absolute terms, the drop among some groups of the rural population in the supply of members of the intelligentsia was merely relative, nevertheless we must explain why the opportunities for joining the ranks of the intelligentsia favored

---

[19] Those who came from families described as "private and retired" were included among those with background in the intelligentsia, since the overwhelming majority were children of retired public employees.

[20] Hanák, op. cit., p. 501.

the urban bourgeoisie.[21]

We must seek the reasons for this phenomenon on two levels: in the transformation of the educational system, and in the peculiarities of the process of embourgeoisement of Hungarian society.

In the first half of the nineteenth century the access to secondary and higher level education was restricted for non-noble groups of society by means of decrees. At the same time, however, those careers in the intelligentsia which were not attractive to children of noble families—e.g., clergy, teaching in primary school—were promoted by means of free instruction or scholarships offered by the denominations, helping the talented offspring of the "lower-classes" into the intelligentsia. The system of public education which evolved after the Compromise, and the liberal policies of the governments left higher education to the individual; hence access to secondary and higher education was limited only by the financial means available to various social classes, their system of values, and their cultural traditions.[22] In other words, opportunities for upward mobility into the intelligentsia were basically determined by the students' degree of embourgeoisement, by their middle-class potential, whether material or mental.

This aspect of the relationship between embourgeoisement and advanced education is reflected in the fact that, in spite of the divergent social structure of the different regions of the country, the children of the same urbanized groups gained access to secondary schools, pretty much in line with the nation-wide average (see appendix 2).

---

[21] In 1889, five of every thousand secondary school students were of peasant origins, 19 whose family were craftsmen, 66 merchants, 151 public servants, and 165 other members of the intelligentsia. Vallás és Közoktatásügyi Minisztérium, *Report 18*, p. 137.

[22] In his study of education policies in the period of the Dual Monarchy, István Balogh states: "In this period we find no attempt to bar members of particular social classes or groups from the opportunity to obtain advanced education, but neither do we find attempts to promote such needs or aspirations by means of financial aid or otherwise." "A paraszti művelődés" [Education among the peasantry], in *A parasztság Magyarországon a kapitalizmus korában, 1848–1914* [The peasantry in Hungary in the age of capitalism] 2, (Budapest, 1965), pp. 541–542.

The shift in the change of opportunities for mobility, during the first three decades of the Dual Monarchy, indirectly reflected the basic traits of the evolution of Hungarian bourgeois class: that is, this evolution was limited to urban centers, the upward mobility of the peasantry stagnated, a significant fraction of the former smallholder and mid-size landowning nobility became impoverished, while the ranks of the rural proletariat, living in misery, expanded further. In this period the peasant population of the villages did not feed the ranks of the intelligentsia to any significant extent, for the "smallholder and lessee" category listed in the statistics did not include peasants, except for the half-peasant half-bourgeois residents of provincial towns.[23]

The peasants of the villages, even if they insisted on education for their children, could at best send them to the free schools, combined with seminaries, under denominational control, or perhaps take advantage of the very limited opportunities of tuition remission, as regulated by the minister of education.[24]

From the turn of the century on, with the inclusion of every institution of secondary learning, our sources enable us to track the changes in the social background of the students joining the ranks of the intelligentsia.

---

[23] We arrived at this conclusion after examining the registries of two secondary schools where the ratio of those classified as "smallholder or renter" was relatively high, and every one of them turned out to be from a local family (from the district of Hajdúböszörmény and Hajdúnánás). Registries of the high school of Hajdúnánás, HBmL, VIII, 61/c. Registries of the high school of Hajdúböszörmény, HBmL, VIII, 54/c.

[24] In the 1880s and 1890s the cost of education for a secondary school student was in the order of 100 to 150 forints (covering tuition, registration fee, textbooks), but the costs doubled if the family did not live in the vicinity. Board at a modest boarding school was around 150 forints, but some charged as much as 400 to 500 forints. Regarding tuition fees, see *Report 25* of the Ministry of Religion and Education, pp. 329–334. Regarding boarding fees, see same, pp. 275–276. Regarding conditions for exemption from payment of tuition, see *Report 6*, p. 775; "For the sake of comparison, someone with an annual expenditure of five thousand forints (or ten thousand crowns) was accounted a very wealthy man in Hungary. At the other extreme, the lowest paid laborers—cottagers—had to survive on wages of as little as one crown a day and usually could not count on more than two hundred working days a year. Skilled workers earned 445 forints (or 890 crowns) a year on average (as shown by a survey conducted in 1906 covering 300,000 people." In András Gerő, *The Hungarian Parliament, 1867–1918: A Mirage of Power* (New York, 1997), p. 121.

TABLE 15

**Distribution of Students in Secondary Schools
According to the Socioeconomic Status of Their Parents**[25]

Social status of parents	1900–1901		1908–1909	
	High school	Middle sch.	High school	Middle sch.
1. Landowner or renter	2.40	9.43	15.33	9.20
2. Smallholder or renter	13.91			
3. Industrialist	1.30	20.85	14.01	20.50
4. Tradesman	15.01			
5. Entrepreneur, wholesaler	1.75	14.81	11.86	13.50
6. Merchant	11.22			
7. Public employee	14.47	15.24	11.16	11.70
8. Private employee	6.25	5.44	8.58	8.10
9. Military	0.9	1.00	1.15	1.30
10. Other intelligentsia	16.24	7.93	17.85	5.90
11. Self-employed	6.71	5.46	8.20	6.60
12. Employed in agriculture	1.61	3.29	2.04	3.50
13. Employed in industry	1.68	4.23	2.07	5.40
14. Employed in commerece	1.52	3.48	3.71	6.60
15. Servants and others	5.03	8.84	4.04	7.70
100 %	59,302	45,213	67,699	69,588

*   Gimnázium or reáliskola.
** Polgári iskola.

25 *Magyar Statisztikai Értesítő,* new ser., 9, pp. 331, 342; new ser., 17, pp. 363, 379.

At the turn of the century, and during the ensuing decade, the trends shift; only the decrease in the ratio of students from families of "landowners and lessees" continues unabated, in fact this trend is accentuated with the rapid increase of students in public schools. The ratios also indicate that the decrease was merely relative; nevertheless, it remains a fact that this category provided an increasingly smaller portion of the intelligentsia, once again growing dynamically as a result of the industrial takeoff.

The more accurate data regarding the social distribution of students in public schools in 1908 show the proportions of actual social groups: 9.2%, formerly identified as students from "landowner and lessee" category of families, are now broken down into 0.5% of owners of large estates, 2% of mid-size landowners, 5.1% of gardener, fisherman, husbandman, etc., and 0.8% of smallholder-day laborer category.

Taking into consideration the differing conditions in the secondary and public schools—that is, among those supplying the intelligentsia—the ratio of students whose social background was in the nobility and landowning class could not have exceeded 6 to 7% in the last two decades of the Dual Monarchy; the ratio of students from families of landowners and peasants must have been in the same range.

The ratio of students from families in the professions rose by only a few percentage points, and did not exceed one third of all students in public schools, even in 1908. The reason for this may be sought in the deterioration of the social position of those in the professions and the decrease in the birthrate (see next chapter).

A completely new trend at the beginning of the century was the advance registered by the strata of petty-bourgeois who were not self-employed, and by the industrial working class. While in 1890 the ratio of children of workers employed in industry and transportation was only 2%, by 1900 their ratio had risen to 3.2% and in 1908 it reached 5.78%; if we include the children of janitorial staff in public institutions this ratio rose to 8.75%! Their advance among students in public schools is even more pronounced: in 1900 their ratio was 7.7%, in 1908 it rose to 12% and, if we include the children of maintenance personnel, altoge-

ther 16.5%. This meant nothing less than that, in the last
decade of the Dual Monarchy, these social groups exceeded all
rural groups taken together in providing reserves for the intelligentsia. An analysis of the ethnic and denominational background of students in secondary and public schools sheds light
not only on these other aspects of the process of reproduction of
the intelligentsia, but also helps provide greater accuracy for
the above analysis.

TABLE 16

Ratio of the Ethnic and Religious Distribution of Students in Secondary Schools[26]

Nationality	1870–1871	1880–1881	1890–1891	1898–1899	1908–1909	1914–1915
	100%: 36,464	100%: 38,567	100%: 42,116	100%: 54,676	100%: 67,699	100%: 76,856
Hungarian	73.56	70.75	72.38	75.55	79.92	83.93
German	12.35	15.30	14.72	12.70	8.83	6.75
Romanian	7.37	6.39	6.42	5.67	6.24	5.37
Slovak	4.13	4.76	3.77	3.27	2.56	1.85
Serbo-Croatian	1.74	2.20	1.89	1.96	1.87	1.45
Ruthenian	0.86	0.60	0.22	0.19	0.12	0.05
Other			0.61	0.66	0.45	0.59
Denomination	**1870–1871**	**1880–1881**	**1890–1891**	**1898–1899**	**1908–1909**	**1914–1915**
Roman Catholic	45.99	44.08	44.50	43.43	43.46	45.39
Uniate	5.30	4.44	4.51	4.32	4.55	4.23
Greek Orthodox	5.74	5.00	5.34	5.06	5.48	4.62
Lutheran	12.37	10.81	10.76	10.05	9.20	8.85
Calvinist	18.36	14.15	14.02	14.30	14.29	13.99
Unitarian	0.97	0.85	0.71	0.71	0.79	0.73
Jewish	11.26	20.26	20.16	22.13	22.23	22.16

[26] Vallás és Közoktatásügyi Minisztérium *Report 1*, pp. 137–166; *Report 11*,
pp. 137–166; *Report 20*, vol. 2, pp. 43–47.

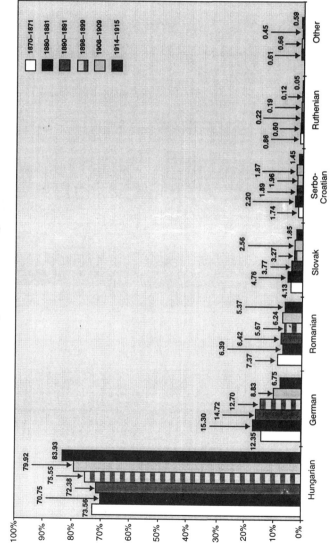

Ratio of Secondary School Students
by Ethnic Background

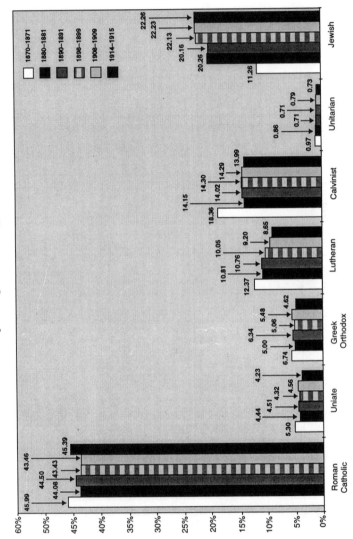

Ratio of Secondary School Students
by Religious Background

TABLE 17

Ratio of the Ethnic and Religious Background of Students in Middle Schools*[27]

	1908–1909	1914–1915
	100%: 69,588	100%: 103,384
Hungarian	81.10	83.13
German	10.70	9.28
Romanian	2.38	2.38
Slovak	2.86	2.67
Serbo-Croatian	1.93	1.59
Ruthenian	0.08	0.09
Other	0.94	0.85
	1908–1909	1914–1915
Roman Catholic	49.70	52.66
Uniate	1.82	2.01
Greek Orthodox	3.41	3.09
Lutheran	7.49	7.38
Calvinist	10.54	11.28
Unitarian	0.33	0.34
Jewish	26.09	23.20

* Polgári iskola.

---

[27] *Magyar Statisztikai Értesítő,* new ser., 9, p. 342; new ser., 17, pp. 362, 383; new ser., 23, pp. 258, 272.

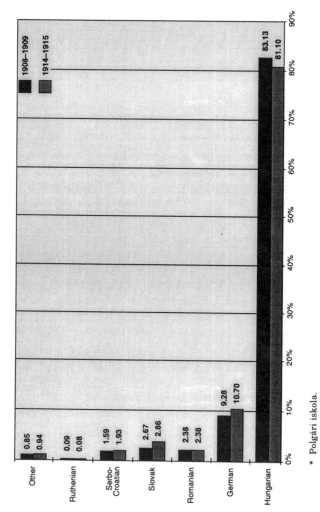

Ratio of Middle School* Students
by Ethnic Background

* Polgári iskola.

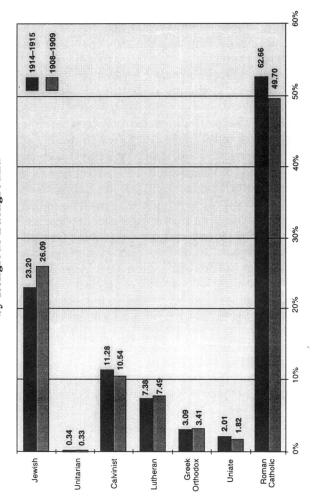

Ratio of Middle School* Students
by Religious Background

1914—1915
1908—1909

Jewish: 23.20, 26.09
Unitarian: 0.34, 0.33
Calvinist: 11.28, 10.54
Lutheran: 7.38, 7.49
Greek Orthodox: 3.09, 3.41
Uniate: 2.01, 1.82
Roman Catholic: 62.66, 49.70

* Polgári iskola.

In the decade following the Compromise Hungarian educational policy was intent on maintaining at least a minimum of the consensus which had resulted from the law on nationalities; therefore, it discarded the notion of placing restrictions on the participation of ethnic or religious groups, trusting that these social groups would not only accept the primacy and hegemony of Hungarian culture, but would accept the social consequences such primacy entailed.

Gusztáv Tarnóczy formulated this concept, not entirely devoid of illusions, in the parliamentary debate on educational policy: "If we wish to see our country powerful, our people materially well off, that is happy and free, we must transform the school into a chemical laboratory which would smooth out national and religious conflicts and combine all elements into a whole..."[28] In the transformation of the educational system, however, the ministry of education saw its hands tied to a large extent by the monopoly enjoyed by the denominations, even if it did succeed in obtaining that these schools open their doors to members of other denominations. The 1870s proved to be the years of "free competition" for ethnic and religious groups, as almost every one of the ethnic groups increased its share of secondary school students. The ratio of German-language speakers increased most; and, since in the same period the ratio of Protestants decreased while that of students of Jewish faith doubled, we assume that this growth was the result of increased participation on the part of the Jewish population, large numbers of whom still spoke German, on its way to joining the ranks of the intelligentsia.[29]

---

[28] *Képviselőházi Napló* [Parliamentary Journal] 5 (1872), p. 60.

[29] The example of the town of Baja, significant because of its commerce in grain, wood and wine, shows how early this process got under way. According to the census of 1857, the mainly German-speaking Jewish population of the town was 8.15% of the total. At the beginning of the 1850s the proportion of Jewish students in the Baja secondary school remained below their ratio among the general population (7.7% in the academic year 1852/53), but from the mid-fifties this ratio rose to slightly above, and in the 1860s it grew to double their ratio among the general population (9.72% in the academic year 1854–1855; 18.75% in 1859–1860; and 18,10% in 1869–1870). Reports from the Royal Catholic Secondary School of Baja, 1852–1853, 1856–1857, and 1869–1870.

After the fusion the overtones of nationalism grew louder not only in general politics, but in educational politics a well. The immediate reason for this was the recognition of the fact that compact ethnic groups could not be assimilated, while certain ethnic groups—especially the Saxon, Serbian and Romanian—educated their intelligentsia in an anti-Hungarian spirit, under the guise of autonomy.[30]

Revision of the ethnic and religious aspects of educational policies was discussed in 1883, during the parliamentary debates about the proposed law on secondary schools. The independentist opposition accused the government partly of "maximalism" partly of weakness in confronting the nationalities, while at the same it defended the autonomy of denominations, the main obstacle to any effective educational policy: "It is the secondary school that offers general culture and prepares for advanced specialization, and those classes of people which carry out the tasks of the nation's intellectual work, receive their training in the secondary school....For me, who view the matter from a practical standpoint, it is clear that it is impossible to Hungarianize compact masses of non-Hungarian people, even if we eliminate the existing constitutional obstacles. But this is no threat to us and does not hinder the creation of a unified national culture. The lower classes live a local existence, greater units, wider communities do not fit into their narrow world-view, and therefore they play no role in launching nationalist movements either....But we must consistently strive, in the education of those classes that perform intellectual work, to ensure knowledge of the Hungarian language and to spread the spirit of patriotism."[31] The government accepted the arguments of the opposition, yet refused to enact discriminatory measures limiting schooling for members of ethnic groups. It sought to carry out its objectives by placing comprehensive restrictions on the

---

[30] Intervention of Béla Grünwald. *Képviselőházi Napló* 11 (1881–1884), pp. 28–29.

[31] Ibid. Grünwald attempted to put pressure on the minister of education with a Cassandra prophecy: "our weakness will cost the lives of many Hungarian citizens, and our future misery will demonstrate how serious a mistake our leniency actually was."

monopoly of denominational schools, and by exercising its right to overall supervision.

The educational system formulated by Act XXX of 1883 functioned to the end of the Dual Monarchy essentially unaltered. The district school superintendents with wide powers but under the guidance of the Ministry of Education, their opportunity to have a say-so in the appointment of teachers, and in charge of ensuring that the Hungarian language, a prerequisite for the high school diploma, has been properly learned, the censorship of textbooks, etc.—all these powers and measures corresponded to the strategy of assimilation of the education policy, far better than the discriminatory legislation and regulations which tended to promote conflict. Thanks to these measures, the assimilatory tendencies of those strata of ethnic and denominational groups that strove to reproduce the intelligentsia were reinforced; in any case, they were pulled by the advantages of belonging to the intelligentsia of the ruling Hungarian ethnic group and pushed by the lack of bilingual education at the high school level (except in the seminaries).

The education policy and the system of assimilation it promoted, were only partly effective; their successes or failures were basically determined by the process of embourgeoisement of particular ethnic and denominational groups, their yearnings for independence, and the difference between the two. Those groups who sought upward mobility along the lines of integration—Jews, ethnic Germans, the Slovaks in part—achieved a higher degree of embourgeoisement in the period of the Dual Monarchy than the Romanian, or Serbian ethnic groups whose tendencies were against integration.

The differences in their degree of embourgeoisement may be measured directly, within the school system, by their participation in primary schooling—without any significant modification at that, for primary schooling was not only mandatory for every social groups, but constituted one of the basic objectives of the educational system.

TABLE 18

Ratio of Those of School Age to Actual Enrollment by Ethnic and Religious Group[32]

Nationality	1869	1880	1890	1896–1900
Hungarian	53.90	82.30	85.60	84.22
German	68.50	86.70	90.80	91.59
Romanian	51.00	84.40	84.70	85.54
Slovak	30.30	53.90	60.80	60.05
Croatian	41.90	59.50	64.40	59.66
Serb	51.40	79.40	83.00	79.21
Ruthenian	36.50	80.80	78.30	77.27
Other (Italian)				93.15
National average	50.40	77.20	81.50	80.24
Denomination	**1869**	**1880**	**1890**	**1896–1900**
Roman Catholic	48.00	86.70	87.30	85.82
Uniate	37.00	56.20	62.20	62.13
Greek Orthodox	29.00	53.90	67.30	64.42
Lutheran	71.00	86.60	88.10	90.79
Calvinist	45.00	80.20	84.40	83.36
Unitarian	41.00	80.70	77.40	83.59
Jewish	37.00	80.40	80.50	82.63
Other				92.23

[32] Vallás és Közoktatási Minisztérium, *Report 25*, pp. 719-720; *Magyar Statisztikai Értesítő*, new ser., 9, pp. 316–317.

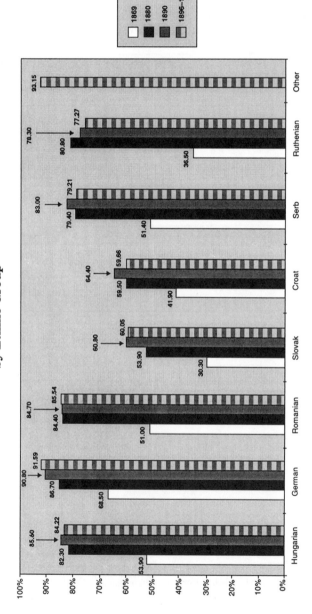

Ratio of Those of School Age to Actual Enrollment
by Ethnic Group

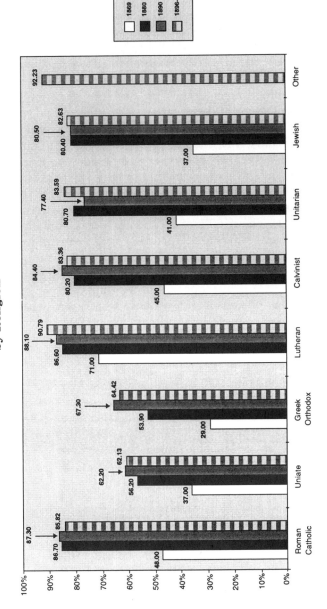

Ratio of Those of School Age to Actual Enrollment by Religion

As a result of the ethnic and religious peculiarities of the process of embourgeoisement and of the educational policy promoting assimilation, from the 1880s the ratio of those of Hungarian mother tongue rose steadily among secondary school students. In 1914, when World War I broke out, their numbers exceeded five-sixth of all those enrolled in secondary schools, while those who did not claim Hungarian as their mother tongue barely amounted to one-sixth. This, however, sheds no light on the true proportions of assimilation, for claiming Hungarian as the mother tongue does not reveal either the actual mother tongue, especially if it was not Hungarian, nor the "degree" of assimilation,[33] nor the proportion and fluency of Hungarian-speaking among those whose mother tongue was not Hungarian. We will try to estimate the degree of assimilation from the scant records bearing on knowledge of language. In 1890, in the midst of the process, about 60% of secondary school students spoke only Hungarian, while the proportion of those who could not speak Hungarian at all hovered around 5%.[34] This indicates that about one third of all students were experiencing a phase of mixed allegiance. It also appears, if we consider the data from public schools, that about 40% of those who became the intelligentsia had been assimilated during the entire period of the Dual Monarchy; for most of them the first decades of the twentieth century were the final stage of assimilation.

The overwhelming majority of those who learned Hungarian came from urban middle-class Jewish and German families (except for Saxons) but there were significant numbers of Slovak and even Serbian and Romanian assimilated among the intelligentsia. The dilemma of the intelligentsia candidates among the latter ethnic groups and the choices they faced are revealed by the data in the records of the the Greek Orthodox Romanian secondary schools. Only one fourth of the students with Romanian as their mother tongue opted for schools where the language of

---

[33] Regarding the internal gradations of the degree of assimilation, see Péter Hanák, "Polgárosodás és asszimiláció a XIX. században" [Embourgeoisement and assimilation in the nineteenth century], *Történelmi Szemle*, no. 4 (1974), pp. 513, 537.

[34] Vallás és Közoktatási Minisztérium, *Report 25*, pp. 420–433.

instruction was Romanian, for these were dead-end streets towards careers in the intelligentsia; three-quarters studied in Hungarian schools. Thus the Greek Orthodox church encountered difficulties even in replacing their clergy and their teachers in primary schools. They were forced to recruit clergymen and teachers from social strata that could not normally afford to send their children to school: the ratio of offspring of peasant families was the highest in the Greek Orthodox secondary schools (21%) while these schools exempted a large proportion from tuition payments (25%) and provided the biggest scholarships.[35]

The Divergent Traits of Social Mobility into the Intelligentsia with Degrees

The main trends in the social relations of secondary school students, in harmony with the social function of those institutions, were to provide reserves for the intelligentsia as a whole, especially where mid-level preparation was required. The analysis of the social relations of students at institutions of higher learning sheds light on the reproduction of the ranks of the intelligentsia with degrees—a much smaller, but all the more influential, stratum of the intelligentsia. We have found it more productive to examine the social background of students at institutions of higher learning in conjunction with the social background of secondary students, for by so doing we obtain an answer to the question, to what extent did the transformations in the social background differ during the period observed.

---

[35] Ibid., pp. 328–329, 344, 404.

TABLE 19

Distribution of Students in High Schools and at Institutions of Higher Education According to the Socioeconomic Status of Their Parents[36]

Socioeconomic status of parents	1880–1891		1900–1901		1908–1909		1914–1915	
	High sch.	Inst. of higher ed.	High sch.	Inst. of higher ed.	High sch.	Inst. of higher ed.	High sch.	Inst. of higher ed.
Farmer, smallholder	14.34	10.99	13.91	8.10	15.33	11.00	14.34	10.45
Landowner	3.02	6.27	2.40	6.00		3.60		4.67
Artisan, merchant	26.55	21.57	26.32	16.30	25.87	21.30	25.46	17.88
Industrialist, merchant	3.02	2.71	3.05	2.40		2.20		4.49
Elem. and middle sch. teacher, clergyman	23.07	8.33	22.95	12.20	9.78	12.80	9.79	14.04
Physician, lawyer, pharmacist, engineer		7.83		10.30	16.27	7.00	16.33	14.26
Other intelligentsia, professions	14.96	19.10	14.47	13.20	11.16	12.40	10.48	
Civil servant in state administration		9.28		12.70		13.60		12.82
Civil servant in county government		2.75		4.50				
Civil servant in community government		2.94		4.00				
Private administrator	5.72	4.62	6.25	5.70	8.33	5.70	10.43	12.73
Military	1.06	0.94	0.90	0.50	1.15	0.70	1.45	1.19
Superintendent, worker, servant	3.61	0.46	4.81	2.00	10.80	1.70	10.56	6.61
Adult student, unknown, other	4.65	2.20	5.03	2.10	1.12	8.00	1.18	0.78
	1880–1891		1900–1901		1908–1909		1914–1915	
	High sch.	Inst. of higher ed.	High sch.	Inst. of higher ed.	High sch.	Inst. of higher ed.	High sch.	Inst. of higher ed.
Total number of students (100%):	42,115	4,765	59,302	9,350	67,699	13,413	76,856	10,536

36 Vallás és Közoktatási Minisztérium, *Report 20*, vol. 2, pp. 245, 282, 305. *Magyar Statisztikai Értesítő*, new ser., 9, p. 349; new ser., 17, p. 404; new ser., 23, pp. 290–291.

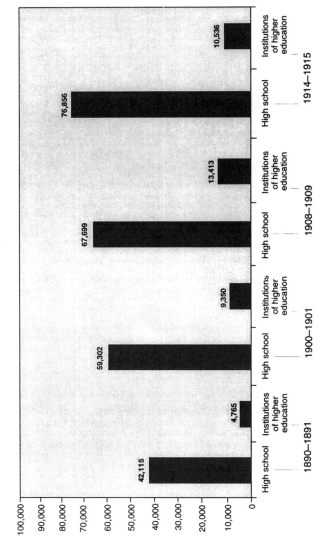

Number of Students in High Schools and at Institutions of Higher Education

	1890–1891	1900–1901	1908–1909	1914–1915
High school	42,115	59,302	67,699	76,856
Institutions of higher education	4,765	9,350	13,413	10,536

Although the records do not consistently include the total number of students attending institutions of higher learning, we can nevertheless safely assert that the intelligentsia with degrees—at the end of the nineteenth century and the beginning of the twentieth—was a rather closed stratum as regards its reproduction: 54.85% in 1890, 62.6% in 1900, 51.5% in 1908, and 54.21% in 1914 were offspring of the intelligentsia. Within the intelligentsia in general, one third were the offspring of parents themselves who had earned degrees, one seventh were the offspring of public employees, predominantly civil servants, whereas employees of private companies provided no more than one twentieth of all university students, far below their percentage among secondary school students. The rapid growth of white collar employed in private enterprise was not felt, at the university level, until just before the World War: in 1914 the ratio of university students whose parents belonged to this category just about doubled, reaching 12.2%.

The middle class and the petty bourgeoisie also played a lesser role in reproducing the intelligentsia with degrees: while they provided over one-fourth of the students in secondary schools (in fact over one-third of students in public schools in this period), they only provided one-sixth to one-fifth of the students in higher institutions. Although the categories listed in the records are not very helpful, it seems that the ratio of those from noble families—in harmony with those whose background were mid-size or large landowners—was about 150% of their representation in secondary schools: they may have provided about 10 to 12% of all university students in the decades of the Dual Monarchy, while those of peasant background provided only about half the ratio of students they provided to secondary schools.

The new trend in social mobility into mid-level intelligentsia—students whose family belonged to maintenance personnel or the unskilled clerical staff, as well as those of blue-collar background—made their presence felt at the university level belatedly: only about 1 to 2% of all university students came from such a background at the turn of the century and only in the last few years of the period did their ratio reach 5%. While we have been unable to show the ratio of participation by specific occupations and professions in the case of the reproduction of the intelligentsia without degrees—we can do so for the intelligentsia with degrees, given the data contained in the records, for most institutions of higher learning, except for law schools, were "career specific." We have selected the academic year 1908–1909 from the records pertaining to the early part of the century.

TABLE 20

Students at Institutions of Higher Learning in the Academic Year 1908–1909 According to the Socioeconomic Status of Their Parents[37]

Socioeconomic status of parents	Total Students	Theology	Law	Medicine	Philosophy	Pharmacy	Engineering
Farmer, smallholder	11.00	33.60	7.00	6.50	9.30	5.20	3.10
Landowner	3.60	0.90	4.90	3.00	2.20	6.30	3.50
Artisan, merchant	21.30	17.60	18.70	30.60	19.20	19.00	27.90
Industrialist, merchant	2.20	0.60	2.20	2.90	1.10	2.60	5.30
Professor, teacher, clergyman	12.80	27.50	8.10	10.60	19.80	6.00	7.50
Physician, lawyer, pharmacist, engineer	7.00	3.10	6.70	11.80	5.10	14.90	8.00
Other intelligentsia and professions	12.40	3.90	15.70	11.60	11.90	18.10	11.60
Civil servant in state administration	13.60	3.50	11.60	7.20	10.40	6.60	16.00
Civil servant in county government			2.50	1.40	1.50	1.70	2.20
Civil servant in community government			2.80	1.90	2.40	3.70	0.60
Private administrator	5.70	3.80	5.30	5.40	6.20	7.20	9.70
Military	0.70	0.20	0.80	0.60	0.90	0.60	0.90
Superintendent, worker, servant	1.70	3.70	1.10	1.30	2.70	0.90	0.70
Other occupation	1.10	1.50	1.20	0.40	0.10	0.30	2.60
Adult student, unknown, other	6.90	0.10	11.40	4.80	7.20	6.90	0.40
Total number of students (100%):	13,413	2,138	6,093	1,964	1,521	348	1,349

[37] *Magyar Statisztikai Értesítő*, new ser., 17, pp. 400–404.

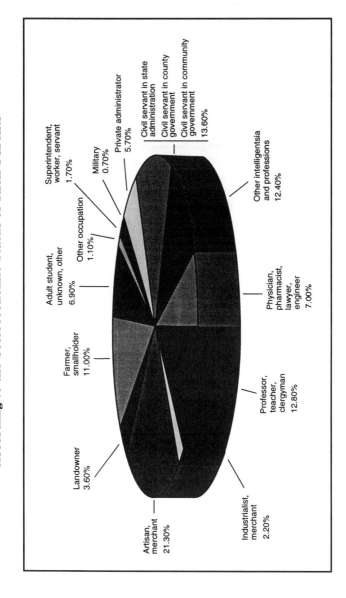

Students at Institutions of Higher Learning in the Academic Year 1908–1909 According to the Socioeconomic Status of Their Parents

Superintendent, worker, servant 1.70%

Military 0.70%

Private administrator 5.70%

Civil servant in state administration

Civil servant in county government

Civil servant in community government 13.60%

Other occupation 1.10%

Other intelligentsia and professions 12.40%

Adult student, unknown, other 6.90%

Physician, pharmacist, lawyer, engineer 7.00%

Farmer, smallholder 11.00%

Professor, teacher, clergyman 12.80%

Landowner 3.60%

Industrialist, merchant 2.20%

Artisan, merchant 21.30%

The tables reveal clearly what the averages do not: among all careers requiring a degree, the clergy was the most open one. In other words, besides careers in elementary school teaching, careers in the clergy were the most receptive to students of peasant or petty bourgeois background. Students whose background was among the landowning and land-renting class gravitated, beyond the median, towards careers that required preparation in law (including political roles). On the other hand, the traditional view of this stratum is contradicted by the fact that over one half of such students chose careers in the professions (medicine, pharmacy, engineering)—although we have to concede that the above-mentioned category included the offspring of capitalist entrepreneurs.

The middle class and petty bourgeoisie, at the beginning of the century, were attracted by careers in the professions: they provided 18.7% of all law students, 30.6% of all medical students, 27.9% of all students in engineering. In accordance with its own social status, the upper-middle class preferred to send its offspring to engineering and medical schools.

The ratio of students whose parents belonged to the professions was the highest at the corresponding faculties, indicating the formation of "dynastic traditions," the growth of the tendency to self-reproduction. Public servants provided the second largest group supplying law students, following the middle class and petty bourgeoisie. While the latter classes aimed for a career as lawyers, the offspring of public servants had the same career in mind as their parents.[38]

The career choice made by the offspring of privately employed white collar offers the most consistent results, but even for them career in the professions was the next step in social climbing. The great, almost magnetic attraction of the professions, was due to what may have appeared as fabulous incomes at a

---

[38] This conclusion may be reached, in part, on the basis of the choice of careers of students from middle-class and petit bourgeois backgrounds. Moreover, between 1890 and 1910 the number of Jewish lawyers rose from 918 to 3,049, while the number of lawyers of all other faiths combined rose merely from 3,084 to 3,694; on the other hand, the ratio of Jews among civil servants did not exceed 4.5%. *Magyar Statisztikai Értesítő*, new ser., vol. 64, pp. 205–206.

time when the intelligentsia of the white-collar strata was becoming impoverished. It was also the hope of independence from institutions of official culture; yet the outcome was overcrowding in the schools offering degrees, oversupply of graduates, and the large number of students described in the statistics as "adults," probably implying lack of resources for completing studies on time.[39]

Data regarding the religious and ethnic distribution of students at institutions of higher learning are provided here, broken down by schools.

TABLE 21

Distribution of University Students by Ethnic Group and Religion in Hungary[40]

Nationality	1870–1871	1880–1881	1890–1891	1900–1901	1908–1909
Hungarian	88.24	70.01	71.76	82.41	84.82
German	4.33	10.17	7.49	6.67	5.35
Romanian	4.73	8.40	11.06	6.05	5.96
Slovak	1.83	3.54	3.48	2.14	1.95
Croatian		0.52	1.25	0.77	0.45
Serb	0.53	2.28	3.59	1.10	0.85
Ruthenian	0.34	5.08	1.36	0.53	0.20
Other				0.32	0.36
Denomination	**1870–1871**	**1880–1881**	**1890–1891**	**1900–1901**	**1908–1909**
Roman Catholic	53.89	43.04	42.57	41.71	40.45
Uniate	2.39	6.41	5.19	5.04	4.70
Greek Orthodox	3.47	3.82	6.09	4.74	4.47
Lutheran	19.20	18.00	13.37	15.45	15.87
Calvinist	9.39	9.94	9.88	8.69	8.95
Unitarian	0.55	0.74	0.73	0.81	0.93
Jewish	11.38	18.05	22.16	23.56	24.57
Non-denominational					0.04

[39] Béla Bosnyák, "A budapesti diáknyomor" [Student misery in Budapest], *Huszadik Század* 13, no. 26 (1912), pp. 224–244.

[40] Vallás és Közoktatásügyi Minisztérium, *Report 1*, pp. 182–183, 200–201, 217; *Report 11*, pp. 329, 332, 351, 362, 370; *Report 20*, vol. 2, pp. 243, 279–280, 309, 320–321. *Magyar Statisztikai Értesítő*, new ser., 9, p. 349; new ser., 17, pp. 400–404; new ser., 23, p. 289.

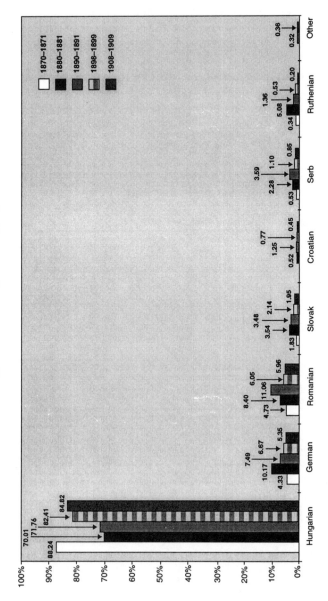

Distribution of University Students
by Ethnic Group in Hungary

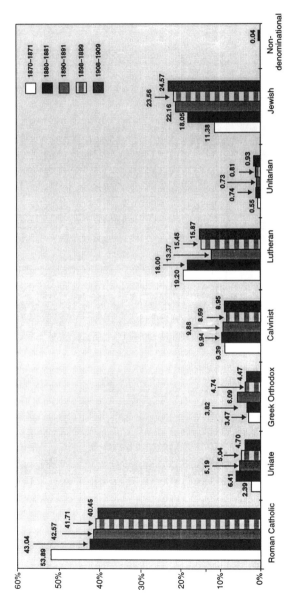

Distribution of University Students
by Religion in Hungary

TABLE 22

Distribution of University Students by Faculty, Ethnic Group and Religion in 1908[41]

Nationality	Theology	Law	Medicine	Philosophy	Pharmacy	Engineering
Hungarian	64.50	90.70	83.70	86.80	90.00	89.80
German	8.23	2.90	7.80	8.50	3.70	5.00
Romanian	18.07	4.20	5.10	2.20	2.60	1.10
Slovak	7.59	0.70	1.50	0.80	0.90	0.90
Croatian	0.64	0.20	0.10	0.20		1.80
Serb		1.00	1.40	0.70	2.30	1.00
Ruthenian	0.83	0.10	0.10	0.10		
Other	0.15	0.20	0.30	0.70	0.50	0.40

Denomination	Theology	Law	Medicine	Philosophy	Pharmacy	Engineering
Roman Catholic	41.68	41.90	28.00	48.70	37.60	41.20
Uniate	12.09	3.60	2.80	3.10	2.60	0.10
Greek Orthodox	9.60	3.90	4.60	1.80	4.60	2.40
Lutheran	11.46	7.70	8.50	12.00	5.70	9.40
Calvinist	23.70	16.40	9.10	19.10	14.70	9.30
Unitarian	0.58	1.10	0.60	1.60	0.90	0.60
Jewish	0.18	25.40	46.30	13.70	33.90	36.90
Non-denominational						0.10

41 *Magyar Statisztikai Értesítő*, new ser., 23, p. 289.

Distribution of University Students by Faculty
and Ethnic Group in 1908

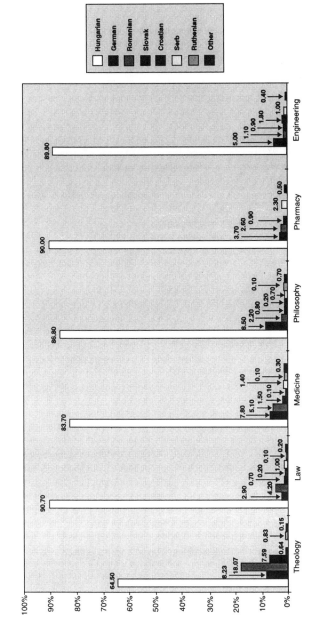

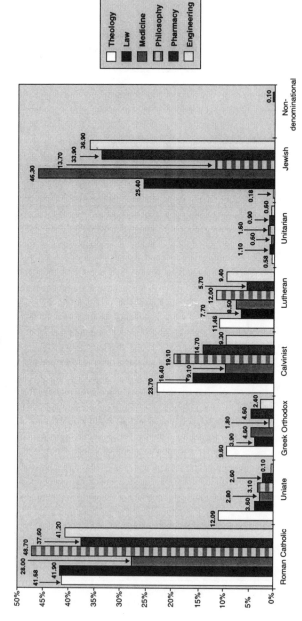

Distribution of University Students by Faculty and Religion in 1908

Among those reproducing intelligentsia in the professions, shifts in religious and ethnic distribution, much as in the case of secondary students, show gains by those with Hungarian as their mother tongue. We see a relationship in the fact that the gains by Hungarian-speakers among the university students corresponds, from the 1890s on, to the increase in the number of Jews among secondary school students. If we analyze distribution by faculty, especially the widely divergent ratios among Romanian and Slovak students, we must conclude that the policy promoting assimilation was successful, whereas instruction in the language of the nationalities led to a dead-end. The growth in the number of Jewish students, albeit with an unbalanced distribution in the various schools, indicates differences in choice of careers, or rather the limitations in job opportunities which encouraged the majority of the Jewish intelligentsia to opt for degrees in the professions.[42]

---

[42] In his analysis of the census of 1910 Péter Hanák demonstrated that the social origins of the intelligentsia among various groups of white collar was extremely polarized: while the bulk of those in public service came from the landowning nobility, the majority of the privately employed white collar and the professionals came from the Jewish middle class; the other places were occupied by white-collar, of middle-class, and petit bourgeois background, extremely heterogeneous as regards religion, ethnicity, and social traditions. Hanák, "A tisztviselő és értelmiségi réteg" [The stratum of the intelligentsia and government employees], in *Magyarország története, 1890–1918*, ed. Hanák, pp. 452–457.

CHAPTER V

The Standard of Living of the Intelligentsia in the Age of Dualism

The Evolution of the Income of the Intelligentsia

The determining factors in the stratification of the social status of the intelligentsia—apart from the place occupied in work relations and the level of training—was their income level and standard of living. The examination of these factors could provide us with information as to what occupations may have attracted, or may have been at least acceptable to certain social groups, to what extent did the income of occupation categories motivate mobility into the intelligentsia, and to what extent these enabled for the children of certain groups of the intelligentsia to opt for an intellectual career. When we undertake the analysis of the income relations of the intelligentsia in the Dual Monarchy we take as our premise that, from mid-century, the traditional intelligentsia lost ground, moreover the roles of the "nobile officium" disappeared altogether: income from his or her occupation was the only thing that made it possible for the overwhelming majority of the intelligentsia to make ends meet.

These conclusions are also supported by the series of data regarding the census of real estate ownership in 1900 and 1910.

TABLE 23

Home and Land Ownership by Members of the Intelligentsia in 1900 and 1910[1]

Categories of intelligentsia	1900				1910			
	Employed males	Home-owners (%)	Land-owners (%)	Estate of 100 holds* (%)	Employed males	Home-owners (%)	Land-owners (%)	Estate of 100 holds* (%)
Civil servants in state administration	8,633	14.20	10.00	2.60	13,017	16.10	8.80	1.70
Civil servants in county government	4,471	25.10	19.70	7.00	4,094	28.30	19.00	6.00
Civil servants of chartered towns	2,962	22.40	12.80	1.20	4,319	21.20	10.90	0.50
Municipal civil servants	2,520	41.50	28.70	1.80	2,771	41.90	25.60	1.60
District notaries	4,925	30.90	47.50	3.10	5,313	29.60	41.60	2.80
Judges and prosecutors	2,779	24.20	20.70	6.20	2,893	25.30	16.50	3.50
Court clerks	4,676	15.20	9.00	0.50	4,933	19.30	8.70	0.60
Public notaries	317	52.00	41.30	13.90	300	53.30	42.70	13.30
Lawyers	4,507	47.20	35.30	9.00	6,743	40.90	27.90	6.40
Clergymen	11,105	27.40	36.80	1.70	11,413	25.40	32.70	1.60
Professors	446	29.10	18.40	3.40	657	26.30	16.10	2.90
Physicians	4,805	33.90	18.20	2.30	5,514	37.10	18.20	2.20
Pharmacists	1,639	42.40	20.70	1.00	1,850	46.00	20.60	1.60
White collar in industry					27,687	7.90	3.90	0.15
White collar in banking and commerce					39,727	12.60	7.50	0.48
White collar in transportation					22,446	15.70	7.60	0.41

[1] *Magyar Statisztikai Közlemények*, new ser., vol. 64, pp. 231–232.   * 100 holds=142 acres

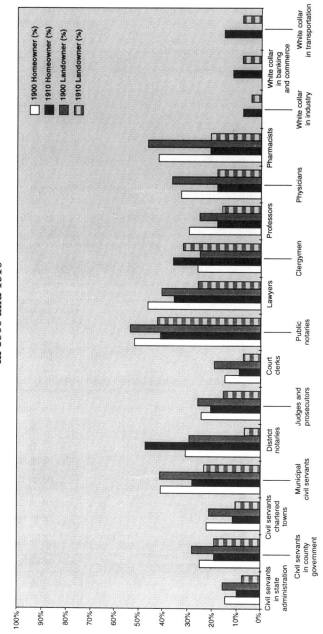

Home and Land Ownership by Members of the Intelligentsia
in 1900 and 1910

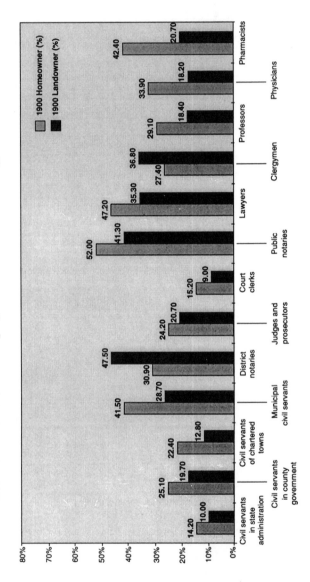

Home and Land Ownership by Members of the Intelligentsia in 1900

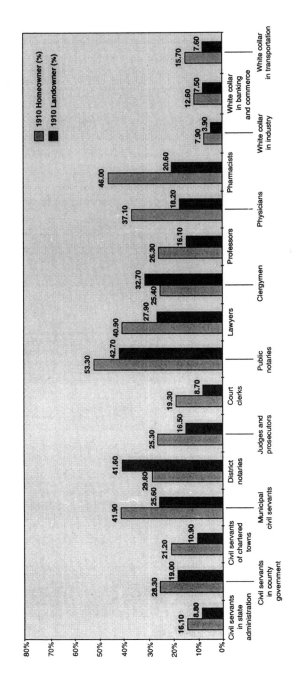

Home and Land Ownership by Members of the Intelligentsia in 1910

About 1% of all members of the intelligentsia owned a significant amount of land—that is, over one hundred *holds*—at the turn of the century and in 1910; while only about one hundred to 150 members of the intelligentsia owned over one thousand *holds* of land. About one sixth of all intelligentsia owned land that was significant from the point of view of income, that is between one and one hundred *holds*. The percentage of landowners was relatively high among public servants, notaries and lawyers, whereas the masses of white collar workers in the economic sector rarely owned any land at all.

We would be hard put to determine to what extent the increasingly significant cash reserves in the last decades of the Dual Monarchy modified the income relations of the intelligentsia, as compared to their earnings in salaries; nevertheless, we must assume that such wealth, derived from inheritance, from contracting an advantageous marriage, or from savings, did affect their standards in the case of a fraction of the intelligentsia.[2]

From the point of view of work relations and source of income, the intelligentsia in this period may be divided into three major groups: public employees, private employees, and members of the so-called professions, even though these categories do not imply either income level nor actual social status.

The records pertaining to these three groups vary in quality and quantity. In addition to the so-called average income of public employees, determined mainly on the basis of the budgets, we may consider the income levels on the official government scale; infact, it is even possible to estimate the real value of the income with regard to two points of reference. As regards the income of private employees, we are only able to indicate the theoretical average within a short span of time, around the turn of the century; even so, the figures do not apply to the entire group. As for income in the professions, we have only indirect evidence. Thus

---

[2] One figure that may serve as an indication of the extent of private wealth accumulated from earnings may be that 14% of the deposits in the postal savings services, catering to small depositors, were held by members of the intelligentsia in 1886–1888: namely, 8,188 white-collar workers and 4,080 other categories of intelligentsia. *Közgazdasági és Statisztikai Évkönyv* [Yearbook of economics and statistics], vols. 3–4, p. 530.

Thus we can only *sketch* the evolution of income among the intelligentsia and the income relations within the three categories in the period of the Dual Monarchy, comparing them, in some instances, to outside points of reference, such as the income of day laborers and workers. We feel, however, that we may at least approximate our original goal, which was to determine to what extent income relations motivated upward mobility into the intelligentsia.

Income Relations of Public Employees

It helps to consider, in the first instance, the income of teachers within the category of public employees, since this group of the intelligentsia is a good example of the enormous social distances within the same group; the primary school teachers, who were the majority—"the day laborers of the nation"—may presumably be considered as a basis for internal comparison.

The Teachers

Lines of division within the category of teachers may be drawn according to type of school, as well as between town and village, and especially between the capital and the provinces.[3]

At the bottom we find the teachers in the public elementary schools. Their salaries were determined by a shortage of professionally qualified teachers necessary for the upgrading of public education: for instance, according to the Ministry, in the academic year 1870–1871 they would have needed at least 27,315 teachers for effective teaching, at the rate of eighty pupils per teacher, as opposed to the 19,297 who were actually so employed.[4] As a first step to overcome the dearth of teachers, the public education bill of 1868 set the minimum pay of full

---

3 Ottó Szabolcs, "A pedagógusok élete az első világháború előtti félszázadban" [The life of teachers during the fifty years preceding World War I], *Pedagógiai Szemle*], no. 9 (1968), p. 830.

4 Vallás és Közoktatásügyi Minisztérium, *Report 2* (Buda, 1872), p. 68.

time teachers at 300 forints, in addition to the "official lodging and a garden of at least one quarter *holds*," whereas teachers' helpers received 200 forints. The bill, however, did not apply to over 90% teachers, employed by the denominations, except by way of recommendation, and thus, in the years after the Compromise "the majority of teachers remained victims of the lack of sympathy on the part of the population, which insisted on maintaining their public school teachers at the same level of misery determined by their ancestors in the previous century."[5] Although the minimum salaries of teachers at higher grades was set at 550 forints for full-time teachers and 250 forints for teachers' assistants, whereas the minimum for public school teachers was raised to 800 forints (or 400 for assistants), the average pay of all teachers in the three types of schools, fifteen years after the bill was passed, was merely 368 forints.[6] This was about twice the income of the average day laborer.[7]

During the first decade of the Dual Monarchy there was no comprehensive legislation regulating the pay of teachers at the secondary level; indeed, the bill on secondary schools was adopted only after protracted gestation, because of opposition from the denominations. Thus we encounter a wide range of salary levels by denomination and by region. In the academic year 1870–1871, the average of 600 forints for the 947 full-time teachers concealed incomes ranging from a minimum of 367 forints to a maximum of 1,750 forints. The average pay of a high school principal was 1,000 forints: while the principal with the lowest pay received 630 forints, the one with the highest pay received 2,000 forints, and he was stationed in Buda. Substitute and assistant teachers numbered 555 in that academic year, and their average pay was 350 forints.[8]

According to another source, two years later, in 1874, the average pay of teachers in Protestant secondary schools, who

---

5 Ibid.

6 Szabolcs, op. cit., p. 834.

7 Sándor Matlekovics, *Magyarország közgazdasági és közművelődési állapota ezeréves fennállásakor* [The economy of Hungary and its public education at the time of its first millennium] (Budapest, 1897), pp. 464–474. (Assuming 200 workdays a year, as an average).

8 *HStK*, vol. 7, part 3, pp. 104–136.

received the lowest salaries reached 699 forints.[9]

Although it is not clear whether our sources included fringe benefits, amounting to a significant portion of the incomes, in their calculations of averages, it remains clear that in the decade following the Compromise the yearly income of public school teachers was barely double that of the poorest stratum of Hungarian society, the day laborers. As for the salaries of secondary school teachers, ranging widely, they were two to three times the income of teachers in grade schools.

The ministerial report containing the data for the academic year 1887–1888 offer us the opportunity to make the first more comprehensive assessment of the income of teachers.

---

[9] Samu Wéber, "A protestáns középiskolai tanárok díjazása" [Remuneration for the services of teachers in Protestant secondary schools], *Magyar Tanügy* (1874), pp. 118–119.

TABLE 24

Income of Teachers in the Academic Year
1887-1888[10]

Category of educators		Effectives	Average income
			in forints
1. PUBLIC ELEMENTARY SCHOOL	(total)	24,379	454.52
Regular		21,557	468.81
Assistant without certification		2,822	345.33
Government employee		1,240	522.85
2. TWO-GRADE MIDDLE SCHOOL		280	559.29
Government employee		74	688.11
3. FOUR-GRADE MIDDLE SCHOOL	(total)	1,109	785.65
Government employee		269	886.61
4. GIRLS' HIGH SCHOOL		162	885.56
Government employee		119	1,114.79
5. HIGH SCHOOL	(total)	2,862	1,000–1,100
State-administered institutions		981	
Budapest—regular			1,800 +100.00 fifth-year bonus
Budapest—substitute			900.00
Country—regular			1,400 +100.00 fifth-year bonus
Country—substitute			800.00
Other institutions		1,881	
Regular			500–1,900
Substitute			500–1,600
6. UNIVERSITY PROFESSOR			
University of Budapest		180	2,122.00
University of Kolozsvár		66	
Polytechnic University of Budapest		47	3,204.00

---

[10] Average earnings computed on the basis of the budgets of different types of schools. For extensive details regarding the pay scale of secondary school teachers, *see* VKM, *Report 18*, pp. 150–154. For details regarding teachers in the capital city, see Gyula Dausz, *A székesfővárosi oktatók fizetésügye (1873–1933)* [The issue of salaries for teachers in the capital city] (Budapest, 1934).

The average incomes, deduced mainly from the budgets, reflect accurately the stratification of teachers' society by level of income, twenty years after the passage of the act on public education. The average income of teachers in primary schools, that is 90% of all teachers, was 454.52 forints; teachers in state-supported schools, mostly in towns, earned 25 to 30% more than their colleagues in denominational schools. In general the theoretical average earning of primary schools teachers was about 2.5 times the average income of day laborers. Five years later, in 1893, in his intervention during the debate on the bill to regulate the pay of denominational and communal teachers, Géza Polonyi, the future minister of justice, compiled the annual expenditures of a public school teacher with three to four children. According to this assessment, although Polonyi was very frugal regarding the needs of a teacher's family (see appendix 3), the expenses of the family would amount to 543 forints and 80 kreuzer.[11] If we assign 43.80 forints to cover the rate of inflation, we may consider 500 forints as the real earnings necessary for survival for a family of the intelligentsia in the years preceding 1890; and this sum does not include the expenses of basic schooling for the children! This sum was not attained by primary school teachers, except in the public schools. Hence it should come as no surprise that the majority of teachers in denominational schools were forced to take on moonlighting jobs as cantors or bellringers for a second, if meager, income.[12]

The teachers at middle schools, which eventually did not survive, were more like the primary school teachers as regards their income; while the teachers at public schools and schools for girls were about midway between primary school and secondary school teachers; the situation of the latter was not regulated, hence their average income of about 1,100 forints concealed a range of twofold and three fold difference.

---

[11] Mihály Pásztor, *Az eladósodott Budapest* [Budapest in the red] (Budapest, 1907), pp. 201–202.

[12] It is a sad reflection on the fate of teachers that in 1888 the minister of religion had to issue a special ordinance regarding collecting dues for the choirmaster, for those in charge of the schools did not provide adequately. See VKM, *Report 18*, pp. 10–11.

The actual income of university professors, at the apex of all personnel in education, is difficult to determine because of income from tutoring; the average pay, as can be determined from the budget, does not reflect the level of income, nor the dispersion from the average. Directive 1429/1889 issued by the minister of religion and education sought to remedy the confused situation; it states that "since the income professors derive from tutoring has increased commensurately not only with the number of hours of lectures but also with the number of students registered, perhaps *ad infinitum* [italics by author], unusual disproportions appear in the incomes of professors with equal course-loads."[13] In spite of the disproportions, the average income professors derived from their teaching position was eight to ten times the income of primary school teachers, and two to three times the income of secondary school teachers; we may estimate it at about 3,000 to 4,000 forints in the years before 1890. While the average income of secondary school teachers was on a level with that of a sheriff, that of the university professor corresponded to the pay of a governor or section chief in a ministry.

On the basis of Act XXVI of 1893, which extended the minimum pay of 300 or 200 forints for primary school teachers to the schools maintained by denominations, ten percent of denominational school teachers had to receive state subsidies to attain that minimum.[14] Between academic years 1887–88 and 1896–97 the pay of teachers increased by 20 to 30% (see appendix 4), but this barely exceeded the rate of increase in the cost of living. And since the increase in salaries was about the same for each category of teachers, the gaps we have outlined within the society of teachers merely became wider. From the turn of the century sources regarding the actual income of teachers are scarcer.

Althugh Act XXVI of 1907 stipulated that every primary school teacher was to be considered a civil servant, and the uniform base pay increased automatically during thirty years of service, with five year supplements (see appendix 5), the justificaprovided by the ministry during the debate on the bill intimates a deterioration in the standard of living of public school teachers.

---

[13] *Report 18* of VKM, p. 168.
[14] *Report 27* of VKM, p. 163.

TABLE 25

Income Distribution of Teachers in State Primary Schools in 1907[15]

Average income in crowns	Number of teachers	Percentage
2,600	5	0.09
2,500	12	0.21
2,400	61	1.08
2,300	26	0.46
2,200	123	2.18
2,100	88	1.56
2,000	255	4.52
1,900	32	0.57
1,800	321	5.69
1,700	277	4.91
1,600	1,344	23.81
1,500	190	3.37
1,400	1,130	20.02
1,200	92	1.63
1,100	204	3.61
1,000	1,484	26.29
Total:	5,644	100%

---

[15] Justification presented by the minister for Act XXVI of 1907 (parliamentary records no. 410). Until the time of the bill the teachers in public schools received varying base pay (800, 1,000, 1,200, or 1,400 crowns), and a seniority benefit of 100 crowns, granted five times, as stipulated in paragraph 2 of Act XXVI of 1893. Moreover, there was a personal bonus of 200 crowns for ten years of service, 300 crowns for 10 to 15 years, and 400 crowns for fifteen years. Thus, the maximum pay earned by a teacher in a public elementary school after fifty-five years of service was:

     1,400 crowns base pay
      500 crowns of bonus (for every five years)
      400 crowns of personal bonus

Total: 2,300 crowns, plus housing allowance, or rent money equal to that earned by civil servants at grade level eleven.

Division of Teachers in State Primary Schools by Income
in 1907 (in Crowns)

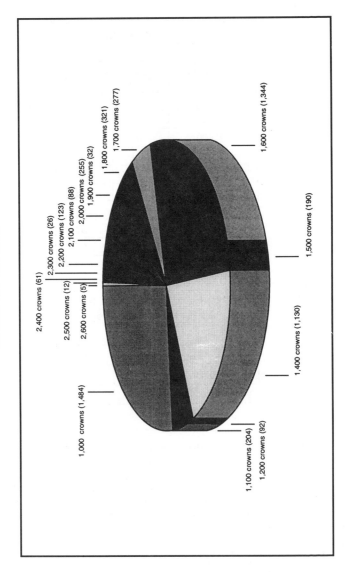

If we compare the income relations of state public school teachers to the price index, we get the following picture: in 1906 the expenses deemed essential by Géza Polonyi for maintaining a teacher's family amounted to 959.81 forints, or 1919.62 crowns (see appendix 3), and thus 89.9% of primary school teachers employed by the state, the highest paid among all primary school teachers, fell below the level of income deemed necessary for a family in the intelligentsia.

The state tried to compensate for the high rate of inflation and the rapid decline in the standard of living by regulating incomes in Acts XV and XVI of 1913 (see appendix 6), which introduced for teachers the same pay as for civil servants at levels eleven to nine with automatic promotions; yet even these measures did not suffice to halt the decline in the standard of living of the teachers. The teachers in the schools of the capital city, although their theoretical income was 20 to 30% higher than in the case of their colleagues in the provinces, were the hardest hit by the rise in the cost of living: their pay scale had to be regulated three times at the beginning of the century, and several times they had to be granted cost of living increases to their pay.[16]

Public Servants

The income relations of the civil servants, whether in the service of the state or of the courts, present a rather complex picture until the passage of Act IV of 1893. Wide divergences appeared in the income of government employees with similar assignments, even within the same region; the two components accounting for these differences were salaries and fringe benefits (housing allowances, travel expenses, etc.,). A significant number of civil servants received fringe benefits in kind; therefore, wherever the records allow, we will attempt to separate this source of income from money in cash.

In the first full year after the autonomy of the counties was restored the average pay of county and district employees was

---

[16] Dausz, op. cit., pp. 20–30.

621.60 forints. The pay of over forty percent of government employees did not attain 500 forints, while only 17.6% received salaries of above 1,000 forints. The average pay of veterinarians was the lowest (207 forints), while deputy physicians received 354 forints, although they could engage in private practice. The average pay of clerks was 368 forints, and those clerical employees who were paid by the day received 300 forints on the average. The average pay of engineers employed by the county, who had little opportunity for moonlighting, was also rather low (577 forints). The only categories who earned salaries above a thousand forints were the governors and deputy governors (1,547 and 1,357 forints), the chief notaries (1,128 forints), the sheriffs (1,006 forints), as well as clerks of the court and public prosecutors (1,109 and 1,091 forints respectively). forty percent of government employees fell within the 500 to 1,000 forint range.

TABLE 26

Income Distribution of County and District Employees in 1866[17]

Annual income in forints	Number of staff	Percentage
201–300	225	4.80
301–400	1,027	21.90
401–500	739	15.77
501–600	831	17.73
601–700	301	6.42
701–800	660	14.08
801–900	79	1.69
901–1,000		
1,001–1,100	260	5.55
1,101–1,200	459	9.79
above 1,200	106	2.26
Total:	4,687	100%

(For average pay according to job category see appendix 7.)

---

17 *HStK*, vol. 1, part 1, p. 40.

The records of the budgets pertaining to local government, prepared before the introduction of uniform pay, shed light on the regional differences behind the averages, as well as on the ratio of pay in cash to fringe benefits.

TABLE 27

Income Distribution of Local Government Civil Servants in 1888 by Level of Government[18]

Government	Effectives	Salary (%)	Other income (%)	Average income (in forints)
1. COUNTIES	7,786	82.51	17.49	723.88
Central	2,580	81.51	18.49	884.91
District	2,411	74.54	25.43	759.01
Municipalities	2,795	93.56	6.44	544.95
2. CHARTERED TOWNS	2,704	88.95	11.05	841.49
Budapest	818	80.35	19.65	1,033.72
Other 24 counties	1,886	94.04	5.96	758.11
3. COMMUNITIES	5,563	71.09	28.91	703.56
Notaries	4,381	66.64	33.36	743.80
Community physicians	1,182	88.41	11.59	639.03
Total:	16,053	79.97	20.03	736.65

---

[18] *Közgazdasági és Statisztikai Évkönyv*, vol. 3–4, p. 566.

In 1888, among all local authorities, it was the employees of chartered municipalities, especially Budapest, who earned the highest incomes; in the case of Budapest the housing allowance added over 20% to their salaries. The lowest incomes were earned by the employees in municipalities under county authority, governed by councils, where the housing allowance was negligible. The salaries of community and district notaries reached a level close to the average because of the value of the land placed at their disposal as part of their office. The budget figures reveal details regarding the largest groups of local employees— 65.16% of the total, or 10,626 persons, not including those in the forestry service, customs officials, etc. We have determined the distribution of average income in their case on the basis of these records.

TABLE 28

Income Distribution among the Major Categories of Local Government Employees in 1888[19]

Annual income in forints	Number of staff	Percentage
301–400	569	5.36
401–500	128	1.20
501–600	2,286	21.51
601–700	199	1.87
701–800	4,644	43.70
801–900	730	6.87
901–1,000	286	2.69
1,001–1,500	1,047	9.58
1,501–2,000	609	5.73
2,001–3,000	107	1.01
above 3,000	21	0.20
Total:	10,626	100%

Thus, in 1888, over one-fourth of local government employees earned incomes at or near the income deemed minimum for a

---

[19] Ibid., pp. 567–570.

**Income Distribution among the Major Categories of
Local Government Employees in 1888**

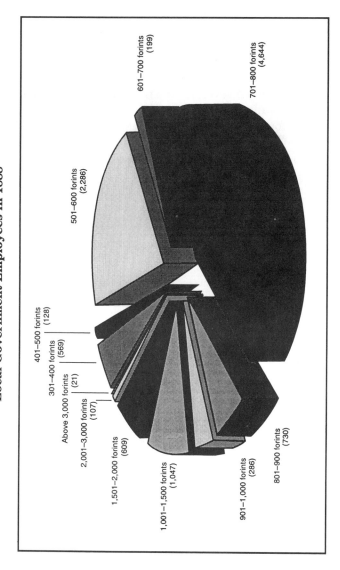

601–700 forints
(199)

701–800 forints
(4,644)

501–600 forints
(2,286)

401–500 forints
(128)

301–400 forints
(569)

Above 3,000 forints
(21)

2,001–3,000 forints
(107)

1,501–2,000 forints
(609)

1,001–1,500 forints
(1,047)

901–1,000 forints
(286)

801–900 forints
(730)

family in the intelligentsia—the kind of income which hardly made it possible for them to pay for the schooling of their children. This category included, among others, albeit only temporarily, trainees who were paid by the day, councilors with municipalities (except chartered towns), clerks and comptrollers in the orphans' courts, community and district doctors, as well as veterinarians.

We may estimate the number of those who earned minimal incomes far higher, however, for the majority of those about whom we have no details, a total of 5,427 persons, were clerks and trainees with low pay. Because of the lack of uniform regulations it was not unusual to find a dispersion of 80 to 100% from the norm in any given category (for details, see appendix 8).

We have calculated the average income of government employees by grade level on the basis of the budget of 1888.

TABLE 29

**Average Income of State Administrators
in 1888 by Grade Level[20]**

Grade level	Number of state administrators		Average annual income in forints
	Number	Percentage	
1. Prime minister	1	0.01	32,000.00
2. Minister	11	0.07	14,181.82
3. State secretary	11	0.07	7,818.18
4. Deputy state secy'	13	0.09	6,930.77
5. State councillor	202	1.35	4,866.11
6. Section chief	398	2.67	3,103.33
7. Secretary	344	2.31	2,115.67
8. Clerk	2,051	13.74	1,705.59
9. Assistant clerk	3,586	24.03	1,158.35
10. Various	3,555	32.82	932.78
11. Various	2,184	14.64	764.45
12. Various	2,566	17.20	620.47
Total:	14,922	100%	1,175.43

[20] The totals for civil servants do not include teachers and professors, white collar employed by the railroads, officials working on estates and industrial plants belonging to the state, but they do include judges and other officials working with the courts. Ibid., p. 572.

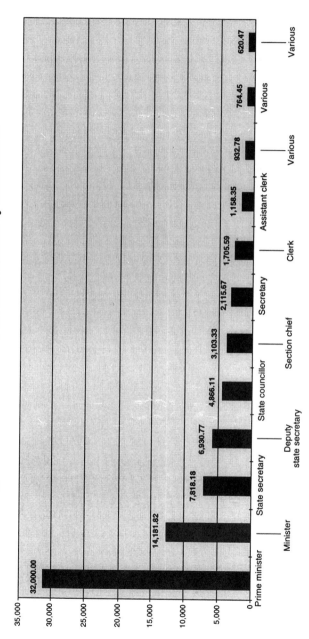

Average Income of State Administrators in 1888 by Grade Level

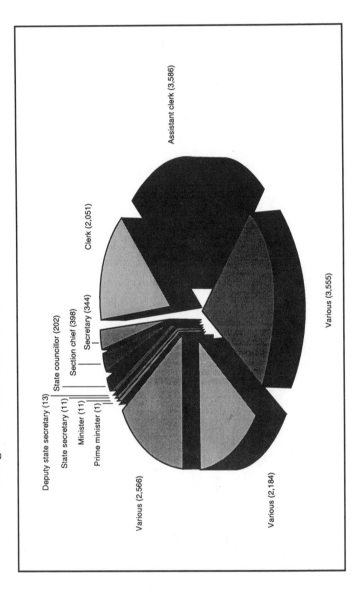

Average Income of State Administrators in 1888 by Grade Level

Assistant clerk (3,586)

Clerk (2,051)

State councillor (202)

Section chief (398)

Secretary (344)

Deputy state secretary (13)

State secretary (11)

Minister (11)

Prime minister (1)

Various (2,566)

Various (3,555)

Various (2,184)

The average income of civil servants employed directly by the government was about sixty percent higher than the average income of those employed by the courts, and exceeded the income of municipal employees as well, mainly because of the averages at grade levels one through five.

But even the average salary of the lowest rank was comparable to the average earned by community and district physicians. We have little information regarding the range of salaries within the same grade levels but, in any case, the range was narrower than in the case of civil servants employed by the courts, precisely as a result of the introduction of grade levels (see appendix 9 for grade levels I-IX). It was probably at grade levels ten, eleven, and thirteen that we find the greatest discrepancies in salaries, for these levels included, in addition to apprentice and part-time clerks, those maintenance personnel whose pay was on a level with salaries at grade eight.[21]

Only about 10% of state civil servants—the categories of trainees and clerks—failed to attain the 500 forint minimum income level, while almost half received salaries commensurate with those of teachers at public and girls' secondary schools, and over one third received salaries comparable to that of teachers in regular secondary schools. About 5% received salaries on a level with those of university professors, while the salaries at grade levels one through five were at the apex of the incomes received by the entire intelligentsia.

Act IV of 1893 introduced uniformity in the salaries of state civil servants, while the courts were allowed to regulate the salary structure of their own employees (although, in practice, the latter eventually conformed as well). The Act set up eleven grade levels and determined what ranks should correspond to what pay-grade (appendix to the Act IV of 1893). Point "b" in paragraph 3 of the Act applied to the salaries of secondary school teachers as well, set at grade levels eight and nine. In order to reach a higher grade level, one had to be appointed; once appointed, the person was entitled to a housing allowance appropriate to the grade level, which took local conditions into consideration (see appendix 5 and 6).

---

[21] Ibid., p. 571.

Referring to inflation, the civil servants were dissatisfied with the provisions of the Act of 1893 and, after 1906, they obtained automatic cost of living increases based on seniority within each grade level.[22]

The county budgets of 1909 contain data regarding the evolution of the average pay of government employees by pay-grade.

TABLE 30

**Evolution of the Pay of State Employees by
Pay-Grade between 1889 and 1909[23]**

Pay-grade	Average income in 1909 in crowns	Raise (Base year 1889)
6.	7,300	32.70
7.	5,200	57.60
8.	4,000	110.50
9.	2,900	141.70

The data in the table make it evident that the automatic pay raises resulted, first of all, in a significant increase in the nominal salaries of lower ranking civil servants, although in real value this signified merely keeping well abreast of the rise in the cost of living. Thus the wage policies of the governments seem to have been aimed at ensuring that the social conditions of lower income employees do not become unbearable. The various cost-of-living bonuses and government welfare had the same objective.

The salaries of county and municipal employees within the same pay-grades increased significantly; hence the gap between their salaries and the salaries of state civil servants narrowed somewhat by the turn of the century. But since the cost of living over a period of fifteen years increased by almost 90%, there was no real improvement in the pay of local government employees.

---

[22] I. Gábor Kovács, "Az értelmiségi keresetek változása (1920–1975)" [Changes in incomes earned by the intelligentsia], in *Értelmiségiek*, p. 228.

[23] *MStK*, new series, vol. 40, p. 15.

TABLE 31

**Distribution of County and Municipal Employees
by Pay-Grade in 1909–1910[24]**

Annual income in crowns	Municipal civil servants in % (with govt. subsidies)	Municipal civil servants in % (without govt. subsidies)	County civil servants in %
up to 1,000	5.10	8.40	9,11
1,001–2,000	24.50	33.20	15,71
2,101–3,000	34.30	29.50	30,00
3,001–4,000	19.60	14.90	26,35
4,001–5,000	7.10	6.60	
5,001–6,000	4.20	3.20	6,17
6,001–7,000	1.80	1.50	11,49
above 7,000	3.40	2.70	1,16
Total: (100%)	18,388	18,388	5,412

In 1909 around one-fourth of county employees still earned salaries below the poverty line, while this ratio among municipal employees had risen to above 40%. This unbearable situation compelled the government to disburse two million crowns of state aid to the municipalities, thanks to which the number of civil servants earning less than 2,000 crowns dropped by over ten percent. Act LVIII of 1912, regarding the development of towns and cities, institutionalized the system of state aid, as a consequence of which towns and cities received five million crowns in aid in 1913, and eight million crowns in 1916.

At the beginning of the century it was still the income of the trainees and part-time clerks, as well as that of the growing mass of white-collar employees in branch agencies still remained below the poverty line (for detals, see appendix 10).

The rate of inflation increased during the war—according to some sources prices rose from 400 to 600% between 1914 and 1917[25]

---

24 *MStK*, new series, vol. 40, pp. 8, 17; vol. 58, 47, 63 and 40–69.

25 Károly Jancsó, *A magyar köztisztviselők* [Civil servants in Hungary] (Budapest, 1917), vol. 2, pp. 21–31.

but even the majority of civil servants, who earned between 2,000 and 4,000 crowns, saw their "middle class" prosperity, consisting of a "three room apartment, second class travel (as opposed to third class) on the railways, and three course meals" whittled away, and they had to compromise regarding schooling for their children, for the rise in their pay level in the same period was merely 25 to 35%.[26]

We have very limited information regarding the income relations of white collar workers with the railways, who also counted as state employees. The budgets only enabled us to determine average salaries for all employees for the years around the turn of the century. According to these, in 1894 the average pay for the 5,536 railroad employees was 1,227 forints, while the average for the 5,965 employees in 1896 was 1,287 forints.[27] In 1902 their numbers increased to 6,674 and their average pay hovered around 2,754 crowns,[28] indicating a slight rise in nominal wages, not commensurate with the rise in the cost of living index. Their average pay level placed them a condition similar to the mass of civil servants, and they were to experience an identical fate as a result of the steep rate of inflation during the war.

Income Relations of Privately Employed White-Collar Workers

While the income relations of civil servants were determined by the capacity of the state budgets, the social policies and the power politics of governments, those of privately employed white collar workers were shaped by supply and demand, modified at times by the competition of careers in the civil service.

White-Collar Employees with Private Railroads

At the turn of the century the number of white-collar workers employed by privately owned railroad companies, after extensive

---

[26] Dezső Buday, "Magyarorszaág honoratior osztályai" [Classes of intelligentsia in Hungary], *Budapesti Szemle* 165, pp. 228–249.

[27] *MStK*, new series, vol. 21, p. 173.

[28] *MStK*, new series, vol. 28, p. 177. At the same time, by 1904, the amount of pay garnished for white-collar employees on the railroads amounted to 9 million crowns. Pásztor, op. cit., p. 94.

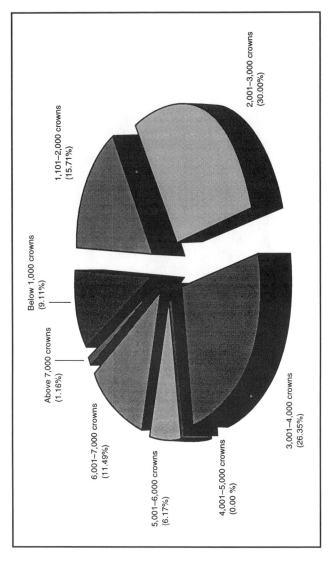

Distribution of Civil Servants in County Government
by Pay-Grade in 1909–1910

2,001–3,000 crowns
(30.00%)

1,101–2,000 crowns
(15.71%)

Below 1,000 crowns
(9.11%)

Above 7,000 crowns
(1.16%)

6,001–7,000 crowns
(11.49%)

5,001–6,000 crowns
(6.17%)

4,001–5,000 crowns
(0.00 %)

3,001–4,000 crowns
(26.35%)

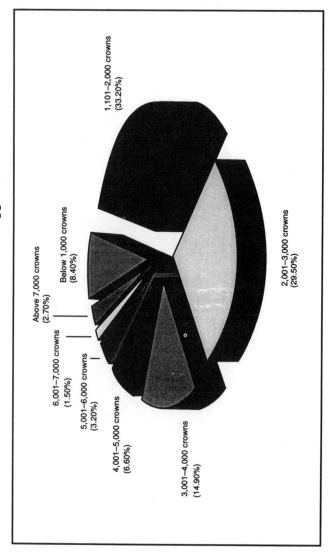

**Income Distribution of Municipal Civil Servants
in 1909–1910 (with State Support)**

1,101–2,000 crowns
(33.20%)

2,001–3,000 crowns
(29.50%)

3,001–4,000 crowns
(14.90%)

4,001–5,000 crowns
(6.60%)

5,001–6,000 crowns
(3.20%)

6,001–7,000 crowns
(1.50%)

Above 7,000 crowns
(2.70%)

Below 1,000 crowns
(8.40%)

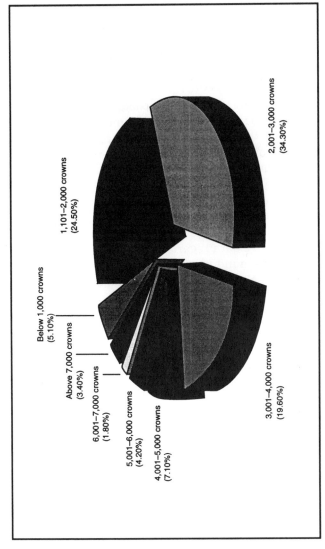

Income Distribution of Municipal Civil Servants
in 1909–1910 (without State Support)

Below 1,000 crowns
(5.10%)

Above 7,000 crowns
(3.40%)

6,001–7,000 crowns
(1.80%)

5,001–6,000 crowns
(4.20%)

4,001–5,000 crowns
(7.10%)

1,101–2,000 crowns
(24.50%)

2,001–3,000 crowns
(34.30%)

3,001–4,000 crowns
(19.60%)

nationalization, increased but slightly. In 1894 there were 913 employees, 950 in 1896, 1,075 in 1900, and 1,178 in 1902. The income level of these employees exceeded those of their colleagues on government-owned railroads by about 15%. In 1894 their average pay was 1,394 forints (as opposed to 1,227 for state employees), in 1896 it was 1,499 (1,287 for state employees), while in 1900 it was 3,111 crowns (2,642 crowns for state employees).[29] In addition to the higher pay-scale, they benefitted from more favorable retirement conditions and several minor fringe benefits, such as better fitting uniforms.

Because of the similarity in training and activities they sought social contacts and identification with those employed by the state, rather than with private employees in industry and commerce.[30]

Employees in Industry

Comprehensive data regarding the income relations of white-collar employees in industry may be found in the census of 1900. At the end of the nineteenth century the income of white-collar employees in industry was considerably below that of any segment of the intelligentsia in public employ; in fact, they were not regarded as part of the "real" intelligentsia by their contemporaries, and did not receive housing allowances, half-fare railroad tickets, or discounts on purchases—perks which constituted part of the middle-class way of life. The increasing demand for labor in the last decade of the century, however, resulted in a rise in their income level: in 1900 the average income of employees in industry was 1,620 crowns, which corresponded roughly to the average income of teachers in the primary schools, and was almost three times the average income of industrial workers.[31]

---

[29] *MStK*, new series, vol. 21, p. 173; vol. 28, p. 177.

[30] Buday, op. cit.

[31] *MStK*, new series, vol. 14, pp. 490–532. Analyzed by Vilmos Fenyő, "A középosztályok dinamikája és a magántisztviselők" [The dynamics of the middle classes and privately employed white-collar workers], *Huszadik Század* 7, no. 14 (1906), pp. 51–73. The same census examined the earnings of industrial workers as well, their average income being 568 crowns a year, not including supervisors and technicians.

TABLE 32

Income of White-Collar Workers Employed by Industry in 1900[32]

Total white collar		White collar		
		Female	Male	Male in B'pest
Number (100 %) of white collar	17,386	2,364	15,022	6,748
Number of white collar surveyed	11,699	1,384	10,315	5,926
Income	In percentages			
Below 1,000 crowns	25.09	95.09	16.67	14.02
1,001–1,200 crowns	12.08	2.60	12.72	10.45
1,201–1,500 crowns	8.09	1.81	8.83	7.30
1,501–2,000 crowns	18.10	0.43	20.28	19.42
2,001–2,400 crowns	12.41		14.01	15.73
2,401–3,000 crowns	8.07	0.07	9.15	10.28
3,001–4,800 crowns	9.94		11.27	14.06
4,801–6,000 crowns	2.69		3.05	3.51
Above 6,000 crowns	3.54		4.02	5.23

The primary reason why the incomes were so scattered, not unlike other groups of the intelligentsia, were differences in training and assignments: the group of employees with salaries in the 4,801 to 6,000 crown range was made up exclusively of technicians with diplomas, while those with incomes above the 6,000 level were 'executives and members of boards.[33] Another reason was the differences in income level between various branches of industry: in similar assignments employees in the machine industry, the food processing industry and manufacturing of luxury products, as well as the chemical industry, received higher pay. A third reason was the low salaries earned by female employees: their income was less than two thirds of the average income for males.

---

[32] The census interpreted the data bearing on 11,699 of the 17,382 white-collar personnel employed in industry (not including mining, smelting and cottage industry, or in the itinerant trades while they were unable to gather information about the remainder. Ibid.

[33] Fenyő, op. cit.

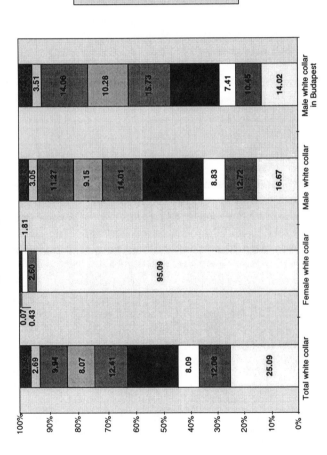

The Income of White-Collar Workers Employed
by Industry in 1900

All in all, almost two-thirds of the white collar in industry earned less than 2,000 crowns which, incidentally, was considered at that time to be the minimum income for a family in the intelligentsia.

White-Collar Employees in Commerce and Banking

There is not a single comprehensive collection of data illustrating the income relations of these major segments of private employees. Nevertheless, as regards the early part of the century, we may accept the statement of Vilmos Fenyő, according to whom: "It is common knowledge that, as regards working hours as well as salaries, conditions in commerce are even worse" than in industry.[34] On the basis of individual research we can examine in detail, even if not the group in its entirety, the income relations and social conditions of employees of some of the major banks and grain trading companies, better off than the masses of others in these categories.

In 1906 Mihály Pásztor, examining the consequences of inflation, analyzed the personal budget of twenty-six employees of a large credit institution and seven employees of a wholesale grain trading company[35] (see appendices 11, 12, and 13).

The income of the bank clerks ranged from 900 to 26,000 crowns, the latter being the salary of the candidate for director. Among the employees who participated in the analysis salaries between 4,800 and 6,000 crowns was the norm. Thirteen of them had personal wealth, among which 300,000 crowns was the largest, 20,000 the smallest, the average being 80,000 crowns. The other bank clerks had no wealth of any kind. In spite of their relatively high incomes, several were indebted, although this was not the result of the drop in their real income, as in the case of other categories of employees, but rather because of their expensive "gentlemanly" passions.

Only three of the employees were spending on the education of their children!

---

[34] Ibid.
[35] Pásztor, op. cit.

The seven employees of the grain trading company earned between 1,800 and 14,000 crowns. A pay of 3,600 to 4,000 crowns was the norm, although only one of them did not have a significant second job. Three of the seven had their pay garnished because of debt before or during the analysis, and only one was without significant indebtedness, even though the greater part of their expenses was spent on the necessities of life (food, shelter, clothing).

The employees of large banks and trading companies—although their average income exceeded that of civil servants and of other private employees—could not avoid the main trends marking the income of intelligentsia groups at the beginning of the century, the decrease in their purchasing power; although, in their case, this merely forced them to give up a non-essential expense, or of incurring additional debts, without endangering their well-to-do middle class way of life. Only about one fifth of all employees in commerce and banking, out of a total numbering 47,892 in 1910, worked with the large institutions and earned salaries at the level mentioned.

The Income Relations of those in the Professions

The task of shedding light on the income relations of those in the professions may well be the hardest because, by the very nature of their profession, they did not earn a steady income from a single source, while the tax structure encouraged them to conceal their true income, that is, to disclose an income smaller than what they actually earned. We may rely on only two kinds of data: the rosters of virilists, which refer to the income relations of certain professions only indirectly but may be considered relatively reliable, for inclusion on the rosters offered political advantages; and notes by contemporaries which contain general and less precise observations regarding the income of small groups of professionals.

The professions in the period of the Dual Monarchy were severed from the umbilical cord of dependence on the magnates as a result of the embourgeoisement in the 1840s, when their clientele became the evolving middle class in the urban centers. The golden age of private practice for the professions were the two decades following the Compromise, when it seemed that the increasing masses of the middle class could afford to resort to their professional services. It is characteristic of the income opportunities in the professions in this period that a significant number of the members of committees on local government were recruited from the professions. In 1889, 6.03% of the members of committees at the county level were lawyers, whereas 4.93% belonged to other professions (in absolute numbers, 1,389, that is 11.37%). Their percentage on committees in the municipalities was even more significant: in Budapest 14.25% (57) were lawyers, and 10.73%, (or 315), in the twenty-four other chartered municipalities; members of other professions amounted to 12.57% (or 51) in Budapest, and 4.66% in the other municipalities (137).[36]

From the end of the 1880s, however, their income opportunities narrowed because the upward mobility of the peasantry came to a halt, and because of the concentration of capital following the industrial revolution and the gradual impoverishment of the white-collar workers.[37] Their condition was aggravated at the beginning of the twentieth century, because those who were unable to prosper in the professions could no longer find alternative positions in government or private institutions. All this led to the sharpening of competition among members in the professions, and extremes in income distribution.

In 1906 the distribution of lawyers practicing in Budapest according to income was as follows:

annual income of 50 lawyers	above 40,000 crowns
" " of 200 "	between 16,000 and 40,000
" " of 300 "	between 8,000 and 16,000
" " of 500 "	between 4,000 and 8,000
" " of 300 "	below 4,000 crowns[38]

The rapid growth in the number of paralegals, mostly lawyers with degrees unable to find the capital necessary to open their

---

[36] *Közgazdasági és Statisztikai Évkönyv*, vols. 3–4, pp. 564–565.

[37] *MStK*, new series, vol. 64, p. 191.

[38] Pásztor, op. cit., p. 89.

own practice, was part of the same trend; while they numbered only 1,846 in 1900 by 1910 there were 4,364.[39]

The situation of the physicians was no better than that of the lawyers. In the same period there were 1,300 physicians who made a living from their private practice in Budapest; some of them, according to a contemporary assessment, "had a large, sometimes excessively large income, while others made five to ten thousand forints (i.e. 10,000 to 20,000 crowns—note by author) a year from their practice, but the majority of them were poor and indebted."[40]

The Main Peculiarities of the Income of the Intelligentsia and Some Consequences

Of all the sources of income land, the traditional source for the noble intelligentsia, had become insignificant by the turn of the century; hence their income was predominantly derived from their pay. There were significant differences, of up to ten or fifteen times, in the averages of the highest earning group contrasted with that of the lowest earning group, and between various occupation groups, sometimes even within the same group. In the first decades of the Dual Monarchy about one-sixth or one-fifth of the intelligentsia earned just enough to ensure minimal livelihood for his or her family, without covering the educational expenses of their children at the secondary or tertiary levels, in spite of the fact that even their low income was two to four times the income of the agrarian proleteriat or of the industrial worker. The masses of intelligentsia, about three-quarters of them, earned five to eight times as much as the industrial worker—which also distinguished the intelligentsia socially, making it possible for them to live a "middle class" way of life, including sending their children to decent schools.[41]

---

[39] *MStK*, new series, vol. 64, pp. 166–67 (including Croatia-Slavonia).

[40] Pásztor, op. cit., pp. 89–91. According to his data, at the opposite poles of the medical profession we find professors who are owners of clinics, with incomes around 100,000 crowns a year, and the "poor majority," who had difficulty making even 200 crowns a year.

[41] Béla Bosnyák, op. cit., pp. 224–244; Imre Csécsy, "Diáknyomor" [Students live in misery], *Nyugat*, no. 1 (1914), pp. 581–582; same, "Az értelmiség túltengése" [Excesses of the intelligentsia], *Szabadgondolat* 4, no. 3 (1914), pp. 83–86.

A small percentage of the intelligentsia—including the highest ranking civil servants, university professors, successful lawyers, doctors, engineers, artists—were able to earn the price of an estate of 500 or 1,000 *holds* in one year; if they were not in a position to inherit, they might purchase such an estate, along with a freshly designed coat of arms, to increase their social prestige.

The rapid economic growth in the aftermath of the industrial revolution not only the created the conditions for the rapid spread of the intelligentsia, especially in the economic sector, but also launched the members of the intelligentsia on the path towards impoverishment, towards "proletarianization," with the rise in the rate of inflation. In the last decades of the Dual Monarchy about half of the intelligentsia sunk to or below the level which we may regard as the minimum livelihood for the intelligentsia.

The process of proletarianization of the intelligentsia entailed several consequences that are important from the point of view of the reproduction of this stratum:

1) The process of women joining the ranks of the intelligentsia accelerated. While this process resulted in increased earnings for the families concerned, it also brought about competition for men, and tended men, and tended to reduce real wages.[42]

2) The number of dependents within the ranks of the intelligentsia decreased. This process was caused, to a lesser extent, by women joining the work force, and to a greater extent by a reduction in the birthrate.[43] This meant nothing less than that, in the last decades of the Dual Monarchy, the intelligentsia was increasingly unable to provide for its own rapidly expanding reproduction.

3) Education at the secondary and higher levels ceased to be exclusive. A decrease in support from the family necessitated a system of self-dependence on the part of students, such as tutoring, part-time clerical work, etc. This process placed higher edu-

---

[42] Regarding the advances made by women see *MStK*, new series, vol. 64, pp. 168–169.

[43] *MStK*, new series, vol. 64, p. 105.

cation within the reach of certain social strata who, in former times, could not think of sending their children to school.[44]

Certain phrases of Dezső Buday's monograph describe the deterioration in the social position of the Hungarian intelligentsia in the period preceding World War I, during the last phase of impoverishment, in fitting language: "First it was the small pleasures of life that were left out of the life of the Hungarian honoratior class: travel, the theater, social life. With their consumer cooperatives they were able to fight against the windmill for an extended period, but now the time had come when they could obtain the necessities of life only at the expense of stored energies. They became indebted, their health would suffer, daily worries would accompany this sad phenomenon. What happened to the old dream of officialdom: a modest apartment for old age they could call their own, or a small villa on Lake Balaton for the persons from Budapest who could save up from their housing allowance, and where they might spend their vacations? What happened to the education of the sons for the professions, or the dowry for giving the daughter in marriage?"[45]

The Structure of Intelligentsia Households

A significant problem of research on the structure of society in the period of the Dual Monarchy is that the sources do not enable the researcher to reconstruct the basic units of society—the family or, more exactly, the household—in a way to make them relevant to the data on society in general. Thus we can only shed light indirectly, and often only very partially, pertaining to small segments (by examining individual careers, particular families), on the actual processes behind the abstract and general notion of social evolution: that is, by shedding light on the units actually spending the incomes, the units responsible for consumption, units which evolved their particular way of life and behavior, strategies of life, within specific apartments or houses.

---

[44] Bosnyák, op. cit.
[45] Buday, op. cit., p. 245.

We can do no better in the case of the intelligentsia than to try, on the basis of indirect sources, to draw a somewhat more nuanced picture which, however, does offer some basis for comparison and a more concrete understanding of income relations and housing.

TABLE 33

Evolution of the Ratio of Earners and Dependents in the Main Occupations of the Intelligentsia between 1900 and 1910, as well as the Family Condition of Earners in the Intelligentsia in 1910[46]

Occupational groups	Number of dependents per 100 employes			Of 100 employed in 1910							
				Male				Female			
	1900	1910	Decr. in %	Single	Married	Widow	Divorced	Single	Married	Widow	Divorced
1. White collar in farming	218.50	198.30	20.20	32.90	64.00	2.70	0.40	85.20	3.70	9.30	1.80
2. White collar in forestry	243.20	227.80	15.40	24.20	72.30	2.90	0.60	66.70		33.30	
3. White collar in mining	188.20	182.90	5.30	32.40	65.40	2.00	0.20	86.00	2.00	6.00	6.00
4. White collar in industry	129.10	113.50	10.60	44.00	53.70	1.70	0.60	88.60	5.50	4.00	1.90
5. White collar in commerce	144.30	117.30	27.00	46.00	51.30	2.00	0.70	89.30	6.10	3.10	1.50
6. White collar in transport	160.10	132.80	27.30	35.20	62.40	2.10	0.60	65.80	20.80	10.80	2.60
7. Public service and profess.	160.70	143.30	17.40	37.60	58.80	2.80	0.80	56.60	28.70	13.00	1.70
Total:	157.20	136.10	21.10								

Evolution of the Ratio of Earners and Dependents in the Main Occupations of the Intelligentsia between 1900 and 1910, as well as the Family Condition of Earners in the Intelligentsia in 1910 (Continued)

Occupational groups	Number of dependents per 100 employes			Of 100 employed in 1910							
				Male				Female			
	1900	1910	Decr. in %	Single	Married	Widow	Divorced	Single	Married	Widow	Divorced
Some sub-groups under 7											
a) Administration		172.10		34.45	62.09	2.52	0.94	78.68	10.56	8.49	2.27
Officials		195.30		28.31	68.22	2.51	0.96	75.29	8.25	11.76	4.70
Consultant		79.60		61.19	35.34	2.59	0.88	79.81	11.66	5.32	3.21
b) Lawyers		192.60		29.75	65.76	3.25	1.24				
c) Paraleg. and candidates	No data available	20.20	No data available	91.59	7.86	0.34	0.21				
d) Education		133.10		33.28	64.22	1.95	0.55	73.67	19.82	5.09	1.42
Public element. school teacher		172.60		27.06	70.63	1.88	0.43	65.98	28.42	4.31	1.29
middle school teacher		93.30		34.78	65.06	2.47	0.69	63.71	30.22	4.81	1.26
High school teacher		164.30		44.01	52.12	1.25	0.62	87.50	12.50		
e) Physician		200.30		26.43	69.83	2.65	1.09	82.35	15.69		1.96
In private practice		217.10		23.25	72.40	2.76	1.59	78.95	15.79		5.26
On hospital staff		84.80		63.83	34.61	1.23	0.33	82.15	17.85		
f) Pharmacist		229.00		15.83	80.05	3.29	0.83	9.09	5.05	85.86	
g) Literature, art		86.80		43.28	92.40	2.61	1.81	57.53	30.82	6.88	4.17
h) Scientific institutions		128.60		35.17	60.94	2.86	1.03	74.64	10.60	12.88	1.82

The first conclusion to be drawn from the table, regarding the ratio of salary-earners to dependents among the intelligentsia, and regarding their marital status, is that the inflation in the first decade of the twentieth century resulted in a decrease of 21% on the average in the number of dependents; while in 1900 there were 157.2 dependents for every 100 salary earners, this ratio dropped to 136.1 by 1910. A detailed analysis of the data allows us to draw some conclusions regarding the processes involved. The first and, in our estimation, the most basic process, was the extension of the years preceding marriage among the intelligentsia, to allow for a firmer financial foundation; consequently, by 1910, the ratio of unmarried among the lower income groups of the intelligentsia was around 50%. Furthermore, as a result of the same process, and in consideration of age relations not included in the table, the number of those young or not so young members of the intelligentsia who lacked the means to found a family became massive. The distinction between civil servants as opposed to clerical personnel paid by the day, and the distinction between lawyers as opposed to assistant lawyers or paralegals were typical of this process.

The other important process which explains the decrease in the number of dependents was the decrease in the birthrate. This process was particularly noticeable among lower income intelligentsia (mainly white-collar employees in industry and commerce), resulting in an increase in families without children, or with only one or two children, at the expense of the traditional family model. Among those groups of the intelligentsia where it was possible to attain an average annual income, or higher, as a matter of seniority (especially higher ranking civil service jobs that required advanced preparation) we find a large proportion of bachelors, but also a relatively high rate of dependents, indicating that, after the delayed marriage, families with two or three children became the norm. The most typical example is that of teachers in the secondary schools; almost half of female and male teachers had not yet founded a family in 1910, while the other half of the group had an average of over three dependents; in other words, in this category a family with two or three children appears to be the norm. A third reason that may explain the decrease in the number of dependents among the intelligentsia is the acceleration in the rate of employment of women—mostly, of course, in the intelligentsia. This also implied that, by the end of the first decade of the twentieth century, the middle-class family ideal had been significantly eroded: partly because, in addition to the head of the family, one of the female members of the family (wife or grownup daughter) became a wage earner—thereby increasing the family's standard of living—and partly because households consisting of single women became common in Hungarian society.[47] The fact that, on the average three quarters of them remained unmarried in 1910 indicates that the income relations of women in the intelligentsia were well below those of men, while their chances of getting married were almost hopeless.

Among the data indicating a strong correlation between income relations and size of family, the data regarding grade school teachers seem somewhat of an exception because, despite their low levels of income, few of them remained unmarried; the number of their dependents is also relatively high in comparison with other groups of intelligentsia at the same income level. This may be explained by the fact that most grade school teachers were employed in village schools—while white collar in industry and commerce lived almost exclusively in cities—where the teachers were given, next to the school building or within it, a service apartment or at least a room, where food, even if at a low level of nutrition, could be procured at lesser expense, and where the traditional family with many children still seemed to be the norm.

All in all, 40 to 45% of the intelligentsia remained unmarried in 1910; in our estimation this meant that about one third of all families (households) in the intelligentsia may have consisted of a single person, while 10 to 12% of all families consisted of two breadwinners. The average size of families among the married urban intelligentsia in the lower income groups was little over three, indicating that families with a single child were typical;

---

[47] As an indication of how widespread this latter phenomenon became at the beginning of the century, see its appearance as a topic in literature: for instance, Sándor Bródy's 1914 play *A tanítónő* [The schoolmistress] (Budapest, 1955), with an introduction by Sándor Róka.

among the village intelligentsia at the same level of income families with two or more children were still the norm. Among intelligentsia with higher income, once married, they could nevertheless maintain a family with two or even more children but, since they tended to marry at a later age, the number of single person households increased considerably. Since their pay increased with seniority, this observation applies particularly to the intelligentsia groups in public service.

Naturally the changes in structure of income and household among the intelligentsia had an impact on housing conditions, for an income with lower purchasing power did not enable them to maintain residence of the same size and quality as they were accustomed to, and smaller apartments were adequate for single households, which were becoming more widespread. In order to verify these relations, or to modify them, we must take a look at the defense mechanisms the intelligentsia developed to fight the impact of the inflation.

The most typical reaction on the part of the intelligentsia was not a reduction of the style of living and level of consumption they were accustomed to, but rather contracting debts in order to bridge the difficulties they conceived of as merely temporary. Mihály Pásztor describes the options faced by the intelligentsia in the following terms: "either they reduce their expenses, eat less meat, move into a smaller apartment, or—if unable to give up the comforts they are accustomed to—incur debts. It is precisely the accustomed comfort that causes the problem, for very few are able to give these up. They enter into debt, therefore, for today when food prices are so high, we still want to live in the same comfort and gentry style as five or ten years ago, when meat, bread and apartment cost less. We believe that we are entitled to this gentry style of life, because we have earned that right with our job, our office. We are entitled to this level of comfort because of our position, this is the *standard of life* [in English] on which we insist, which we cannot give up and for which we make up by incurring debts, not covered by our income."[48] Pásztor documents his description with innumerable examples—in the case of certain intelligentsia groups the total

---

[48] Pásztor, op. cit., p. 29.,

amount of debts as disclosed to the authorities exceeded half of their total income from salaries!—points to the general cause of the phenomenon: "social prejucide has set up a principle: everyone must live in accordance with their position. Let us be clear on this point: the style of life must be in harmony not with income, but with the position. The blue-collar person may wear blue collar, but the teacher in the primary school or the clerical trainee in the ministry may not."[49]

In Hungary at the beginning of the century the intelligentsia's particular way of "incurring debts" was buying on the installment plan; in fact, this practice—and there is no coincidence here—attained its apogee during the first decade of the twentieth century. Buying on installment presented the already indebted member of the intelligentsia with further opportunities for contracting loans: "He buys the encyclopedia or the masterpieces of literature for a hundred forints: makes a down payment without unwrapping the masterpieces from their cardboard coffin; carries it to the used bookstore and sells it for a third of the price."[50]

The growing indebtedness of the intelligentsia entailed the almost natural concomitant, the spread of corruption—to a degree where one was no longer surprised that a judge of the supreme court accepted a bribe, but rather that he could be bribed for as little as three hundred forints.[51]

Another important manifestation of the reaction of the intelligentsia was the chase for additional income, especially in the form of moonlighting jobs. In 1900, 13.6 % of the intelligentsia had a second job.[52]

A third component of the reaction of the intelligentsia was to organize; organizations of public servants lobbied or demonstrated mainly for pay-raises, increases in housing allowance, cost of living allowances, etc. In the case of professionals, however, given their particular market relations, organization often entailed examining and even questioning the essence of social relations in

---

49 Ibid., pp. 28 and 44–45.
50 Ibid., pp. 62–63.
51 Ibid., pp. 50–51.
52 *MStK*, new series, vol. 27, pp. 290–291.

a deeper, political sense.[53]

Finally, we deem reduction in the level of consumption as the last resort manifestation of the reaction of the intelligentsia: this usually signified moving into a smaller or less comfortable apartment.

The defense mechanisms of the intelligentsia indicate that, given the mentality of Hungarian society at the beginning of the century, we can hardly expect a straightforward correlation between the income relations of the intelligentsia and their evolution on the one hand, and the level of consumption, the structure of consumption, particularly the amounts spent on housing, on the other hand.

In order to analyze the peculiarities of this correlation we will examine the structure of the budget of ten typical household belonging to the intelligentsia.

The Consumption Structure of Intelligentsia Households

We attempted to reconstruct, on the basis of rather limited notes and data from private sources, a series which may be considered indicative. Thus, in our table, we find cases all the way from an official with dependents, earning 14,000 crowns and disposing of personal wealth, down to an unmarried civil servant, earning 2,300 crowns, through one or more representatives from groups of the intelligentsia at various levels of income and of varying family status. The data pertain to the year 1906, with the exception of household number 3. The value of our data is diminished by the fact that eight of the ten households resided in the capital city (except 3 and 6), and do not include anyone in the professions, among whom, because of the great dispersion of incomes, structure and habits of consumptions would be the most striking. Since the data are from the same year, we are unable to examine changes in life-style and habits through the

---

[53] It cannot be considered a coincidence that the bourgeois radicals, the Society of the Social Scientists and the circle around the journal *Huszadik Század*, came mainly from the ranks of the professionals. See György Litván and László Szűcs, *A szociológia első magyar műhelye* [The first sociology workshop in Hungary] (Budapest, 1973), vols. 1–2, pp. 5–46.

transformations of the structure of consumption. It is possible, however, to identify some specific aspects of the consumption of families in the intelligentsia that are revealing of the mentality and values that determined their lifestyle, the relationship between their income and housing.

TABLE 34

Households of the Intelligentsia in 1906 or 1909 at Different Levels of Income and Family Status, in Absolute Numbers (Crowns) and in Percentage Distribution[54]

Expenditures	1. MARRIED Private white collar Salary: Cr 1,000 + Cr 4,000 income and in assets Cr 12,000 2 maids		2. MARRIED Bank clerk Salary: Cr 7,600 2 minors 2 maids		3. RETIRED White collar from Pozsony Income: Cr 7,223 family of three 1 maid		4. MARRIED White collar Salary: Cr 4,000 + Cr 3,000 income and in assets Cr 16,000 1 maid		5. MARRIED Bank clerk Salary: Cr 6,000 + Cr 1,000 stipend childless 1 maid	
1. Food	2,400	17.14	2,000	26.32	1,262.88	19.67	2,000	28.37	1,800	24.12
2. Luxury items	50	0.36			271.48	4.23	200	2.84	1,100	14.75
3. Clothing	3,000	21.43	900	11.84	539.19	8.38	1,000	14.18	1,200	16.09
4. Rent	2,000	14.29	1,000	13.16	1,200.00	18.69	1,200	17.02	1,200	16.09
5. Upkeep of home	500	3.57	400	5.26	492.12	7.67	400	5.67	200	2.68
6. Cleaning items	600	4.29			110.42	1.72				
7. Maid and other services	400	2.86	480	6.32	355.69	5.55	240	3.40	240	3.22
8. Entertainment	stays home		200	2.63	197.04	3.07	20	0.28		
9. Leisure activities			600	7.89	907.02	14.13	600	8.51	1,500	20.01
10. Medical	300	2.14	300	3.94	280.07	4.36	200	2.84	100	1.34
11. Tax, legal expenses, pension contribution	820	5.86	160	2.11	348.35	5.42	590	8.36	120	1.61
12. Miscellaneous (gifts, mistress, etc.)	3,930	28.07	1,560	20.52	456.01	7.10	600	8.51		
Totals:	**14,000**	**100%**	**7,600**	**100%**	**6,419.27**	**100%**	**7,050**	**100%**	**7,460**	**100%**
Note: Some of the statistics are estimated.	Debt: Cr 6,000, guarantor for Cr 1,000, for pt. 11 debt servicing, for pt.12 savings. No known children.		For point 12 it is also savings.		1909 income and expenditure data. It excludes one time hospitalization cost.		Cr 6,000 debt, for point 11 it was also debt servicing. He already had a lien against his salary.			

54   Pásztor, *Az eladósodott*, pp. 158–171, 201–202. Imre Illés, "Egy pozsonyi hivatalnok család háztartási számadása" [The household budget of a family of civil servants in Pozsony (Bratislava)], *Közgazdasági Szemle* (1913), pp. 563–576. In his work, *Háztartási statisztika* [Housekeeping statistics] (Kolozsvár, 1914), Illés presents the budget entries of two families of civil servants, pertaining to a few months in the years 1912–1913.

Households of the Intelligentsia in 1906 or 1909 at Different Levels of Income and Family Status, in Absolute Numbers (Crowns) and in Percentage Distribution (Continued)

Expenditures	6. MARRIED Elementary school teacher,* tenant in service housing without maid		7. UNMARRIED Bank clerk Salary: Cr 6,000, without assets, cleaning woman		8. UNMARRIED Bank clerk. Salary: Cr 4,800 + Cr 400 income, without assets, cleaning woman		9. UNMARRIED Private white collar Salary: Cr 1,800 + Cr 1,000 income, Cr 6,000 in assets, cleaning woman		10. UNMARRIED Deputy court clerk Salary: Cr 2,300	
1. Food	968.30	50.43	1,200	20.00	720	13.85	600	21.43	792	29.46
2. Luxury items			110	1.83	100	1.92	20	0.71	200	7.44
3. Clothing	466.26	24.29	1,200	20.00	360	6.92	300	10.71	468	17.41
4. Rent			600	10.00	200	3.85	500	17.85	284	10.57
5. Upkeep of home	181.68	9.46					150	5.35	88	3.27
6. Cleaning items	53.38	2.78							72	2.68
7. Maid and other services			80	1.33	80	1.54	80	2.85		
8. Entertainment	80	4.17	100	1.66	600	11.54			100	3.72
9. Leisure activities			920	15.53	396	7.62	200	7.14		
10. Medical	50	2.60			100	1.92	100	3.57		
11. Tax, legal expenses, pension contribution	90	4.89	400	6.66	700	13.46	320	11.42	514	19.12
12. Miscellaneous (gifts, mistress, etc.)	26	1.35	1,390	23.16	1,944	37.38	530	18.93	170	6.32
Totals:	1,919.62	100%	6,000	100%	5,200	100%	2,800	100%	2,688	100%
Note: Some of the statistics are estimated.	*Minimum budget estimated for legislative proposal.		Savings for point 12, debt servicing for point 11.		Debt servicing for point 11.		Cr 3,000 debt.		Cr 2,000 debt, guarantor for Cr 3,000, lives in rooming house.	

On the surface it appears that the household data confirm our above-stated preconceptions regarding debts and moonlighting. A more detailed examination of the budget or of the pattern of consumption confirms that, within the intelligentsia, the line of division lies between married and unmarried, or single household versus family.

Family households generally required household help—one or two live-in servants, depending on income—whereas in single-person households the norm was to hire someone to do the chores in the daytime or avail oneself of services such as laundry-shop, eating out, etc. The exception from this point of view was the grade school teacher with four children, indicative of the circumstances prevailing for the bulk of intelligentsia families at this low level of income.

The data clearly indicate, furthermore, that the ratio of the income spent on the necessities of life (food, clothing) grows in reverse proportion to the level of income: in the household of the grade school teacher (6) it was close to 90%, in that of the deputy notary (10) it just exceeded half of all expenses. The ratio of expenditures on necessities was strongly affected by the number of dependents—although we do not have exact numbers for all ten households; a comparison of the data from households 2 and 3 confirms the latter ratio: in the case of 2 with four members 2,000 crowns (26.32%) were spent on food, 900 crowns (11.84%) on clothing. In the case of 3, with three members, these same expenses amounted to 1,263 crowns (19.67%) and 538 crowns (8.38%).

A comparative analysis of expenses by household is also confirmed by well-known, or less well known life-styles illustrated in contemporary literature or journalism.

a) In case I, the household had an income well above average, allowing a balanced pattern of consumption, close to that of a member of the upper middle class, and probably including a summer home: "To spend vacations at home" considering the amount of debts and personal wealth and the sum of yearly savings, did not jeopardize the life-style.

b) The structure of household 2, we may suspect, is a type of middle-class family enjoying a relatively high income, living a rational life-style, where the head of family has a good position and can afford to hire two live-in household employees to help his wife with their two small children; they do not spend on dining or luxury items and, in spite of a lack of savings and a lack of debts, can cover the cost of education for the children and an occasional quality summer trip. Household 3 is a variant of the former, where the income from the rent of property valued at 30,000 crowns provides security and allows for the grownup daughter to indulge in her whims and entertainment costs, all the more so since, being of marriageable age, this may count as a rational investment.

c) Households 4 and 5 are two variations of the debt-incurring type of intelligentsia family: the head of the former, in addition to his salary of 4,000 crowns a year earns 3,000 crowns moonlighting; his assets of 16,000 crowns must have derived from inheritance or from an advantageous marriage, because he is unable to save because of overspending; in addition to his deficit he incurred a debt of 6,000 crowns that year, his pay had been garnished on several occasion even before that, though he had no excessive expenses under any particular item, merely attempting to maintain his erstwhile middle-class level of consumption which, of course, included having a mistress. The cause of indebtedness in the other, childless, household, was the significant overspending on representation (luxury items, dining, vacation, country club, but also clothing and apartment), hence the deficit in the annual budget foreshadowed complete bankruptcy for the family.

d) The household budget of the primary school teacher 6 is a sad reflection on the pattern of consumption and life-style of members of the intelligentsia with large families, restricted to the bare essentials. There was precious little left among most of these families for self-improvement or for the education of the children—hence it is no accident that public school teachers and other groups of the intelligentsia living at similar levels were in the forefront of social agitation at the beginning of the century.

e) Single households in the intelligentsia include several types, ranging from the bank clerk with good prospects, able to save from his 6,000 crowns yearly income, to the indebted deputy notary, living in a sublet, with little hope of ever founding a family. The latter was the more typical as regards bachelor or spinster households, whereas the former is the exception that proves the rule.

It was typical of all single households that they spent only about half or one third of what family households had to spend on housing—just enough to cover the rent for bachelor's quarters or a sublet—and, because of their limited housing the pub, coffeehouse or restaurant functioned as practically an organic part of their apartment, replacing kitchen, dining-room, living-room and sometimes even the studio.

Thus the analysis of the budget of the ten intelligentsia households not only confirms the former picture regarding the income relations of the intelligentsia, as regards the relationship between income and life-style, but also offers insights into the varieties of modes of life, of living strategies concealed by averages and general tendencies. Beyond all this they provide opportunities for additional conclusions regarding the household budget.

The opportunities for self-improvement and culture for the intelligentsia decreased proportionately with lower incomes, or with the decrease in the purchasing power of those incomes; by the first decade of the century, for a significant fraction of the intelligentsia this meant sinking not only below the middle-class level, but even below the poverty level.

In the case of family households, the expectations with regard to a middle-class way of life, the matter of social prestige overcame the correlation between income level and size of apartment.

Keeping help was an organic part of the middle-class way of life; in the case of families in the intelligentsia living almost at the upper middle-class level two or more servants were the norm. The budgets shed light on the fact of how even low-income families in the intelligentsia could afford to keep a servant, the explanation being the incredibly low wages paid for housework. In households with families this expense amounted to 3 to 6% of the income, whereas in the case of single households it was no more than 1 to 3% was spent on wages for servants, whether live-in or not. In other words, help cost no more a year than a few cigars or cigarettes or a cup of coffee a day, or the cost of subscribing to a few dailies and periodicals.

Data Regarding Housing Conditions among the Intelligentsia

There is no comprehensive survey of housing conditions of the intelligentsia in the period of the Dual Monarchy, the only significant survey being the one for Budapest in the year 1906,[55] where the residents of apartments were listed by occupation, thus making it possible to identify the circumstances under which groups of the intelligentsia lived.

This collection of data covered almost one-fourth of the intelligentsia of Hungary, since that was the fraction of the intelligentsia which resided in the capital city.[56] Table 35 summarizes the data regarding the housing conditions of the intelligentsia renting apartments under regular terms.

---

[55] *BpStK*, vol. 43.
[56] Thirring, op. cit., vol. 53, pp. 94, 127, and 162–63.

TABLE 35

Distribution of Intelligentsia Households Renting Apartments, by Size of Apartment, Composition of Household, and Amount of Rental in Budapest in 1906[57]

Occupation of head of family	Total Individld.	Total households	Apartments by size								
			Apartments with kichen					Apartments without kichen			
			Spaces 1-3	Spaces 4-5	Spaces 6-10	Spaces from 10	Total:	Space 1	Spaces 2	Spaces more	Total:
1. In absolute numbers											
Education	10,896	2,486	427	884	998	38	2,347	59	37	43	139
Civil service	41,023	9,144	1,771	3,639	3,419	118	8,947	60	60	77	197
Private white collar	47,150	9,671	2,265	3,834	3,258	89	9,446	108	63	54	225
Other intelligentsia	22,498	4,894	667	1,207	2,533	170	4,577	128	87	102	317
Total intelligentsia:	121,567	26,195	5,130	9,564	10,208	415	25,317	355	247	276	878
2. In relative numbers											
Education	No data available	100%	17.18	35.56	40.14	1.53	94.40	2.37	1.49	1.73	5.60
Civil service		100%	19.37	39.79	37.39	1.29	97.85	0.66	0.66	0.84	2.15
Private white collar		100%	23.42	39.64	33.68	0.92	97.67	1.12	0.65	0.55	2.33
Other intelligentsia		100%	13.62	24.66	51.75	3.47	93.52	2.62	1.78	2.08	6.48
Total intelligentsia:		100%	19.58	36.51	38.96	1.58	96.64	1.36	0.94	1.05	3.36

[57] *BpStK*, vol. 43, pp. 202–203.

Distribution of Intelligentsia Households Renting Apartments, by Size of Apartment, Composition of Household, and Amount of Rental in Budapest in 1906 (Continued)

Occupation of head of family	Composition of household									Annual rent by amount			
	Apartments with maid				Apartments without maid				Vacant apartm.	800 crowns	800–2,500 crowns	Above 2,500 crowns	Unknown
	Single person	House-hold*	Mixed house-hold**	Total:	Single person	House-hold*	Mixed house-hold**	Total:					
1. In absolute numbers													
Education	6	1,246	257	1,509	6	769	193	968	9	1,309	1,021	52	104
Civil service	3	4,514	861	5,378	25	3,037	654	3,716	50	5,309	3,398	162	216
Private white collar	3	4,411	1,374	5,778	14	2,927	917	3,858	25	5,756	3,521	126	268
Other intelligentsia	12	2,588	744	3,344	21	1,106	354	1,481	69	1,640	2,626	429	199
Total intelligentsia:	24	12,759	3,236	16,000	66	7,839	2,118	10,003	153	14,073	10,566	776	787
2. In relative numbers													
Education	0.24	50.12	10.34	60.70	3.24	30.93	7.76	38.93	0.37	52.65	41.07	2.09	4.18
Civil service	0.03	49.36	9.42	58.81	0.27	33.21	7.15	40.63	0.55	58.70	37.16	1.77	2.36
Private white collar	0.03	45.61	14.21	59.75	0.14	30.26	9.48	39.89	0.26	59.52	36.40	1.30	2.77
Other intelligentsia	0.25	52.88	15.20	68.33	0.43	22.60	7.23	30.26	1.41	33.51	53.65	8.76	4.06
Total intelligentsia:	0.09	48.70	12.35	61.11	0.25	29.93	8.09	38.26	0.58	53.72	40.36	2.96	3.00

* Includes family members only.
** Includes others (mainly lodgers).

The 2,093 members of the intelligentsia not included in the table owned their own home or houses in Budapest, and 1,959 of them were residents of the capital city. 87.7% of the homeowners among the intelligentsia owned but one house which, however, may have included several apartments. Only 12.28% (257) owned more than one house; among these were 39 lawyers with two houses, 24 with more than two houses, 30 physicians with two houses, 12 with more, 28 government officials with two houses, 10 with more, and 10 bank officials with two houses, 3 with more.[58]

The housing circumstances of those who owned their own homes were most likely better than the housing of the average intelligentsia, whereas those who owned several houses belonged to the upper middle rather than the middle class. Thus, altogether 7.47% of the intelligentsia households in Budapest lived in their own home.

The tables reveal nothing about the so-called "living quarters" or the households inhabiting them; in other words, we have no information regarding apartments designated as service apartments and other places such as shops, offices, etc., which may have served as lodgings. At the time of the data there were altogether 157,007 apartments in Budapest, whereas 31,955 addresses were listed as "living quarters."[59]

Unlike the data collected in the censi, the data from 1906 were concerned with the number of spaces; this causes no problem in the case of bachelor's quarters or apartments of two rooms, including a kitchen, but in all other cases we cannot be certain regarding the number of rooms. According to the experience of those who conducted the survey, the following generalizations seem to apply:[60]

Apartment with kitchen meant one room plus a kitchen.

4 spaces meant two rooms plus side-rooms

6 spaces meant three rooms plus side-rooms

8 spaces meant four rooms plus side-rooms

10 spaces meant five to six rooms plus side-rooms.

[58] Ibid., pp. 100–109.

[59] Ibid., p. 31.

[60] Ibid., p. 86.

Thus we have every right to assume that an above average middle-class apartment fulfilling more than one function consisted of at least six spaces: three rooms, a kitchen, plus any two, whether it be anteroom, bathroom, servants quarters or hall or foyer (the room between the anteroom and the living-room).

The rents were also measured by space; it appears from the text of the survey that the average rent for an apartment of five spaces—that is, not quite three rooms—was 797 crowns. Thus we may conclude that it was not possible to find a comfortable three-room apartment under 800 crowns—and we may consider this sum as the lower limit for an apartment of the middle class. The upper limit would be the rent for ten spaces (or 5 to 6 rooms) —costing an average of 2,462 crowns in 1906, rounded out to 2,500 crowns; above this amount we are dealing with the apartment of a member of the upper middle class.

Considering the above it may be asserted that in the middle of the first decade of the twentieth century almost 60% of the urban intelligentsia surveyed lived in apartments of less than three rooms! A little over one-third of them lived in apartments with two rooms, or four to five spaces, while the rest lived in one or two rooms with kitchen, and a little over 3% lived in efficiency apartments. Since the proportion of households with live-in maids was 61.11%, we may easily conclude that about one fifth of the intelligentsia living in apartments with less than three rooms—probably two rooms—nevertheless had live-in help! Since few of the two-room apartments were remodeled to include separate quarters for the maid we presume that she slept, according to an old custom, in the kitchen. Pásztor describes this phenomenon, with some exaggeration: "...There is an army of maids and servants in Budapest numbering one hundred thousand—exactly as many as skilled workers. Keeping a maid is a luxury, yet every little government employee keeps a maid, as a matter of 'noblesse oblige.'"[61] The proportion of households with maids among the teachers, civil servants, and privately employed white collar was around 60%. This figure rose to around

---

[61] Mihály Pásztor, *Cifra nyomorúság* [Fancy poverty] (Budapest, 1906), p. 16.

70% among professionals, revealing the fact that, because of their situation in the market economy, and unlike salaried persons, they were able to foist the consequences of the inflation onto their clients. The relatively favorable position of persons in the professions is also indicated by the fact that over 50% had apartments of at least three rooms, consequently those who paid the highest rent, between 800 and 2,500 crowns, were also well represented among them. About one tenth of the professionals were able to keep an apartment in the upper-middle class style. Privately employed white-collar employees seldom could afford such apartments; only 36.4% of them paid rent at this level and a little over 1% of them had quarters corresponding to the upper-middle class. We would note the low proportion of civil servants among those who paid the rent of middle-class apartments with surprise, were it not that we are aware of their real income relations. But considering all the factors, it becomes obvious why the municipal council of Budapest felt obliged (much less than in Vienna) to undertake the construction of apartment buildings for government employees and improve their living conditions.[62] In addition to the housing projects with small apartments and the barracks for rent, the council also built four apartment buildings exclusively for government employees. The majority of the apartments in these buildings were of two rooms, some of three and four. The annual rent for these apartments, which included anteroom, kitchen, maid's quarters and bathroom, was 20 to 40% lower than the rent in similar, privately owned apartment buildings.[63]

About 40 to 41% of personnel in education in the capital was able to maintain an apartment at the middle-class level in 1906; this ratio, better than the national average, can be explained by the fact that the ratio of primary and secondary schools was far higher in the capital city, even institutions of higher learning being concentrated in the capital, while the salaries of public school

---

[62] Imre Ferenczi, "A lakásügy és haladása Magyarországon az utolsó három évben" [The housing problem in Hungary and its progress over the past three years], Városi Szemle (1913), pp. 616–735.

[63] Zoltán Sidó, "Budapest székesfőváros lakásügyi intézményei" [Offices dealing with housing in the capital city], Városi Szemle (1912), pp. 729–730.

teachers was also 1.5 to 2 times that of their colleagues included strangers, sublets and lodgers who were not members of the
family, was over 20% among the intelligentsia. This fact com-
pletes the picture we have drawn regarding defense mechanisms. One fifth of the intelligentsia in the capital was able to
foist the hikes in rents onto others whose situation was even
worse: "The family makes do with a single room, while leaving
the other to the lodger or lodgers...thus, in Budapest, one poor
person lives off the poverty of another."[64] Over half of these
mixed households also had a servant, thus preserving the false
appearance of a middle-class way of life, for that was what
prompted the tailor, the waiter, or the grocer around the corner
to grant credit.

The data in the survey do not provide answers to the question, where did the salaried members of the intelligentsia who
did not rent an apartment or own a house, whose numbers were
almost equal to those who did, actually live in the capital. The
best we can do in their case is to assume. But we cannot be far
wrong if we assume their circumstances to be identical with
those of unmarried members of the intelligentsia—whose ratio
exceeded the national average of 30 to 35%, or if we equate them
with the second or third breadwinners in the families of the
intelligentsia, who lived with the head of the family. It was
almost hopeless for single members of the intelligentsia to
obtain a separate apartment, as witnessed by the fact that
3.36% of all one-room apartments had no kitchen.

Only a small fraction of them had access to service lodgings,
for there were no more than 280 apartments so designated in
the city in 1906.[65] Thus they must have been those who rented
rooms or beds, and who were thus obliged to pay a significant
portion of the rent paid by the principal lessee; they were the
ones who rented a room by the month or in a cheap bed and
breakfast in the suburbs, waiting for their fate to improve—an
appointment, a raise, or an advantageous marriage, a bride
with a large dowry. Here again, the municipal council sought to

---

[64] Pásztor, *Cifra nyomorúság*, p. 40.

[65] *BpStK*, vol. 43, p. 31.

improve their hopeless lot by undertaking the construction of a public dormitory in 1911, modelled on the British Rowton institutions. This housing for the masses, built at the corner of Aréna út and Angyalföld út (avenues), had sleeping cubicles of eighteen or nineteen cubic meters on its three floors, and offered lodging at 60 fillérs a night. Those who rented by the week were entitled to a free bath. In the period August 2 to 8, 1913, 26% of its guests were members of the intelligentsia.[66]

Few sources are available regarding general housing conditions in other cities, and fewer yet specifically about the intelligentsia. As regards living and housing conditions in the villages, we have ample information provided by ethnologists, especially for the peasantry.[67]

Since the lack of sources makes it impossible to carry out an analysis at the macro level regarding mid-size and small towns, the next chapter will be a case study of the residents of an apartment building, mainly members of the intelligentsia, in a mid-size city at the beginning of the century. This will also provide us with perspective regarding the above discussed statistical data on housing in the capital city.

---

[66] Imre Ferenczi, "A székesfővárosi VI. kerületi népszálló" [The public dormitory in the sixth district of the capital], *Városi Szemle*, pp. 899–915; same, "A lakásügy állása és haladása..." [Status and progress report on the housing problem], p. 1727.

[67] Regarding this issue, see András Gergely's study, which digests an enormous mass of materials, and the attached bibliography. "A mindennapi élet keretei a századfordulón" [The context of everyday life at the turn of the century] (Manuscript, 1970). An abridged version was printed in *Történelmi Szemle*, nos. 3–4 (1971), pp. 406–441.

CHAPTER VI

A Case Study: The Bishop's Palace in Debrecen and Its Residents between 1912–1914*

The Bishop's Palace, which remains one of the landmarks of downtown Debrecen, admitted its first residents in November 1912—although it was only on January 27, 1913, that the city council issued a permit of use for it.[1]

This period, the "last years of peace," may be considered epoch-making as regards the architectural development of downtown Debrecen. The second great construction wave, which climaxed in the capital towards the end of the first decade of the twentieth century, reached larger towns such as Debrecen by the beginning of the 1910s. The architectural evolution accompanying the temporary boom in investments and marked by Hungarian or Hungarianizing romanticism and by the art nouveau style (referred to as *secession* in the Habsburg Monarchy) disrupted the city-scape that had evolved by the late nineteenth century in the empire style, in which neo-classic public buildings arose side by side with traditional one-story buildings adjusted along an eclectic or empire style for the sake of harmony. In the years from 1907 to 1909 the Debrecen municipal council was prompted by the increasingly urgent need for housing, along with

---

* The contemporary name for the building was "ecclesiastic apartment building." What probably gave rise to the name by which it was commonly known was that the bishop's (Melius's) palace used to stand in that space, the main square of the city, near the Nagytemplom [Great Calvinist Church]. Although the name is inaccurate, since the Reformed Church had no office space in the building other than two service apartments reserved for clergymen, I use the common name: Bishop's Palace.

[1] The Archives of the Reformed Church Diocese East of the Tisza River (TREL), I. 99. d. (P 1907), box 39. Construction records 95.

the evolution in aspirations and the investment boom which manifested itself at this time, to review the earlier zoning and urban construction regulations. The new architectural regulations, as well as the construction of state-of-the-art concrete sewer lines and the expansion of the municipal water and gas networks, created conditions allowing the new buildings, especially apartment buildings, to emulate those of the capital, both with regard to their architecture and their functionalism.[2]

The new buildings (for instance, the First Savings Bank of Debrecen, the Chamber of Commerce and Industry, as well as the apartment buildings of the Debrecen Reformed Church Parish) were not always well received. Lajos Zoltai, the historian of the municipality, summarized the opinion of one side of the issue in impassioned language: "The city, which but a half a century ago was referred to as a big village by many rather than as a metropolis in the international sense of the word, is in a hurry to divest itself of its peasant garb. Palaces rise from the ground and life is rendered easier, more beautiful for everyone by the achievements of modern technology, the hygienic amenities which necessarily accompany modern urban development."[3] But, on the whole, public opinion in Debrecen regarded the disruption of the classicizing cityscape of the city, the radical transformation of the structures and magnitude of the buildings which reflected the particular rationality of the economy and way of life of the peasant bourgeoisie, as entailing some kind of loss of value.[4]

The History of the Construction of the Bishop's Palace

Indicative of the close relationship between the construction waves in Budapest and Debrecen was the fact that the idea of the palace came from the planning and architecture firm László Brothers

---

[2] Lajos Sapi, *Debrecen település és építéstörténete* [The history of the settlement and building of Debrecen], (Debrecen, 1972), pp. 66–78.

[3] *Debreczeni Képes Kalendárium* [Picture calendar of Debrecen] (from here on, *DKK*), 1912, p. 140.

[4] The description of a town dwelling for the well-to-do. Lajos Zoltai, "A legrégibb debreczeni ház története" [The history of the oldest building in Debrecen], *DKK*, 1913, pp. 146–152.

in Budapest. The presbytery of the Reformed Diocese of Debrecen received their proposal on January 7, 1909, to the effect that, on the triple lot next to the Great Church, they offered to build a three-story apartment building which would revert, free of charge, as the property of the diocese after fifty years of usufruct.[5]

The ad-hoc committee of the diocese appointed to discuss the proposal raised the issue: could they derive a profit from doing the construction work themselves? They issued a call for bids to decide this issue—more exactly they asked two local architects and three from the capital regarding the construction of an apartment building under numbers 1–3 of Hatvan utca (street), to include apartments of three, four and five rooms, with quality side-rooms, and taking into consideration the opportunities for profit.[6] From among the bids submitted by the deadline of April 1, 1909, the committee found the one by the architecture and construction company of Kálmán Balogh of Budapest the most appropriate for execution and as regards costs. The final plans and budget were accepted by the committee, now permanent, on November 19, 1909 and, after signing the primary contract with Balogh, presented the case to the presbytery for its approval.[7] The final approval, however, was not forthcoming, for in the meantime the committee decision on the bid was greeted by nationwide indignation on the part of the architectural community. In the *Vállalkozók Lapja* [Paper of Entrepreneurs], Ezrey, an architect accused the committee of religious bias,[8] while the daily *Nap* published an article under the title "Nepotism in Debrecen," stating: "The presbytery, which may well be expert in ecclesiastic matters, but all the less so on architectural issues, came up with a strange decision....Considering that the pre-jury of experts had declared the plan submitted by László Brothers to be the best, awarded first prize and the bid to the candidate in last place."[9] Because of the turmoil and charges, the presbytery

---

[5] TREL, I. 99. d. (P 1907), box 35, V–775/1910.
[6] TREL, I. 99. d. (P 1907), box 35 V–146/1909.
[7] TREL, I. 99. d. (P 1907), box 35 V–775/1910.
[8] *Vállalkozók Lapja*, June 7, 1909.
[9] *A Nap*, July 8, 1909.

reorganized the committee it had entrusted with making the decision, and asked the Association of Hungarian Engineers and Architects (MMEE) to examine the Balogh plan from an expert point of view. The president of the Association confirmed the opinions expressed in the press: "The church would jeopardize its financial interests if it were to carry out these plans. Had the plans been submitted to some sort of expert selection process, they would have been eliminated in the first round. A new call has to be issued, in the preparation of which the Association would be glad to participate...."[10]

Thus the first round of the planning process ended in fiasco, delaying the beginning of construction. The retraction of the hurried award resulted in court action which dragged on until February 1915, at which time a settlement was reached by which the diocese would pay the architect Kálmán Balogh 14,000 crowns in damages.[11]

The way out from the impasse was that the presbytery purchased a fourth lot, next to the three lots, from the Reformed Church Preparatory school, for the sum of 100,000 crowns and, with the help of the MMEE, announced a new contest for construction on the site which now was 6,281.9 square meters. At this same meeting, the leadership of the diocese raised the sum earmarked for construction to one and a half million crowns (to include purchase of the lot), arguing that "it is better to have a plan which, even with expenditures of a million and a half to two million, would earn significantly higher revenues than limit construction by a smaller sum."[12]

The new contest was announced in the fall of 1910, with the active participation of the MMEE, strictly in accordance with the bidding rules formulated in regulation 79049/908 of the Ministry of Commerce. According to the announcement the objective was to build an attractive apartment building of three stories at the corner of Egyház tér (square) and Hatvan utca (street), and the prizes were pegged at 3,500, 1,600 and 900

---

[10]   TREL I. 99. d. (P 1907) box 35 V–9/1910.
[11]   TREL I. 99. d. (P 1907), box 42 136/4.
[12]   TREL I. 99. c. Minutes of the meetings of the presbytery 80 k. 1066–1910. sz.

crowns. Included among the conditions of the contest was that only residents of Hungary may participate, under a code-name, that the budget per square meter may not exceed 200 crowns, while the total cost was not to exceed 1.4 million crowns. It was also specified that there be a large number of stores at ground level, apartments to include three, four, five and six rooms, maybe two-room bachelor apartments as well, with comfortable side-rooms, with indoor plumbing, electricity, gas, elevator and other services bearing in mind that "revenues are the main consideration." To ensure appeal the announcement of the contest also specified that "outside corridors were to be avoided as much as possible."[13]

The jury on which, in addition to the members of the apartment building committee, two representatives from the MMEE were included, met on February 10, 1911, in Budapest. According to the minutes of the session thirty-seven of the forty-two plans submitted were accepted as valid, while four arrived too late and one failed to conform to standards. Of the remaining plans the jury selected by majority vote the one submitted under the code-name "Graphic Perspective" as worthy of the first prize; the party responsible was a firm of architects in Budapest, Bálint and Jámbor (the same firm was responsible for the county administration building in Debrecen, in Hungarian romantic style). The second and third prizes were also won by planners from Budapest.[14] The decision, which was accepted by the consensus of the profession, was followed by a contract issued on May 13, 1911. In August another call for bids was issued to subcontractors, with the proviso that, among other things, "all work is to be performed and the roof of the building is to be erected already within the year, and the building should be ready for occupancy by July 20, 1912."[15]

As a consequence of the outstanding work organization and technical supervision, and in spite of minor slips by sub-contractors—among them local firms and firms from Budapest partici-

---

[13] TREL I. 99. c. (80 k. 448–1910. Psz.)

[14] TREL I. 99. d. (P 1907), box 36. Records relating to the construction of apartment building 4/1.

[15] TREL I. 99. d. (P 1907) box 35 V–103/1911. In addition to the local dailies the announcement was published in the August 16, 1911, issues of *Vállalkozók Lapja* and *Vállalkozók Közlönye* [Bulletin of entrepreneurs].

pated half and half, while the ceramic tiles or faience wall-coverings were manufactured by the Zsolnai plant—the building, of unusual size for Debrecen, was ready fifteen months after the beginning of construction. In fact, the first residents were able to move in beginning November 1.[16]

Good use was made of every square meter of the four lots to build a structure of intricate design. Access to the apartments was facilitated by nine staircases and elevators, making it possible to practically eliminate outside corridors, so common in Budapest. There were three larger forecourts, a rectangular inner courtyard and a *cour d'honneur* along the facade, allowing direct light to reach the apartments from various directions; since the forecourts were connected to the inner courts by broad passes, it became possible to install stores not only along the street but also in the courtyards: thus sixteen stores opened onto the street, fifteen within the courtyards. The cellars included storerooms belonging to the stores as well as storage space for each apartment. The stores and shops were also provided with storerooms on the same level. The stores were equipped with huge store windows and windowpanes of glass as well as ample entrances, and the wide entrances to the building itself were provided with double wrought iron gates such as the people of Debrecen had hardly seen before.

In addition to the space for stores there were five larger apartments on the ground floor, another connected to one of the stores, and three apartments designed for superintendents. There were fifteen apartments on each floor, three lofts or studios above them, five laundry-rooms and space for drying linen. The lobbies leading to the five spacious main staircases were embellished with wrought-iron banisters and yellow, red or cobalt-colored ceramic tiles manufactured by Zsolnai. The toilets for superintendents and servants were placed in the nooks between the floors along the narrower stairwells, as were the service elevators.

The forty-meter high tower with balconies on the facade facing the city's main square elicited much discussion. Károly

---

[16] TREL I. 99. d. (P 1907) box 39. Records relating to the construction of apartment building, 95.

Weichinger, the architect who had planned the lighting fixtures of the central building of the University of Debrecen, as well as the Paulian stone church in Pécs, wrote: "It is surprising that the Reformed church is competing with the steeples of the Great Church of Debrecen, for the tower of the apartment building is not insignificant enough not to detract from the impact of the steeples, but neither is it impressive enough to have a positive impact on the appearance of the church square."[17] There was a simple explanation for the construction of this tower: the water supply for the flush-toilet facilities and the bathrooms required its own water tower, inasmuch as the city's pumps could not provide sufficient pressure for the water to reach the upper levels of the apartment building. This function of the palace's tower became superfluous only after the construction of the municipal water tower. There is no unanimity regarding the architectural designation of this building, combining a variety of styles; at the time of its construction it was referred to as "modernized empire style."[18] Today, because of the peculiarities of its structure, its elaborateness, its busy facade—the statuary of which was designed by András Tóth, the father of the poet Árpád Tóth—its most common designation is: art nouveau incorporating elements of Hungarian romantic style.[19]

The actual expenses of construction reached 2,513,911 crowns, which the diocese covered with the help of mortgages, so-called community loans, and church investments.[20]

The Apartments of the Bishop's Palace

At the beginning of the 1910s there were 18,908 apartments in Debrecen, of which 1,736 (9.2%) were vacant, especially in the suburbs and the surrounding hamlets. Only about one quarter of the apartments, in 8,500 buildings, could be considered urban and modern. 63% of the inhabited apartments had but one room

---

[17] Gyula Kovács, "Debreczen városesztétikája" [The urban esthetics of Debrecen], *DKK*, 1917, p. 25.

[18] *DKK*, 1913, p. 142.

[19] Sapi, op. cit., p. 76.

[20] TREL I. 99. d. (P 1907), box 35 III–650/1911 and III–725/1913.

with or without kitchen, 18.8% had two, 6.3% had three, 3.6% had four, 1.86% had five, and 2.25% had even more rooms.

There was a dearth of less expensive two or three-room apartments in Debrecen; since, with the municipal surtax, the tax on real estate took care of up to 40% of the income from rents, the construction of less expensive small apartments did not pay off for the developers.[21] The demand for large apartments with amenities exceeded the supply somewhat, for the larger apartments carved out of the front sections of traditional urban residences usually lacked modern comfort.

The intent of the builders of the Bishop's Palace was that the apartments would meet the demand of those families that required such comfort. The distribution of apartments was as follows:[22]

Size		Number
2	rooms studio	4
3	rooms studio	4
3	rooms w/maid's room	12
4	rooms w/maid's room	7
4	rooms/anteroom, maid's room	9
5	rooms w/maid's room	4
5	rooms/anteroom, maid's room	3
6	rooms w/maid's room	1
6	rooms/anteroom, maid's room	2
6	rooms/anteroom, 2 maid's rooms	4
	loft	3
	storefront	1
	superintendent's quarter	3
		57

In every one of the regular apartments there was a kitchen, bathroom, anteroom and toilet next to the latter, as well as a pantry attached to the kitchen. In the case of apartments looking

---

21 Miklós Ardó, *A lakáskérdés megoldása Debreczenben* [The resolution of the housing problem in Debrecen] (Debrecen, 1917), pp. 4–5.

22 TREL I. 99. d. (P 1907), box 37. Records relating to the construction of apartment building, 54; TREL I. 99. k. 3.—The basic book and inventory of the apartment building of the diocese.

on the street there were balconies enabling the occupants to spend time in the open air; moreover, assigned to each apartment cellar for storing firewood, and laundry-rooms in the attic.

The ceiling height in the apartments was 3.6 meters, the floor was covered by parquet, the walls with wallpaper, while the walls of the kitchen and of the maid's room were covered with Zsolnai tile and the floors made of cement. Huge, decorated ceramic furnaces and ordinary woodstoves in the maid's room provided heating for the apartments. The tiled bathrooms were provided with a coal fired boilers for heating air and water. The kitchens were provided with woodstoves and burners or stoves operating on municipal gas, as well as plate-warmers.

There were electric bells for communication between the household and the servant in the rooms of those apartments that included maid's quarters. The doors, whether single or double-winged, as in the case of the doors to living quarters, were provided with knobs of yellow copper. The windows were made in one, two, or three sections, but each window was completed at the top by four to twelve sections that did not open; the knobs of the windows and of the doors leading to the balcony were likewise made of copper. The windows and balcony doors opening onto the street were equipped with wooden shutters on the inside, those opening on the courtyard were provided with roll-down blinds of cloth.[23]

The plans for the apartments reflect with crystal clarity the peculiarities of the lifestyle and values of middle-class families at the turn of the century. There were two basic plans: those opening onto the main stairwell were either L or T shaped, with a rectangular anteroom and rooms of about equal size (25 to 30 meters square), usually along a corridor. Most of the rooms in the Bishop's Palace were used as dining rooms, bedrooms, and studies. Only the largest, six-room apartments of the upper middle class were provided with a living room, sewing room, and separate bedroom for children. The rooms were furnished according to their function with fashionable furniture copying a range of earlier styles or with contemporary furniture, but quite often one

---

[23] TREL I. 99. k. 3.

encountered "provincial Biedermeier" style as well. The rooms, however, were often used otherwise than originally intended; in the four-room or smaller apartments only the parents had a bedroom, the children would normally sleep with their parents until three or four years of age and play in the dining room. Bigger children were provided with a so-called child's corner in the dining room where they could study and sleep. On social occasions the row of rooms, except for the bedroom, were used for entertaining. In the five or six-room apartments entertaining usually took place in the living room or the study.[24]

The economic units of the apartments—the kitchen, pantry and maid's room—were separated from the bedrooms and living rooms of the apartment by an inside corridor. The separation was enhanced by a separate entrance which opened from the kitchen to the side stairwell or the outside corridor, providing access to the service elevators. The household help, usually numbering one, sometimes two, brought the provisions, the wood from the cellar or carried the dirty linen to be washed to the attic through this network in the rear. Rinsing was usually done by the maid in the kitchen, some evenings making use of the bathtub as well.[25]

Normally the help was not allowed to use the toilet or the bathroom in the apartment, but had to use the toilets along the stairwells between the floors or the maid's bathroom near the laundry rooms; according to the building rules the maid was entitled to take a bath once a month free of charge—using her own fuel. In addition to the social conventions that evolved the house rules of the Bishop's Palace restricted the movements and behavior of the help in other ways as well: they were not allowed to use the main elevators and it was prescribed that "servants may not sing, whistle, shout from the upper floors, or talk from one apartment to another across the courtyard."[26] The

---

[24] Sámuel Tankó, *A lakóházak tervezése és építése* [Planning and construction of apartment buildings] (Budapest, 1894), pp. 4–21. Iván Kotsils, *A közép- és kislakások alaprajzi megoldásai bérházakban* [Groundplan solutions for small and mid-size apartments in apartment buildings] (Budapest, 1942), pp. 3–9.

[25] Oral communication by Éva Dienes (Mrs. Lajos Némedi). (See note 27.)

[26] TREL I. 99. d. (P 1907), box 38. Records relating to the construction of apartment building, 79/8.

last prohibition, as the written complaints amply reveal, was seldom observed.

We are able to reconstruct the furnishings and use of apartment 53 on the third floor in detail, on the basis of the recollections of a former resident whom we were fortunate enough to track down."[27]

János Dienes, artist and teacher at the girls' secondary school, rented the four-room apartment, with 127 square meters of floor space, from November 1; the actual occupation, however, had to wait until early in January 1913, after his honeymoon. His mother, proud of her noble ancestors, but who had assimilated certain peasant customs while she was the wife of a pastor in the village, was in charge of the household and was instrumental in the interior decorating. The furnishings of the apartment remained essentially unchanged until the late twenties, except that bed space had to be added when the two daughters were born; any significant change could not have occurred before the death of the person in control of the household.

The room at the western end of the series of three rooms opening to the north functioned as the master bedroom (space 5 on the ground plan). The two beds, painted matt beige, of ordinary pine, were placed side by side directly opposite the double winged door, in the center. On the outside of each bed, against the wall were two night tables, each provided with a reading lamp weighted at the bottom. Close against the wall facing the window, in the corner of the main wall stood the wardrobe, with two doors, one half of which had shelves for holding linen, while the other was designed for hanging women's and men's clothing. The remaining piece of furniture in the bedroom was the dresser, placed along the wall between door and window. After the birth of the two daughters—in the last years of the war—furniture had to be added, namely a small sofa along the foot of the two beds and a crib between the tiled stove and the door, as sleep-

---

[27] These data were communicated to me by Éva Dienes (Mrs. Lajos Némedi), the elder daughter of János Dienes. She resided in apartment 53 on the third floor of the Bishop's Palace, with her parents, between 1914 and 1939. The interview took place at her apartment, 12 Dóczy utca (street) Debrecen, on December 16, 1983. I wish to thank her for her valuable contribution.

ing accommodations for the two children. In the mid-twenties the crib was removed from the apartment, the smaller child now slept on the little sofa whereas the older one moved into the dining room.

The built-in appurtenances of the bedroom was the bathroom and, in the corner towards the next room, the large ceramic fireplace, as well as two bells by the head of the beds. The emplacement of the bedroom was determined by the fact that it had but one door other than the door from the anteroom, leading into the bathroom.

The middle room in the row, the largest, also opening onto the anteroom was the dining room. The bedroom and the other room could be approached through the dining room although these rooms had other entrances as well. "Provincial Biedermeyer" was the style of the principal pieces of the dining-room furniture. In the middle of the space was an oval-shaped table which could be extended if necessary, and four upholstered chairs; if there were more than four diners, the folding chairs in the room were brought into use. In the southwestern corner of the dining room stood a simple, undecorated cabinet with a single door, as well as a buffet. In addition to the dinnerware the bread was also kept in the buffet; considered sacred, it remained in the custody of grandmother and could not be handled by the family. In the northeastern corner of the dining room there was a cot which served as grandmother's permanent accommodation, whereas in the space in front of the windows stood the father's easel. (An important consideration in the selection of the apartment was the northern exposure which the father felt would be most appropriate for his work.)

In the years after the war the older daughter slept in the northeastern corner of the dining room. The parquet of the dining room, unlike the other rooms, was not covered by any rug, for that would have hampered regular sweeping. Since the center of the family life was the dining room, which served more than one function, the members of the family did not refer to it among themselves as the dining room, but rather as simply "the room." The last room in the row was the study—the exclusive preserve of the head of family. The central place in this room was occupied by a sofa and two armchairs upholstered in brown leather. Along the wall facing the entrance to the dining room there was a carved and decorated black, bookshelf with a glass front and, between the seats, in the center of the room, there stood a likewise black, small carved table with a square top and four wedge-shaped legs on which were placed, as memorable relics, the two-volume illustrated Golden Bible and an album of Munkácsi paintings. Heating in the study, as in the dining room, was provided by a large stove covered with colored tile.

The fourth room, opening onto the courtyard, may have been the most interesting of all. In addition to its art nouveau style furniture, this room was crowded with the mother's dowry, who came from a Transylvanian Saxon burgher family—it was a second dining-room set, also in art nouveau style, which did not meet with the approval of grandmother in charge of the household. Thus this room was rendered practically useless, it appeared more like a storage place for furniture than a living space. Only on special occasions did the family make use of it—for instance, this was where the Christmas tree would be placed—and it was not heated except on such occasions. Since this room played no real function in the family's everyday life, and could not even serve as a guest room, it could not be named by its function. While the dining-room with its many functions was simply "the room," this fourth space that played no function at all was referred to, almost at random, as the "red room." The reason for this designation was simply that when the apartment was first occupied its walls had been covered with red wallpaper. The peculiarities of naming the rooms are enhanced by the fact that the name "red room" stuck, outliving the wallpaper: it remained the red room long after the wallpaper had been replaced by paper of a different color, since the original wallpaper was the favorite hangout of the bedbugs so common in the building.

Part of the living space was the rectangular shaped water closet, opening from the anteroom, and the bathroom; the latter included a bathtub on lion claws, grey on the outside, white enamel on the inside, a shower above, a square washbasin with a single faucet and the furnace, as well as a Székely laundry basket decorated with nails on the cover.

The utility section of the apartment included the maid's room and the kitchen which, it so happened, opened onto the same corridor as the main entrance. In the southeastern corner of the kitchen there was a stove fired by wood, the "sparhelt," next to which stood a woodbin to store the firewood brought up from the cellar. The most important items of furniture in the kitchen were two simple tables made of pine, one next to the woodbin, the other perpendicularly along the eastern wall. There were chairs next to the latter; this was where the maid took her meals. Water for cooking and for minor laundry performed in the kitchen was drawn from a faucet in the wall beneath the window opening onto the courtyard.

In the maid's room, with 8.8 meters square floorspace and wooden flooring, there was a cast-iron bed and a old pine wardrobe for the maid; in addition there was a large, decorated oak chest in which the family's spare white linen was kept. During the first years of occupancy the maid's room remained unheated; only by leaving the door to the kitchen open could it be kept warm. After the war a small cylinder-shaped iron stove was installed to heat the room. In the Dienes household the grandmother took care of the cooking, while the task of the maid was merely to prepare the ingredients. The weekly laundry, as well as the monthly washday were also the maid's duty, as were serving the meals and washing the dishes. Moreover, she had to take the garbage that could not be burnt out onto the sidewalk twice a week, whence the garbageman's cart, equipped with a bell, would remove it to the city dump. The maid would accompany some family member to the market and it was her task to carry the bags home. Other food and grocery needs of the Dienes family were met by the nearby grocer on the basis of a standing list; the bills were paid monthly. The only exception was the milk, which was brought up from the dairy on Mester utca (street), also nearby—fresh from the cows milked at dawn.

The maid would accompany the family on summer vacations to the banks of the Tisza, where they usually rented a peasant cottage; they did not forego the housekeeping to which they were accustomed.

All in all, the floorspace of the smaller two or three-room studio apartments was 80 to 95 meters square, the three-room regular apartments had 110 to 120 meters square, the four-room apartments were of 130 to 140 meters square, the five-room ones

150 to 170 meters square, and the largest ones, the six-room apartments for the upper middle class, with two maid's rooms and other annexes, were of 290 to 350 meters square.

The diocese owners set the rents in accordance with the quality and size of the apartments: studio apartments rented for 1,000 to 1,100 crowns, 1,400 to 2,200 crowns for regular three-room apartments, 1,600 to 3,000 crowns for four-room apartments, 2,000 to 3,500 crowns for the five-room apartments, depending on their location, the floor, and use. As for the six-room apartments, the rent was 3,800 to 4,500 crowns."[28]

In the same year (1912) the average rent for one, two, or three-room apartments in Debrecen was 600, 1,100, and 1,600 crowns respectively.[29]

The Residents of the Bishop's Palace

The Reformed Diocese of Debrecen issued its first advertisement regarding apartments available in the building in the eighth issue of the 1912 volume of the daily *Debreceni Szemle*:

> The apartment building in construction at the corner of the Hatvan utca (street) and Egyház tér (square) has space for stores, each provided with store-rooms and cellars; moreover, there will be modern apartments on the ground, and on floors 1 through 3, equipped with bathroom and other appurtenances, which may be rented...by paying a non-refundable application fee of 10% of the rental.[30]

The applications came in steadily to the building committee from the beginning of the summer to November 1; yet, in spite of the heavy demand, in most cases the rent stipulated in the leases was below the contemplated amount. The reasons for this, in addition to the waning enthusiasm and the inflation, must have been the fact that rents in Debrecen, unlike Budapest and other

---

[28] TREL, I. 99. d. (P 1907), box 27. Records relating to the construction of apartment building, 54.

[29] Ferenczi, *A lakásügy állása és haladása...*, p. 638.

[30] *Debreczeni Szemle*, no. 8 (1912), p. 11.

cities, did not rise in the period 1909 to 1912, because of extensive construction.[31]

The difference between the contemplated rents and the actual amount was especially noticeable in the case of the larger, five or six room apartments, where the deficit amounted to as much as 600 to 900 crowns, while six of the large apartments were not rented at all by the time the building was completed.[32]

The lease of store space resulted in even greater losses to the diocese. By December 24, 1912, only seven stores in the courtyard had been leased. According to the manager's report, the main reason for the deficit in this case was that the rent for the stores had been determined on the assumption that these were times of boom; the new situation required a reexamination of the rent structure.[33] Eventually, every one of the apartments was leased, even if at a lower rate, but the majority of the store spaces remained available even as late as December 1914.[34]

We were unable to determine the occupation of about 10% of the residents; one fifth of them were middle or big entrepreneurs, and members of their family, and there was a family member from a family of large landowners, while almost 70% of the renters belonged to the city's intelligentsia.

In the first decade of the twentieth century the effectives of the intelligentsia were on the rise in Debrecen. Because of the city's role in administration, the resettlement of the regional centers of infrastructural institutions (e.g., railroads, post office, banks, and insurance companies), the temporary boom in private enterprise, and because of the demand for professional services that normally accompany the process of urbanization (lawyers, doctors, teachers), the ranks of the intelligentsia increased by over 50%.

The number of salaried members of the intelligentsia was 2,446 in 1900, and rose to 3,692 by 1910. The steepest rise was

---

[31] Ferenczi, *A lakásügy állása és haladása...*, p. 634.

[32] TREL, I. 99. d. (P 1907), box 39. Records relating to the construction of apartment building, 95/24.

[33] Ibid., also TREL I. 99. d. (P 1907), box 35, II-1693/1914.

[34] Ibid.

in the ranks of the private sector white-collar employees (80.06%), but the numbers of teachers and lawyers also increased significantly (63.35% and 40.95% respectively).[35]

TABLE 36

Distribution of salaried intelligentsia in Debrecen in 1910[36]

Occupation	Total wage-earning intelligentsia	Percentage of all wage-earners*
1) Agriculture	54	1.46
2) Mining, industry, transport	1,554	42.09
3) Military	205	42.09
4) Public service and professions	1,889	51.16
Some sub-groups under 4		
a) Administration	490	13.27
b) Justice	389	10.53
c) Ecclesiastic service	87	2.36
d) Education	495	13.40
e) Public health	237	16.42
f) Scientific societies and assoc.	69	1.86
g) Art and literature	101	2.73
h) Other intelligentsia	21	0.57

* The wage-earning intelligentsia comprised 8.7% of all the wage earners in Debrecen.

Of course, the residents of the Bishop's Palace did not reflect the distribution of the intelligentsia in the city since, because of the high rent, only those whose annual income—considering the structure of the family budget in the period—reached or exceeded 4 to 6,000 crowns could afford to live there.

The distribution of the occupation of the residents of the 57 apartments in the Bishop's Palace, between 1912 and 1914, was as follows:

---

35 *MStK*, new series, vol. 64, pp. 308, 313.

36 Ibid.

Occupation	Number of staff	Percentage
Civil service	5	7.94
Professions	14	22.21
Lawyer	7	
Physician	4	
Architect	3	
White collar (private)	4	6.34
Clergyman	1	1.58
Teacher	13	20.63
In secondary school	11	
In higher education	2	
Officer in military	4	6.34
Other intelligentsia or family	2	3.17
Total inteligentsia:	43	68.25
Relative of landowner	1	1.58
Entrepreneur and relative	11	17.46
Institution	2	3.17
Occupation unknown	6	9.52

Note: One lawyer cum large landowner was virilis. See text.

The number of private sector white-collar employees was well below their proportion among the intelligentsia in the city as a whole; even so one of them was the director of a corporation. On the other hand, the post office employee was only able to remain by subletting part of his four-room apartment four months after he moved in.

One fifth of the residents were teachers or professors in the secondary schools or institutions of higher learning. A minority of them could only afford to rent apartments with two, three or four rooms, but most of them added to their income by moon-lighting or tutoring. Among them only the professor at the Agricultural College could afford to rent a six-room apartment.

Those who rented the larger, five or six-room apartments were mostly in the professions and used part of the apartment for business or office. Much as elsewhere, in the case of every occupation group of the intelligentsia, the studio apartments were rented primarily by single young men at the beginning of their career; after a raise, a promotion, or a successful marriage they moved from these quarters into a larger apartment where complete housekeeping and keeping a maid were possible.

The treasury paid the rent on two studios, a five-room, and a six-room apartment for the four army officers.

The only clergyman resident occupied the space as a service apartment, combining a three and a four-room apartment.

One fifth of the residents who were not members of the intelligentsia included owners of mid-size enterprises—for instance, a ladies' fashion business, a restaurant, a net-manufacturing plant; as regards representatives from the upper bourgeoisie, these were members of their family living on their own, or working with the firm as the son in "and Son" among the residents. But there was a white elephant, a son of one of the greatest landowners in the area, who rented the six-room apartment with two maid's room.

The residents who belonged to the upper-middle class serve as notches to indicate what strata did the standard of living of families in the intelligentsia (the higher salaried members of the middle class) approximate—their social level, lifestyle, system of values. What the examination of the status of the intelligentsia residents reveals is that very few among them belonged to the city's theocratic elite. This group of the intelligentsia included persons whose background was the well-to-do bourgeoisie who either managed and led the affairs of the city, married into such families, or adapted to their lifestyle and system of values by living in their own homes or striving for it; they regarded renting an apartment as something alien to their system of values, beneath their dignity. The resident of apartment 50 of four rooms, secretary in the office of the mayor, Elek Szabó, the father of the well-known contemporary writer Magda Szabó, was no exception to this rule; he rented an apartment merely while a bachelor, moving to their joint family home once he got married. Since the number of civil servants was also growing in the first decade of the twentieth century there was a dearth of apartments for them. It is no accident, therefore, that one group of municipal employees formed, at the time of the construction of the Bishop's Palace, the Association of the Estate for Debrecen Officials, the purpose of which was to construct an estate with fifty single-family homes in a wooded area of the city, between the Széchenyi and Posta parks. The Association began the construction of single-family homes of three, four, or five rooms, with gardens and small improvements, on lots bought from the municipal council at advantageous prices, at the beginning of the 1910s; the project was completed after the war. [37]

Among other intelligentsia residents in the Bishop's Palace we find a good many engaged in creative activities—their writings appeared in the dailies or in professional journals. There were others known beyond their circle, nationwide. Among them we may note the clergyman Zoltán Jánosi, writer and politician, a member of the National Council at the time of the liberal democratic revolution of 1918–1919, appointed under-secretary of the interior in the Dénes Berinkey cabinet. We have already mentioned the artist János Dienes, teacher at the girls' secondary school, who was awarded the Munkácsy prize in 1953 for his life's work. The fourth-story loft on the side of Hatvan utca (street) was rented for a few years by the Olympic competitor and architect, Alfréd Hajós, with his business partner, having won the bid for the new building of the Arany Bika [Golden Bull] hotel.

The depression which hit the country towards the end of 1913 ruined large numbers of people with little or moderate income in Debrecen. Not only did the expectations of the diocese regarding leasing store space go up in smoke, but also about one third of the families renting apartments were then forced either to relinquish their prestigious quarters or attempt to stay by applying for grace periods in the payment of the rent. The overwhelming majority of them were teachers living on fixed salaries, but there were some among them, such as the self-employed Peter Goldstein who rented a six-room apartment and who, in his letter requesting permission to pay his overdue rent in monthly installments, wrote: "I work as does my whole family, I try hard, yet I am unable to meet my obligations."[38]

---

[37] Lajos Husz, "A debreceni képviselőtelep" [The estate for Debrecen officials], *DKK* (1912), pp. 148–150.

[38] TREL, I. 99. d. (P 1907), box 40. Records relating to the construction of apartment building, III/9. The letter was dated December 22, 1913.

The answer of the management was usually negative. "Since the church feels the burden of today's terrible fiscal situation just as much as individuals, the committee regrets to inform you that it cannot honor your application."[39]

In the last years of World War I it was not merely the turnover among the residents that demonstrated the deterioration in the position of the middle-class intelligentsia of the city, but also the fact that the larger apartments were being split into smaller units.[40]

In Debrecen—and perhaps the situation was similar in other Hungarian towns—only a fraction of the intelligentsia lived in rented apartments like the ones in the Bishop's Palace. Only those families in the intelligentsia who were not tied to the city fathers by their background or their activities, and therefore whose ideal of housing was not to own a single family home, but preferred to rent a larger and more comfortable apartment at the cost of one's year investment.

Until the war broke out there were but five larger apartment buildings in Debrecen similar to the Bishop's Palace, with forty to sixty apartments each. Thus, although we do not have exact data, we must assume that a decisive fraction of the intelligentsia at the beginning of the twentieth century lived either in their own home or part of their own home, or in apartments rented in traditional residences that differed from the ones described in this case study.

Considering the modern apartment building, which made its appearance in Debrecen as well at the end of the first decade of the century, this decade represents historically the last stage of the process of embourgeoisement and urbanization. This process started with the citizen residing in two places—one on the outskirts of the city or on land he owned in the hamlet, where there was no separation between the economic life of the family and its more intimate sphere and which entailed a particular dichotomy of urban-rural existence.

---

40 Ibid., 128/14.

39 TREL, I. 99. d. (P 1907), box 40. Records relating to the construction of apartment building, III/9.

Beyond the housing relations of the more socially mobile elements of the middle-class intelligentsia in the towns, the living conditions described in this case study may also be used as data in interpreting the statistics on the housing relations of the middle-class intelligentsia in the capital city; after all, the history of the construction of the Bishop's Palace makes it clear that the models were the apartment buildings of Budapest.

CONCLUSION

The Tracks of Development of the Intelligentsia in Hungary—the Gentrified and Educated Middle Class

This title requires explanation: why have we singled out this class? Where are the headings regarding other classes?

The intelligentsia in Hungary covered a lot of ground from the mid-nineteenth century until the last decade of the Dual Monarchy: it increased over fivefold in numbers, it changed basically in its functions, it modernized in its occupational structure and, with the changes in techniques of social organization, the circumstances and particulars of organization changed as well, as did the role and importance of various social formations in its reproduction. In accordance with its rapid growth, the intelligentsia necessarily became open: the traditional intelligentsia could not possibly provide for its own "expanded reproduction." Thus doors opened to members of other social groups; after sparse beginnings, from mid-century the children of the urban bourgeoisie and, to a lesser extent, the children of other strata were streaming in, in increasing dimensions. At the turn of the century, along with the first and second generation bourgeois intelligentsia, they provided a decisive fraction of the intelligentsia's supply line, whereas those who came from the so-called historic classes provided only about one-tenth, while the peasantry, over half of Hungary's population, provided little more than one twentieth. In the last two decades of the Dual Monarchy—although in a subordinate role and proportions—the lower ranks of the petty bourgeoisie and the working class joined in the process of mobility into the intelligentsia. The radical structural transformation of the system of reproduction of the intelligentsia was helped by the fact that the basically liberal education policies of the regimes did not attempt to administratively restrict the social mobility of any social group. The opportunities for mobility of particular classes, ethnic groups and denominations were determined basically by the degree of their embourgeoisement and the educational system, which had evolved historically to some extent, provided unlimited opportunities for joining the ranks of the intelligentsia only to those who chose assimilation. As a result, the overwhelming majority of the career intelligentsia at the beginning of the twentieth century spoke Hungarian or had learned to speak it; the ratio of those assimilated from other ethnic groups among them must have been about 50%.

Because of the social and economic backwardness of Hungary, the state power created by the Compromise—building on the experience and traditions of the state of enlightened absolutism—not only organized and managed the network of political institutions; as part of the strategy of catching up, it organized administrative technical and infrastructural institutions—either integrated into its political bureaucracy, directed by it or modeled upon it—the task of which was to create conditions favorable to the capitalist transformation of the economy and to modernization. Moreover, it often played the role of organizer itself, as a substitute for the as yet undeveloped market.

On the other hand, the fact that, within the framework of the market of the Dual Monarchy, the financing of the modernization of the Hungarian economy, from the Compromise to 1900, came largely from investments from foreign sources, entailed the consequence that the professional tasks of the Hungarian economy were carried out and operated by great capitalist multinational organizations even in the early stages of the transformation.

Thus it should not appear strange that the preponderant majority of the rapidly professionalized intelligentsia, in its main types, came about as an organized intelligentsia of bureaucrats, integrated by state and economic organizations.

If we add to all this that the evolution of the bureaucratic intelligentsia and its rapid growth took place under extremely backward educational conditions in Hungary, and that the income level of the bulk of the intelligentsia—in spite of its considerable differentiation—was many times that of the "lower classes of the population," then we have found a point of reference to explain why the comprehensive social organization of the intelligentsia and its separation from other classes got under way early.

We have striven not to jump to any conclusions beyond those justified by our sources and included in our analysis, thus avoiding the possibly false stereotypes found in the literature on the history of the Hungarian intelligentsia. We cannot avoid, however, given the results of the research we have accepted—primarily that of Ferenc Erdei, István Bibó, Tibor Huszár and Péter Hanák—and, reviewing our own work,[1] formulating, albeit schematically and partly as a hypothesis, certain issues and interpretations regarding the more general evolution of the intelligentsia before World War I. We are also, thereby, pointing out the road for further research.

The analysis of processes of social structure in a narrower sense uncovered several contradictions, or failed to provide answers to questions raised earlier. The most important among these: the factors for stratification do not explain why the Hungarian intelligentsia did not organize as professionals according to their function in the system of production, as they had in the case of most West European societies; why was it that the formation we usually call the middle class became the all-encompassing framework and determining factor of its position, its social integration and lifestyle? Why was it that, while there was a significant shift in the intelligentsia's social composition and origins towards bourgeois strata, this shift did not show up in commensurate proportions in its lifestyle, system of values, its political attitudes? Nor does it help in resolving this issue if we accept the correct observation that, after the bourgeois revolution, social evolution notwithstanding, the Hungarian feudal order and relations had not completely dissolved—

---

[1] Péter Hanák, "A magyar 'középosztály' fejlődésének problémájához" [The problem of the development of the Hungarian "middle class"], *Valóság*, no. 3 (1962), pp. 23–39; István Bibó, *Értelmiség és szakszerűség* [Intelligentsia and professionalism] (Szeged, 1947).

unless we seek the reasons for these remnants.[2]

In other words, we are asking: what factor or factors beyond the processes of change in social structure in a narrower sense influenced social evolution and, within it, the evolution of the intelligentsia, in the period of the Dual Monarchy? We may find the answer in the impact the political regime and power structure of the Dual Monarchy exercised on social evolution. By means of the Compromise the ruling elite, made up of owners of mid-size estates, created a system of political institutions built from top down, the basic task of which was to eliminate social and ethnic autonomies which, in any case, were only fledgling, given the backwardness and the lack of integration of Hungarian society, or rather societies; and, by the same token, to repress the formation of social and national self-rule, for this was the only way in which the hegemony of the traditional Hungarian ruling classes could be preserved. Within the framework of a bourgeois liberal constitutionalism and with the changes in social legitimation, it was no longer possible to base the reconstitution and operation of political power as social power on the noble "middle order" organized along privileges of birth; in any case, this middle order of the nobility was no longer adequate in the new historical situation for filling the functions demanded by power and modernization. (Nor was it possible to base this rule on a strong national bourgeoisie, since there was no such thing.) The Hungarian liberal theoreticians of the period of Compromise were well aware of this vacuum. Recently Béla G. Németh has demonstrated that the middle class ideologies enunciated in this period were systematic attempts at bridging this gap. [3] It was not for lack of good will on the part of those who developed these theories that the landowning nobility which has accepted embourgeoisement and the bourgeois ethic, along with Hungarian national traditions and objectives,

---

[2] Pierre Bourdieu, "Az értelmiségi hagyomány és a társadalmi rend meg-őrzése" [The preservation of intellectual tradition and social order], in Pierre Bourdieu, *A társadalmi egyenlőtlenségek újratermelődése* [The reproduction of social inequality] (Budapest, 1978), p. 46. He wrote: "The surviving remnants do not explain a thing if we do not explain why some traditions are still practiced."

[3] Németh, op. cit., pp. 280–181.

and the technocrats who joined their ranks, were not the ideal combination for fulfilling this function. The framework of the middle class, outlined in theory, was filled by the intelligentsia, rapidly expanding because of the successes of economic modernization; it was within this framework that it met with the noble landowning class which, losing its estates, was compelled to intellectualize. Accepting the antidemocratic and national content of the system of rule ensured by the Compromise, it was the functions required by the development and operation of this system in all its breadth that was complemented by the intelligentsia; thus, within the "gentrified and educated middle class," it could continue to act as bulwark for the existing structures of class power, hegemony and personal relations. This explains why those groups of the intelligentsia which originated in the middle class and which became numerically preponderant at the turn of the century could not make their social traits prevail over the tradition-preserving gentry, and thus, within the intelligentsia, "the gentry consciousness and the tendency to preserve the existing social order prevailed over the role of the intelligentsia."[4]

It appeared that the system of selection of the new middle-class intelligentsia was perfectly adequate for the legitimation requirements of the period: instead of privileges of birth, there was the system of education which ensured an adequate level of training. In addition to this mechanism of selection, however, there was a comprehensive second system, which Péter Hanák referred to as the mechanism of socialization of the middle class.[5] Certain elements of this mechanism are obvious: the ideological content of secondary and higher education; the double taxation; the census on education; titles and ranks, manners of approaching people, the familiar versus the formal form of address, style of clothing, behavior, the complicated symbolism pertaining to every aspect of life; the ability to obtain credit and to fight duels, etc. In addition to all this there were the public and cultural institutions, the network of clubs, casinos and other social organizations and associations which filled the social-

---

4 Bibó, op. cit., p. 4.
5 Hanák, op. cit.

ization requirements of the intelligentsia. The impact, character, significance, practical operations and interaction of these
components, which would bring us closer to an understanding of
the phenomenon of middle-class, remain to be analyzed.[6]

The formation of a "gentrified and educated middle class"
remains one of the major unclarified aspects of the social evolution of Hungary in the period of the Dual Monarchy, the track
the intelligentsia followed in its development, a tradition which,
in some of its structures and attitudes, has been preserved to
this day.

---

[6] For a still useful analysis, see Geiza Farkas, *Az úri rend* [The gentry estate]
(Budapest, 1912).

APPENDICES

APPENDIX 1

Distribution of the Intelligentsia by Type of Settlement and by Region in 1910

Area, type a settlement	Total population	Total gainfully employed	Public serv. and profess.	White collar in agriculture	White collar in industry	Total* intelligents.	Intelligents. per 1,000 inhabitants
I. West of Danube							
A. Towns with municipal councils and settlements of over 10,000 inhabitants	195,189	87,758	5,988	113	541	6,642	34.03
B. Chartered towns	164,679	78,339	5,930	52	936	6,918	42.01
C. Settlements of less than 10,000 inhabitants	2,702,159	1,125,372	20,196	1,935	1,016	23,147	8.56
Totals:	3,062,027	1,291,469	32,114	2,100	2,493	36,707	11.99
II. North of Danube							
A. Towns with municipal councils and settlements of over 10,000 inhabitants	207,626	93,781	6,564	110	923	7,597	36.59
B. Chartered towns	93,408	48,838	3,534	42	811	4,387	46.97
C. Settlements of less than 10,000 inhabitants	1,874,390	771,828	14,596	1,384	1,371	17,351	9.25
Totals:	2,175,924	914,447	24,694	1,536	3,105	29,335	13.48
III. Between Danube and Tisza							
A. Towns with municipal councils and settlements of over 10,000 inhabitants	888,997	361,054	15,006	267	1,860	17,133	19.27
B. Chartered towns	427,432	187,538	8,882	88	936	9,906	23.17
C. Settlements of less than 10,000 inhabitants	1,572,858	610,172	13,498	937	745	15,180	9.65
D. The municipality of Budapest	880,371	492,975	43,753	270	14,961	58,991	67.01
Totals:	3,769,658	1,651,739	81,139	1,562	18,509	101,210	26.85
Greater Budapest (including suburbs)	1,069,040	571,763	47,945	290	16,416	64,651	60.47
IV. West of Tisza							
A. Towns with municipal councils and settlements of over 10,000 inhabitants	192,660	81,909	6,352	70	383	6,805	35.32
B. Chartered towns	95,670	46,057	3,529	20	499	4,048	42.31
C. Settlements of less than 10,000 inhabitants	1,481,351	603,988	12,798	1,014	808	14,620	9.86
Totals:	1,769,681	731,954	22,679	1,104	1,690	25,473	14.39

Area, type a settlement	Total population	Total gainfully employed	Public serv. and profess.	White collar in agriculture	White collar in industry	Total* intelligents.	Intelligents. per 1,000 inhabitants
V. East of Tisza							
A. Towns with municipal councils and settlements of over 10,000 inhabitants	442,980	178,778	8,795	189	420	9,404	21.23
B. Chartered towns	191,790	89,383	6,802	107	837	7,746	40.39
C. Settlements of less than 10,000 inhabitants	1,960,154	761,227	14,924	1,293	436	16,653	8.49
Totals:	2,594,924	1,029,388	30,521	1,589	1,693	33,803	13.02
VI. Between the Tisza and Maros Rivers							
A. Towns with municipal councils and settlements of over 10,000 inhabitants	205,344	92,526	4,786	66	583	5,435	26.47
B. Chartered towns	183,899	91,179	6,112	50	1,061	7,223	39.27
C. Settlements of less than 10,000 inhabitants	1,752,526	741,163	14,005	742	529	15,276	8.72
Totals:	2,141,769	924,868	24,903	858	2,173	27,934	13.04
VII. Beyond the Király Pass							
A/ Towns with municipal councils and settlements of over 10,000 inhabitants	276,136	134,172	11,030	127	1,064	12,221	44.25
B/ Chartered towns	86,325	43,064	4,311	26	346	4,683	54.25
C/ Settlements of less than 10,000 inhabitants	2,315,906	1,002,790	17,659	756	889	19,304	8.34
Totals:	2,678,367	1,180,026	33,000	909	2,299	36,208	13.52
VIII. Fiume (Rijeka) and district	49,806	25,152	1,938	3	517	2,458	49.35

* Not including white collar employed in commerce, banking and transportation.

APPENDIX 2

The Distribution of Secondary School Students by Religion, Ethnic Group and Social Background, by School District and Type of School in Academic Year 1890–1891

School district	1. Religious categories							2. Ethnic categories						
	Catholic	Uniate	Greek Orth.	Lutheran	Calvinist	Unitarian	Jewish	Hun.	German	Roman.	Slovak	Serbo-Croat	Ruthene	Other
Budapest	2,595	13	47	414	404	11	1,922	4,928	418	9	13	17	1	20
Suburbs of Budapest	2,329	8	62	95	553	2	686	3,358	260	24	56	33		4
Debrecen	832	61	52	387	1,760		798	3,748	79	40	7	14	2	
Székesfehérvár	1,778	5	10	86	209	1	718	2,650	123	3		29	1	3
Győr	1,702	1	5	558	241	2	549	2,420	363		22	47		3
Pozsony (Pressburg, Bratislava)	1,908	2	5	319	109	2	790	1,617	968	4	539	2		5
Besztercebánya (B. Bistrica)	1,477	43	6	978	334	1	574	1,880	873		667		1	2
Kassa (Košice)	1,401	610	4	213	469		810	2,706	316	135	249		84	8
Nagyvárad (Oradea)	1,326	180	593	142	224	1	666	1,767	629	581	24	124		7
Kolozsvár (Cluj)	806	828	166	275	909	239	195	2,083	291	985	3	3		43
Nagyszeben (Sibiu)	967	147	750	944	588	39	158	1,574	1,127	882				10
Szeged	1,501	13	548	116	105	3	661	1,729	549	41	7	516	3	57
Fiume (Rijeka), state sec. sch.	130		3	3	1		7	20	17			12		95
Totals for Hungary:	18,742	1,902	2,250	4,530	5903	299	8,489	30,483	6,201	2,702	1,587	795	92	256
Totals for secondary schools:	15,724	1,857	1,940	3,751	5457	278	5,795	25,389	4,413	2,451	1,495	724	90	240
Totals for middle schools:	3,018	45	310	779	447	21	2,694	5,094	1,788	251	92	71	2	16

3. Social background categories

School district	Large landown.	Small-holder	Empl. in agricult.	Industri-alist	Artisan	Empl. in industry	Whole-saler	Retailer	Empl. in comm.	Civil servants	Private w. collar	Military	Oth. prof. with dipl.	Consult.	Self-em. & retir.	Totals:
Budapest	206	124	49	161	610	134	274	607	153	969	507	83	838	297	394	5,406
Suburbs of Budapest	105	577	51	23	705	29	54	443	26	453	190	21	657	211	190	3,735
Debrecen	145	713	84	27	557	53	90	329	42	558	166	12	771	166	174	3,890
Székesfehérvár	75	238	95	31	562	32	44	414	15	358	199	32	388	154	169	2,806
Győr	1,411	549	83	32	486	36	52	353	35	295	185	12	451	145	144	3,055
Pozsony (Pressburg, Bratislava)	69	446	53	36	547	56	28	442	22	447	207	50	429	166	137	3,135
Besztercebánya (B. Bistrica)	178	340	35	21	672	26	34	384	9	482	263	15	626	234	94	3,413
Kassa (Kosice)	109	480	51	33	488	39	39	368	17	583	195	42	770	136	148	3,498
Nagyvárad (Oradea)	60	401	55	47	380	11	73	414	20	480	155	34	710	119	164	3,132
Kolozsvár (Cluj)	121	823	64	14	346	9	48	132	4	524	105	35	930	96	157	3,408
Nagyszeben (Sibiu)	83	910	8	30	610	21	48	310	15	544	100	73	660	104	77	3,593
Szeged	32	436	40	11	495	13	27	524	20	423	114	36	457	118	156	2,902
Fiume (Rijeka), state sec. sch.	2	4		3	13	6	2	10	10	56	21	1	5	11		144
Totals for Hungary:	1,272	6,040	668	459	6,444	465	813	4,738	388	6,302	2,407	446	7,692	1,957	2,024	42,116
Totals for secondary schools:	1,142	5,407	462	337	5,161	282	502	3,323	182	5,524	1,870	340	6,165	1,493	1,255	34,802
Totals for middle schools:	123	564	138	183	1,386	170	223	1,428	174	703	576	127	710	412	377	7,314

APPENDIX 3

The Minimum Household Budget of a Teacher's Family with Three to Four Children in 1893 and 1906

1893	forint	1906	forint
1. Milk, coffee and sugar	73.00	Milk, coffee and sugar	83.95
2. Half a kilo meat	88.10	Half a kilo meat	131.40
3. Noodles, eggs, seasoning.	25.55	Noodles, eggs, seasoning.	51.10
4. Vegetables for stewing	65.70	Vegetables for stewing	65.70
5. Fat	14.60	Fat	73.00
6. Vinegar	0.60	Vinegar	1.00
7. Soap	11.53	Soap	11.53
8. Bleach	0.10	Bleach	0.96
9. Starch	0.80	Starch	8.32
10. Oil (for lamp)	6.48	Oil (for lamp)	24.84
11. Polish	0.72	Polish	2.08
12. Brush	0.20	Brush	1.00
13. Brooms	–	Brooms	1.80
14. Combs	–	Combs	1.00
15. Bread	73.00	Bread	78.00
16. Linen for the year	20.00	Linen for the year	30.00
17. Two pairs of shoes for husband	10.00	Two pairs of shoes for husband	12.00
18. Two pairs of shoes for wife	8.00	Two pairs of shoes for wife	10.00
19. For repairs	3.60	For repairs	10.00
20. A summer suit for husband	6.00	A summer suit for husband	12.00
21. Children's shoes	8.00	Children's shoes	20.00
22. Fabric for a dress	25.00	Fabric for a dress	28.00

1893	forint	1906	forint
23. One winter coat to last 3 years, purchased at 25 forints	8.33	One winter coat to last 3 years, purchased at 25 forints	8.33
24. One straw hat, one felt hat	5.20	One straw hat, one felt hat	5.20
25. One black formal suit to last 6 years, purchased at 36 forints	6.00	One black formal suit to last 4 years, purchased at 36 forints	9.00
26. Four neckties	1.20	Six neckties	3.00
27. Two kerchiefs for wife	0.60	Four kerchiefs for wife	4.40
28. One woolen dress	10.00	One woolen dress	14.00
29. A summer and a winter coat	8.00	A summer and a winter coat	16.00
30. Dresses for the children	12.00	Dresses for the children	40.00
31. Children's hats		Children's hats	8.00
32. Stationery and journals	10.00	Stationery and journals	40.00
33. Doctor, medicine	15.00	Doctor, medicine	25.00
34. Contribution to pension	6.00	Contribution to pension	8.00
35. Income tax	3.00	Income tax	5.00
36. Road tax	1.50	Road tax	1.50
37. Membership dues	2.00	Membership dues	2.00
38. Church tax		Church tax	5.00
39. Eötvös fund	1.50	Eötvös fund	1.50
40. Insurance		Insurance	24.00
41. Charity	2.00	Charity	5.00
42. Firewood	25.00	Firewood	60.00
43. Replacement of kichen utensils		Replacement of kichen utensils	6.00
44. Gloves		Gloves	3.20
45. Textbooks		Textbooks	8.00
Totals:	559.51		959.81

APPENDIX 4

Teachers' Salaries in Academic Year
1896–1897

Category of educators	Effectives	Average income (in forints)
1. KINDERGARDEN	1,247	380.47*
2. PUBLIC ELEMENTARY SCHOOL (total)	27,150	480.00**
Government employee	1,668	545.59*
3. TWO-GRADE MIDDLE SCHOOL (total)	128	507.46*
4. FOUR-GRADE MIDDLE SCHOOL (total)	1,922	823.81***
Government employee	581	928.44*
5. GIRL'S HIGH SCHOOL (total)	625	913.26*
Government employee	242	1,001.20*
6. HIGH SCHOOL (total)	3,454	1,089.88*
Regular teacher	1,904	
Substitute	344	
Resident teacher of religion	144	
Non-resident teacher of religion	579	
Other non-resident teacher	105	
Physical education teacher	136	
Special subject teacher	242	
7. UNIVERSITY PROFESSOR		
University of Budapest	187	2,940.00
University of Kolozsvár	71	3,516.00
Polytechnic University of Budapest	64	3,536.00

*   From the budget.
**   On the basis of ratios in academic year 1887–1888.
***   Some less than 500 forints annual salary.

APPENDIX 5

Pay Categories for Public Elementary School Teachers According to Act XXVI of 1907

Elementary school teachers	Group I	Group II	Group III*
	in crowns		
Base salary	1,200	1,100	1,000
5 years later	1,600	1,500	1,400
10 years later	1,800	1,700	1,600
15 years later	2,000	1,900	1,800
20 years later	2,200	2,100	2,000
25 years later	2,400	2,300	2,200
30 years later	2,600	2,500	2,400
Subject teachers	Male		Female
Base salary	1,400		1,200
5 years later	1,800		1,500
10 years later	2,100		1,800
15 years later	2,400		2,000
20 years later	2,600		2,200
25 years later	2,800		2,400
30 years later	3,000		2,600
Salary supplement for housing			
I. housing category (group I: salary Cr 600)			
II. housing category (group I: salary Cr 420)			
III. housing category (group II: salary Cr 360)			
IV. housing category (group III: salary Cr 300)			
V. housing category (group III: salary Cr 200)			

* Salary supplements were set according to housing categories which were supposed to take the cost of living in particular locations into consideration.

APPENDIX 6

Pay Categories of Public Elementary School Teachers According to Act XXVI of 1913, and Pay Categories of Community and Denominational Elementary School Teachers According to Act XVI of 1913

A.

Public Elementary School Teachers

Pay		Annual salary in crowns	Annual housing allowance (in crowns) by housing category						
Category	Grade		I.	II.	III.	IV.	V.	VI.	VII.
Base salary		1,200	600	540	480	420	360	300	240
III.	3	1,400							
	2	1,600	800	720	640	560	480	400	320
	1	1,800							
II.	3	2,000							
	2	2,200	900	810	720	630	540	450	360
	1	2,400							
I.	3	2,600							
	2	2,900	1,000	900	800	700	600	500	400
	1	3,200							

B.

Community-Employed and Denominational Elementary School Teachers

Pay		Annual salary in crowns	Annual housing allowance (in crowns) by housing category in every pay category and grade						
Category	Grade		I.	II.	III.	IV.	V.	VI.	VII.
Base salary		1,200	600	540	480	420	360	300	240
III.	3	1,400							
	2	1,600							
	1	1,800							
II.	3	2,000							
	2	2,200	600	540	480	420	360	350	240
	1	2,400							
I.	3	2,600							
	2	2,900							
	1	3,200							

APPENDIX 7

Average Annual Pay of County and District Officials in Hungary in 1866

I. Administrative personnel	Average pay/ year in forints
1. First deputy sheriff	1,547
2. Second deputy sheriff	1,357
3. Chief notary	1,128
4. Deputy notary	704
5. Chief magistrate	1,006
6. Magistrate	755
7. Juror	471
8. Comptroller	829
9. Accountant (bookkeeper)	685
10. Archivist	500
11. Cashier	510
12. Clerk	368
13. Clerk, temporary	300
14. Printer	384
II. Medical and technical personnel	
1. Head physician	603
2. Physician	354
3. Veterinarian	207
4. Engineer	577
III. Personnel of the judicial court	
1. Assessor	1,109
2. Chief judge, juror	686
3. Cashier, registrar, comptr., clerk	385
4. Chief prosecutor	1,091
5. Assistant prosecutor	727
6. Registrar of real estate	515
7. Official of the orphans' court	663
8. Gendarme	517
9. Castellan	447

The overall average for county and district officials: 621.60 forints.

APPENDIX 8

Average Annual Salary of Administrators in Local Government, and Their Range of Incomes in Hungary in 1888

I. Counties	Highest	Lowest	Average
	in forints		
A. OFFICIALS AT THE COUNTY SEAT			
1. Deputy sheriff	4,200	2,300	2,875
2. Chief notary	3,300	1,340	1,796
3. Deputy notary	1,680	700	1,066
4. Assistant prosecutor	2,200	720	1,375
5. President wards' court	3,000	1,240	1,699
6. Assessor, wards' court	1,800	1,000	1,295
7. Head physician	1,600	800	1,107
8. Physician	800	500	588
9. Veterinarian	850	400	593
10. Head comptroller	2,400	900	1,293
11. Assistant comptroller	1,800	800	1,020
12. Comptroller, wards' court	2,100	900	1,288
13. Auditor	1,300	600	968
14. Chief accountant	2,100	900	1,266
15. Assistant accountant	1,800	700	975
16. Management trainee	500	360	361
B. DISTRICT OFFICIALS			
1. Chief magistrate	2,340	1,000	1,698
2. Magistrate	1,100	600	874
3. District physician	1,098	100	503
4. Veterinarian	1,098	200	537
5. Management trainee	480	360	361
C. MUNICIPAL EMPLOYEES (TOWNS WITH COUNCILS)			
1. Mayor	3,000	700	1,302
2. Councillor	1,522	50	549
3. Chief notary	1,522	400	858
4. Deputy notary	1,400	200	638
5. Prosecutor	1,500	40	399
6. Assessor, wards' court	1,400	100	583
7. Chief of police	1,800	200	859
8. Deputy chief of police	1,250	50	536
9. Physician	1,014	100	486
10. Assistant physician	763	100	370
11. Veterinarian	1,000	50	302
12. Comptroller	1,522	80	648
13. Auditor	1,200	150	596
14. Architect and engineer	1,522	100	726

II. Chartered Municipalities	Highest	Lowest	Average
	in forints		
A. BUDAPEST OFFICIALS			
1. Mayor	7,000	7,000	7,000
2. Deputy mayor	6,000	5,000	5,500
3. Councillor	4,000	3,300	3,370
4. Chief notary	3,300	3,300	3,300
5. Notary	2,650	1,700	1,858
6. Chief prosecutor	3,300	3,300	3,300
7. Assistant prosecutor	2,050	1,700	1,850
8. Aide to prosecutor	1,093	1,093	1,093
9. President, wards' court	4,000	4,000	4,000
10. Assessor, wards' court	2,500	2,500	2,500
11. Notary, wards' court	2,050	1,700	1,850
12. Clerk, wards' court	1,220	1,000	1,107
13. Stenographer, wards' court	3,300	3,300	3,300
14. Head physician	4,132	4,132	4,132
15. Aid to head physician	1,800	1,800	1,800
16. District physician	1,400	600	1,293
17. Veterinarian	1,000	1,000	1,000
18. Treasurer	3,000	3,000	3,000
19. Cashier	2,050	1,600	1,762
20. Auditor	2,500	2,500	2,500
21. Chief accountant	4,000	4,000	4,000
22. Accountant (bookkeeper)	2,800	2,800	2,800
23. Chief engineer and dir. of publ. builds.	9,000	9,000	9,000
24. Engineer	2,500	1,600	2,007
25. Engineering aide	1,500	1,220	1,487
26. Engineer trainee	500	500	500
27. Director of statistical office	3,300	3,300	3,300
28. Clerk trainee	600	600	600
B. OFFICIALS OF OTHER MUNICIPALITIES			
1. Mayor	3,300	1,509	2,785
2. Councillor	2,600	1,000	1,432
3. Chief notary	1,800	1,000	1,511
4. Notary assistant	1,210	720	904
5. Chief prosecutor	1,700	600	1,066
6. Assistant prosecutor	1,400	600	892
7. President, wards' court	2,200	400	1,396
8. Assessor, wards' court	1,880	900	1,238
9. Chief of police	2,640	900	1,693

II. Chartered Municipalities	Highest	Lowest	Average
	In forints		
(Cont.)			
10. Deputy chief of police	1,210	600	976
11. Head physican	1,200	500	799
12. Assistant physican	1,050	300	525
13. Veterinarian	1,100	240	514
14. Chief treasurer	1,600	980	1,200
15. Auditor	1,200	150	862
16. Comptroller	1,700	800	1,263
17. Assistant comptroller	1,200	560	851
18. Engineer and architect	1,980	600	1,103
III. Communities			
1. District and community notaries	3,000	120	727
2. District and community physicians	1,400	200	526

APPENDIX 9

White-Collar Civil Service Salary Categories in 1888 According to Grade Level, and Compared to Austrian Categories

Rank	HUNGARY			AUSTRIA		
	Salary in forints	Rent in forints	Total	Salary	Fringe benefits	Total
I. Prime minister	20,000	12,000	32,000	12,000	14,000	26,000
II. Minister	12,000	4,000	16,000	10,000	10,000	20,000
III. Under secretary	6,000	1,000	7,000	7,000	3,000	10,000
IV. Deputy under secretary	6,000	600	6,600			
V. Minister councillor	5,000 4,000	600 600	5,600 4,600	6,000 5,500 4,500	1,000 1,000 1,000	7,000 6,500 5,500
VI. Section chief	3,000 2,500	500 500	3,500 3,000	3,600 3,200 2,300	800 800 800	3,100 2,900 2,700
VII. Secretary	1,800 1,500	400 400	2,200 1,900	2,400 2,200 2,000	700 700 700	2,400 2,200 2,000
VIII. Clerk	1,000 900	300 300	1,300 1,200	1,800 1,600 1,400	800 600 600	2,400 2,200 2,000
IX. Assistant clerk	600	200	800	1,300 1,200 1,100	500 500 500	1,800 1,700 1,600

APPENDIX 10

Average Annual Salary of Administrators of Chartered Municipalities in 1909–1910

	Number of governm. employees	Average pay in crowns
I. COUNTIES		
1. Central staff	1,754	3,004.50
Of whom: officials	1,419	3,465.66
clerks	335	1,051.10
Breakdown of government employees		
a) Administrative department		
Deputy sheriff	63	8,951.71
Chief notary	63	6,160.98
Deputy notary	260	3,807.92
Administrative trainee	183	1,353.00
b) Legal department		
Chief prosecutor	63	6,693.17
Assistant prosecutor	23	3,824.35
c) Heath department		
Head physician	63	5,836.03
Deputy physician	3	3,030.00
d) Archives department		
Chief archivist	63	3,697.03
Deputy archivist	19	2,768.42
e) Branch office		
Director of branch office	28	3,736.43
Clerical staff	393	2,284.90
Other support staff	161	2,929.60
f) Miscellaneous department		
Castellan, warden of barracks	34	2,410.59
2. Personnel of orphan's court	1,010	3,234.63
Clerk, temporary	119	3,771.40
Official	811	
Judge, orphans' court	63	6,670.95
Assessor, orphans' court	271	5,012.51
Prosecutor, orphans' court	10	3,810.50
Notaries	76	2,976.05
Trainee	20	1,335.00
Other personnel grades (VIII–IX)	6	3,557.00
Other personnel grades (X–XI)	365	2,651.00

	Number of governm. employees	Average pay in crowns
3. District personnal	2,648	3,075.67
Officials	2.155	3,537.22
Clerk, temporary	493	950.71
Chief magistrate	433	6,890.00
Magistrate	602	3,033.00
Management trainee	113	1,324.00
District physician	431	3,368.00
White-collar, branch officer	576	2,098.00
II. MUNICIPALITIES		
All white collar and clerk	18,338	2,253.40
Of whom: officials	16,010	2,424.32
clerks	2,378	1,102.73
Breakdown of government employees		
1. Actual administrative personnel	2,144	3,195.00
Clerk, temporary	933	1,128.00
Mayor	138	6,710.00
Deputy mayors, councillors	291	4,565.00
Chief notary	138	4,257.00
Deputy notaries, clerks	280	3,507.00
Other administrative personnel	75	2,219.00
Personnel in prosecutor's office	152	3,155.00
Archival personnel	68	3,022.00
Branch office personnel	733	2,268.00
Miscellaneus personnel	269	1,906.00
2. Personnel of orphan's court		
Official, white-collar	296	3,152.00
Clerk, temporary	84	1,064.00
Of whom: official		
clerk	122	4,366.00
other administ. personnel	90	2,381.00
personnel in the court	5	2,718.00
barnch office personnel	79	2,183.00
3. Comptroller's office personnel		
Official, white-collar	836	3,075.00
Clerk, temporary	192	973.00
Of whom: comptroller of the treasury	128	3,727.00
accountants	101	3,766.00
cashiers, auditors	241	2,990.00
bookkeepers of finances	366	2,712.00

	Number of governm. employees	Average pay in crowns
4. Health service		
Officials	566	2,900
Clerk, temporary	19	751
Of whom: head physician	126	3,197
district physician	224	3,223
hospital administrators	23	2,581
veterinarians	129	2,209
other health officials	64	2,698
5. Educational and cultural personnel	7,849	1,936
Secondary school	303	3,620
Four grade middle school (polgári isk.)	756	3,244
Vacational school	312	1,804
Four grade (public) elemetary school	4,457	2,130
Trade school	769	438
Other schools	23	735
Kindergarten	578	926
Libraries, museums	21	1,843
6. Law enforcement		
Official	865	2,785
Clerk, temporary	390	950
7. Forestry management personnel	211	2,590
8. Technicians		
Official	433	3,894
Clerk, temporary	113	1,955
Of whom: official superv. chief eng.	76	6,603
engineer and ass. engineer	203	3,999
other officials	154	2,416
9. Internal revenue personnel		
Official	1.092	2,368
Clerk, temporary	464	946
Treasurer	48	3,836
Official, head bookkeeper	89	3,966
Cashier, accountants	542	2,391
White-collar, branch office	413	1,825
10. Sales and income-tax personnel		
Official	518	1,896
Clerk, temporary	19	1,089

	Number of governm. employees	Average pay in crowns
11. Municipal plants		
Supervisor	190	4,072
Official	593	2,606
Clerk, temporary	109	1,330
12. Personnel paid from municipal funds		
Official	1,047	1,674
Clerk, temporary	47	1,012

APPENDIX 11

Housekeeping Budgets of the Unmarried Administrators of a Major Bank in 1906

	I.	II.	III.	IV.	V.	VI.	VII.	VIII.
1. Salary	26,000	7,600	6,000	6,000	6,000	5,200	4,800	4,800
2. Extra income								400
3. Assets	80,000					300,000	120,000	
4. Rent	2,400	w. mother and sister, 1,200	600	480	600	800	360	200
5. Food	2,400	1,400	1,200		760	1,200	1,200	720
6. Clothing	800	500	1,200	1,600	300	500	600	360
7. Gambling expenses				Cr 10–12 wins or losses	cards		small bets	
8. Expensive hobbies	horseriding, travel, 3,600							books periodicals
9. Coffee house	infrequent visit		twice a week	daily, 1 crown	3x daily		2x daily	for breakfast
10. Theater	premieres		opera/concert				every premiere	free tickets
11. Vacation	summer travel	800	800	360	400	1,200	2,400	360
12. Debts								600
13. Medical		1,200						100
14. Retirement	480	160	400	120	130	130	100	100
15. Clubs	300	yes, about	120		160			36
16. Mistress	1,200	1,200	1,000	1,000	1,200	1,000	year-long affair, 2,400	occasional liaison

	IX.	X.	XI.	XII.	XIII.	XIV.	XV.	XVI.
1. Salary	4,000	4,000	3,600	3,200	1,500	1,200	1,000	900
2. Extra income								
3. Assets	120,000				40,000		160,000	
4. Rent	lives at home	1,200	support from home			lives at home		
5. Food	eats at home				eats at home			from home
6. Clothing	600	600	360	800	500	260		
7. Gambling expenses	200	gambling	1,200	chess, 200	races, 800		300	
8. Expensive hobbies			carousing ca. 2,000/year		carousing 4,000	sports, 120		
9. Coffee house	every evening	pool	occasional		once daily			
10. Theater	opera daily	premieres	premiere at musicals				opera, 100	
11. Vacation	1,000						400	
12. Debts		2,000	ca. 2,000	2,000				
13. Medical		200						
14. Retirement	100		60	100	24			
15. Clubs	100	120	100	100	80	40	40	
16. Mistress		yes	yes		2,000			

APPENDIX 12

Housekeeping Budgets of Administrators at a Major Financial Institution in 1906

	I.	II.	III.	IV.	V.	VI.	VII.	VIII.	IX.	X.
1. Salary	26,000	12,000	11,000	7,600	7,600	7,600	6,000	6,000	6,000	4,000
2. Assets	140,000	200,000		200,000		60,000	50,000	30,000	20,000	
3. Rent	owns home	2,000	1,400	2,600	1,000	1,400	800	800	1,200	700
4. Housekeeping	4,400	3,800	2,400	4,000	2,400	2,800	2,400	1,600	2,000	1,600
5. Clothing	400	400	400	500	400	600	300	400	400	200
6. Wife's clothing	400	900	400	900	300	500	200	600	800	200
7. Number of children	3	3	1	1	2		3			
8. Schooling	1,000		260				300			
9. Clothing for children	360	500	140		200		360			
10. Gambling expenses				small bets					300	
11. Coffee house		200		breakfast		400	200	200	800	100
12. Theater	200	400		premieres	200	200	200			100
13. Cigars		360	180	240		100	200		300	
14. Expensive hobbies				Soirées						
15. Summer vacation	1,600	560		1,600	600	700		400	1,200	
16. Medical	400	200	100	600	300	50			100	100
17. Club dues	400					80	80			
18. Pension	480	200	170	160	160	160	120	120	120	80
19. Number of maids	2	2	2	3	2	1	2	2	1	1
20. Their wages	720	600	560	1,000	480	360	480	360	240	180

APPENDIX 13

Housekeeping Expenses of the Administrators of a Wholesale Grain Company in 1906

	I.	II.	III.	IV.	V.	VI.	VII.
1. Income	14,000	10,000	6,000	4,000	3,600	2,400	1,800
2. Married or single	married	married	single	married	single	single	single
3. Extra income	2,000	4,000	1,000	3,000	500		1,000
4. Assets	30,000	12,000	18,000	16,000	8,000	100,000	1,600
5. Rent	3,000	2,000	1,200	1,200	1,000	1,600	500
6. Food	2,800	2,400	1,600	2,000	1,800	1,000	600
7. Clothing	2,000	3,000	600	1,000	600	600	300
8. Gambling	stock mark.	bridge	races	casino		stock mark.	some cards
9. Expensive hobbies	wife	buys books		women	travels	social life	
10. Coffee house	Cr 100/ mo.	50	80	200	20	80	10–20
11. Theater	50–60/ mo.	80		20	60	100	
12. Summer vacation	1,000	home	600	400	at parents	500	200
13. Debts	15,000	6,000	8,000	6,000		12,000	3,000
14. Guarantees		1,000		1,000		4,000	
15. Interest payments	500	270	380	290		600	200
16. Lien against salary	no	no	no	not now	formerly	yes	no
17. Club	200		occasional	200		300	
18. Taxes	800	600	400	300	300	180	120
19. Mistress		1,000		600		2,000	

APPENDIX 14

The Educational System

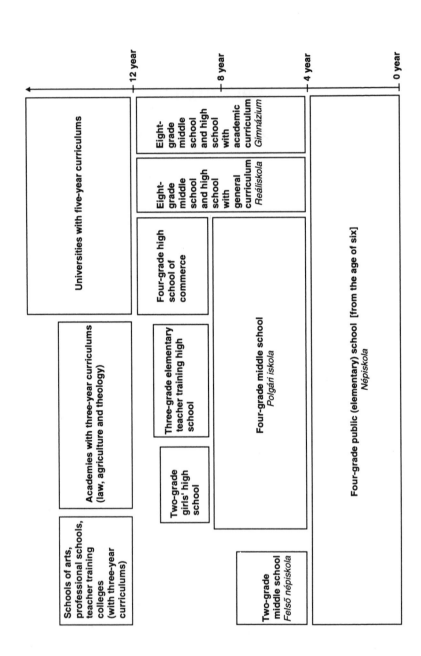

APPENDIX 15

Map:
Nineteenth-Century Hungary

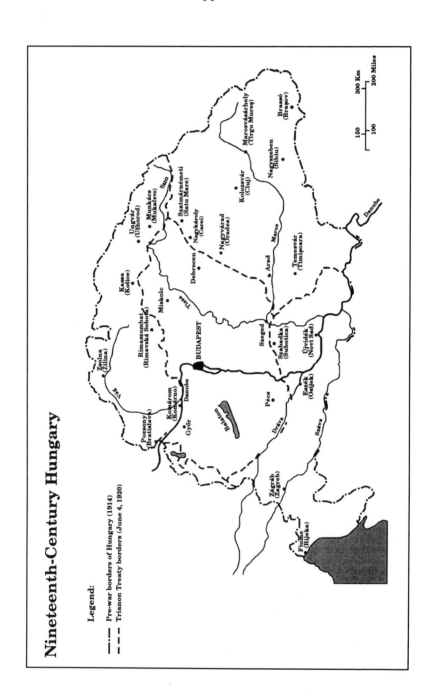

Nineteenth-Century Hungary

Legend:

--·-- Pre-war borders of Hungary (1914)
----- Trianon Treaty borders (June 4, 1920)

APPENDIX 16

Color Charts:

1. Distribution of the Intelligentsia by Occupation and by Region in 1869

2. Careers Chosen by High School Graduates in Hungary in Percentages

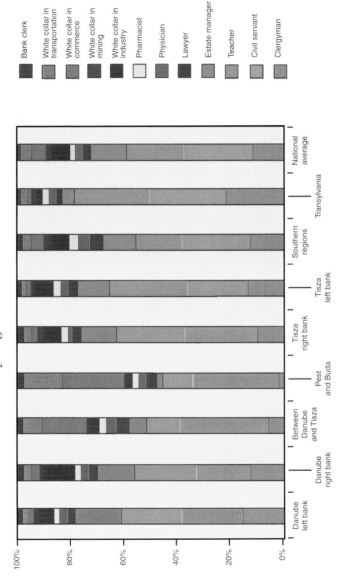

Distribution of the Intellegentsia by Occupation and by Region in 1869

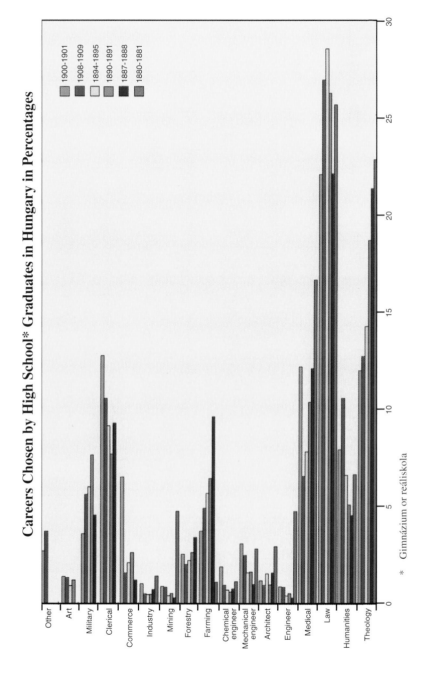

Careers Chosen by High School* Graduates in Hungary in Percentages

1900-1901
1908-1909
1894-1895
1890-1891
1887-1888
1880-1881

Other
Art
Military
Clerical
Commerce
Industry
Mining
Forestry
Farming
Chemical engineer
Mechanical engineer
Architect
Engineer
Medical
Law
Humanities
Theology

* Gimnázium or reáliskola

NAME INDEX

PLACE INDEX

Volumes Published in
"Atlantic Studies on Society in Change"

No. 1   *Tolerance and Movements of Religious Dissent in Eastern Europe.* Edited by B. K. Király. 1977.

No. 2   *The Habsburg Empire in World War I.* Edited by R. A. Kann. 1978.

No. 3   *The Mutual Effects of the Islamic and Judeo-Christian Worlds: The East European Pattern.* Edited by A. Ascher, T. Halasi-Kun, B. K. Király. 1979.

No. 4   *Before Watergate: Problems of Corruption in American Society.* Edited by A. S. Eisenstadt, A. Hoogenboom, H. L. Trefousse. 1979.

No. 5   *East Central European Perceptions of Early America.* Edited by B. K. Király and. G. Bárány. 1977.

No. 6   *The Hungarian Revolution of 1956 in Retrospect.* Edited by B. K. Király and Paul Jonas. 1978.

No. 7   *Brooklyn U.S.A.: Fourth Largest City in America.* Edited by Rita S. Miller. 1979.

No. 8   *Prime Minister Gyula Andrássy's Influence on Habsburg Foreign Policy.* János Decsy. 1979.

No. 9   *The Great Impeacher: A Political Biography of James M. Ashley.* Robert F. Horowitz. 1979.

No. 10   *Special Topics and Generalizations on the Eighteenth*
Vol. I*   *and Nineteenth Century.* Edited by B. K. Király and Gunther E. Rothenberg. 1979.

* Volumes no. I through XXXVI refer to the series War and Society in East Central Europe.

No. 11
Vol. II
East Central European Society and War in the Pre-Revolutionary 18th Century. Edited by Gunther E. Rothenberg, B. K. Király, and Peter F. Sugar. 1982.

No. 12
Vol. III
From Hunyadi to Rákóczi: War and Society in Late Medieval and Early Modern Hungary. Edited by János M. Bak and B. K. Király. 1982.

No. 13
Vol. IV
East Central European Society and War in the Era of Revolutions: 1775–1856. Edited by B. K. Király. 1984.

No. 14
Vol. V
Essays on World War I: Origins and Prisoners of War. Edited by Samuel R. Williamson, Jr. and Peter Pastor. 1983.

No. 15
Vol. VI
Essays on World War I: Total War and Peacemaking, A Case Study on Trianon. Edited by B. K. Király, Peter Pastor and Ivan Sanders. 1982.

No. 16
Vol. VII
Army, Aristocracy, Monarchy: War, Society and Government in Austria, 1618–1780. Edited by Thomas M. Baker. 1982.

No. 17
Vol. VIII
The First Serbian Uprising 1804–1813. Edited by Wayne S. Vucinich. 1982.

No. 18
Vol. IX
Czechoslovak Policy and the Hungarian Minority 1945–1948. Kálmán Janics. Edited by Stephen Borsody. 1982.

No. 19
Vol. X
At the Brink of War and Peace: The Tito-Stalin Split in a Historic Perspective. Edited by Wayne S. Vucinich. 1982.

No. 20
Inflation Through the Ages: Economic, Social, Psychological and Historical Aspects. Edited by Edward Marcus and Nathan Schmuckler. 1981.

No. 21
Germany and America: Essays on Problem of International Relations and Immigration. Edited by Hans L. Trefousse. 1980.

Vol. XIII   *Great War: The Rise of Communist Parties in East Central Europe, 1918–1921.* Edited by Ivo Banac. 1983.

No. 33
Vol. XIV   *The Crucial Decade: East Central European Society and National Defense, 1859–1870.* Edited by B. K. Király. 1984.

No. 35
Vol. XVI   *Effects of World War I: War Communism in Hungary, 1919.* György Péteri. 1984.

No. 36
Vol. XVII   *Insurrections, Wars, and the Eastern Crisis in the 1870s.* Edited by B. K. Király and Gale Stokes. 1985.

No. 37
Vol. XVIII   *East Central European Society and the Balkan Wars, 1912–1913.* Edited by Béla K. Király and Dimitrije Djordjevic. 1986.

No. 38
Vol. XIX   *East Central European Society in World War I.* Edited by B. K. Király and N. F. Dreisziger, Assistant Editor Albert A. Nofi. 1985.

No. 39
Vol. XX   *Revolutions and Interventions in Hungary and Its Neighbor States, 1918–1919.* Edited by Peter Pastor. 1988.

No. 41
Vol. XXII   *Essays on East Central European Society and War, 1740–1920.* Edited by Stephen Fischer-Galati and B. K. Király. 1988.

No. 42
Vol. XXIII   *East Central European Maritime Commerce and Naval Policies, 1789–1913.* Edited by Apostolos E. Vacalopoulos, Constantinos D. Svolopoulos, and B. K. Király. 1988.

No. 43   *Selections, Social Origins, Education and Training* Vol. XXIV *of East Central European Officers Corps.* Edited by B. K. Király and Walter Scott Dillard. 1988.

No. 44
Vol. XXV   *East Central European War Leaders: Civilian and Military.* Edited by B. K. Király and Albert Nofi. 1988.

No. 46   *Germany's International Monetary Policy and the European Monetary System.* Hugo Kaufmann. 1985.

No. 47   *Iran Since the Revolution—Internal Dynamics, Regional Conflicts and the Superpowers.* Edited by Barry M. Rosen. 1985.

No. 48   *The Press during the Hungarian Revolution of 1848–* Vol. XXVII *1849.* Domokos Kosáry. 1986.

No. 49   *The Spanish Inquisition and the Inquisitional Mind.* Edited by Angel Alcala. 1987.

No. 50   *Catholics, the State and the European Radical Right, 1919–1945.* Edited by Richard Wolff and Jorg K. Hoensch. 1987.

No. 51   *The Boer War and Military Reforms.* Jay Stone and Vol. XXVIII Erwin A. Schmidl. 1987.

No. 52   *Baron Joseph Eötvös, A Literary Biography.* Steven B. Várdy. 1987.

No. 53   *Towards the Renaissance of Puerto Rican Studies: Ethnic and Area Studies in University Education.* Maria Sanchez and Antonio M. Stevens. 1987.

No. 54   *The Brazilian Diamonds in Contracts, Contraband and Capital.* Harry Bernstein. 1987.

No. 55   *Christians, Jews and Other Worlds: Patterns of Conflict and Accommodation.* Edited by Philip F. Galagher. 1988.

No. 56   *The Fall of the Medieval Kingdom of Hungary:* Vol. XXVI *Mohács, 1526, Buda, 1541.* Géza Perjés. 1989.

No. 57   *The Lord Mayor of Lisbon: The Portuguese Tribune of the People and His 24 Guilds.* Harry Bernstein. 1989.

Atlantic Studies on Society in Change

No. 58   *Hungarian Statesmen of Destiny: 1860–1960.* Edited by Paul Bődy. 1989.

No. 59   *For China: The Memoirs of T. G. Li, Former Major General in the Chinese Nationalist Army.* T. G. Li. Written in collaboration with Roman Rome. 1989.

No. 60   *Politics in Hungary: For a Democratic Alternative.* János Kis, with an Introduction by Timothy Garton Ash. 1989.

No. 61   *Hungarian Worker's Councils in 1956.* Edited by Bill Lomax. 1990.

No. 62   *Essays on the Structure and Reform of Centrally Planned Economic Systems.* Paul Jonas. A joint publication with Corvina Kiadó, Budapest. 1990.

No. 63   *Kossuth as a Journalist in England.* Éva H. Haraszti. A joint publication with Akadémiai Kiadó, Budapest. 1990.

No. 64   *From Padua to the Trianon, 1918–1920.* Mária Ormos. A joint publication with Akadémiai Kiadó, Budapest. 1990.

No. 65   *Towns in Medieval Hungary.* Edited by László Gerevich. A joint publication with Akadémiai Kiadó, Budapest. 1990.

No. 66   *The Nationalities Problem in Transylvania, 1867–1940.* Sándor Bíró. 1992.

No. 67   *Hungarian Exiles and the Romanian National Movement, 1849–1867.* Béla Borsi-Kálmán. 1991.

No. 68   *The Hungarian Minority's Situation in Ceauescu's Romania.* Edited by Rudolf Joó and Andrew Ludanyi. 1994.

No. 69   *Democracy, Revolution, Self-Determination. Selected Writings.* István Bibó. Edited by Károly Nagy. 1991.

No. 70   *Trianon and the Protection of Minorities.* József Galántai. A joint publication with Corvina Kiadó, Budapest. 1991.

No. 71   *King Saint Stephen of Hungary.* György Györffy. 1994.

No. 72   *Dynasty, Politics and Culture. Selected Essays.* Robert A. Kann. Edited by Stanley B. Winters. 1991.

No. 73   *Jadwiga of Anjou and the Rise of East Central Europe.* Oscar Halecki. Edited by Thaddeus V. Gromada. A joint publication with the Polish Institute of Arts and Sciences of America. New York. 1991.

No. 74   *Hungarian Economy and Society during World War*
Vol. XXIX *Two.* Edited by György Lengyel. 1993.

No. 75   *The Life of a Communist Revolutionary, Béla Kun.* György Borsányi. 1993.

No. 76   *Yugoslavia: The Process of Disintegration.* Laslo Sekelj. 1993.

No. 77   *Wartime American Plans for a New Hungary. Docu-*
Vol. XXX *ments from the U.S. Department of State, 1942–1944.* Edited by Ignác Romsics. 1992.

No. 78   *Planning for War against Russia and Serbia. Austro-*
Vol. XXXI *Hungarian and German Military Strategies, 1871–1914.* Graydon A. Tunstall, Jr. 1993.

No. 79   *American Effects on Hungarian Imagination and Political Thought, 1559–1848.* Géza Závodszky. 1995.

No. 80   *Trianon and East Central Europe: Antecedents and*
Vol. XXXII *Repercussions.* Edited by B. K. Király and L. Veszprémy. 1995.

No. 81   *Hungarians and Their Neighbors in Modern Times, 1867–1950.* Edited by Ferenc Glatz. 1995.

No. 82 *István Bethlen: A Great Conservative Statesman of Hungary, 1874–1946.* Ignác Romsics. 1995.

No. 83 *20th Century Hungary and the Great Powers.* Edited
Vol. XXXIII by Ignác Romsics. 1995.

No. 84 *Lawful Revolution in Hungary, 1989–1994.* Edited by B. K. Király and András Bozóki. 1995.

No. 85 *The Demography of Contemporary Hungarian Society.* Edited by Pál Péter Tóth and Emil Valkovics. 1996.

No. 86 *Budapest, A History from Its Beginnings to 1996.* Edited by András Gerő and János Poór. 1996.

No. 87 *The Dominant Ideas of the Nineteenth Century and* Eötvös. Translated, edited, annotated and indexed with an introductory essay by D. Mervyn Jones. 1996.

No. 88 *The Dominant Ideas of the Nineteenth Century and Their Impact on the State.* Volume 2. *Remedy.* József Eötvös. Translated, edited, annotated and indexed with an introductory essay by D. Mervyn Jones. 1997.

No. 89 *The Social History of the Hungarian Intelligentsia, 1825–1914.* János Mazsu. 1997.

No. 90 *Pax Britannica: Wartime Foreign Office Documents*
Vol. XXXIV *Regarding Plans for a Postbellum East Central Europe.* Edited by András D. Bán. 1997.

No. 91 *National Identity in Contemporary Hungary.* György Csepeli. 1997.

No. 92 *The Hungarian Parliament, 1867–1918: A Mirage of Power.* András Gerő. 1997.

No. 93 *The Hungarian Revolution and War for Independence*
Vol. XXXV *1848–1849. A Military History.* Edited by Gábor Bona. 1997.

No. 94   *Academia and State Socialism: Essays on the Political
History of Academic Life in Post-1945 Hungary and
East Central Europe.* György Péteri. 1997.

No. 95   *Through the Prism of the Habsburg Monarchy:*
Vol. XXXVI   *Hungary in American Diplomacy and Public Opinion
during World War I.* Tibor Glant. 1997.